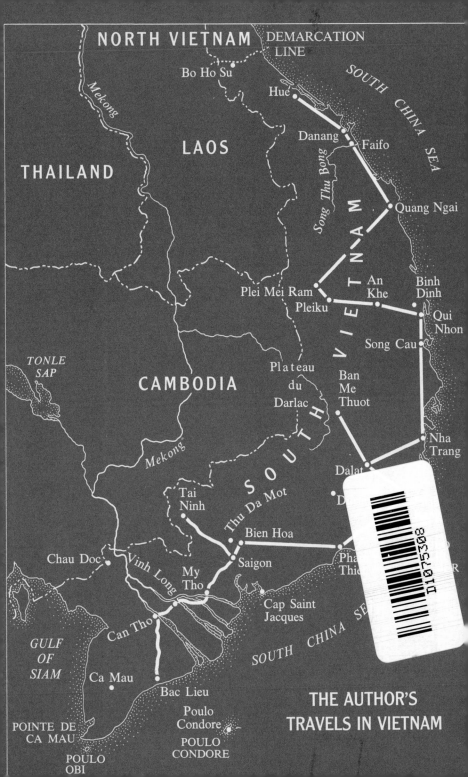

THE AUTHOR'S
TRAVELS IN VIETNAM

Our Vietnam Nightmare

Books by Marguerite Higgins

Our Vietnam Nightmare

Tales of the Foreign Service
          (*with Peter Lisagor*)

Jessie Benton Fremont

Red Plush and Black Bread

News Is a Singular Thing

War in Korea—Report of a Woman Combat Correspondent

MARGUERITE HIGGINS

Our
Vietnam
Nightmare

HARPER & ROW, PUBLISHERS

NEW YORK

Grateful acknowledgment is made to the following for permission to use quoted material:

"The Buddha and the Occident," by Irving Babbitt from the book *The Dhammapada,* translated by Irving Babbitt. Copyright 1936 by Edward S. Babbitt and Esther B. Howe. Reprinted by permission of the publisher, New Directions.

The Smaller Dragon: A Political History of Vietnam, by Joseph Buttinger, published by Frederick A. Praeger, Inc., Publishers, New York, 1958.

The Washington *Evening Star* for permission to use quoted material by Crosby Noyes, foreign editor, and Richard Critchfield, Asian correspondent.

Frederick E. Nolting, Jr., former Ambassador to Vietnam.

Mission in Torment, by John M. Mecklin. Copyright © 1965 by John Mecklin. Reprinted by permission of Doubleday & Company, Inc.

Viet-nam: The First Five Years, An International Symposium, edited by Richard W. Lindholm. Copyright © 1959 by the Michigan State University Press.

The White House Years: Mandate for Change, 1953–1956, by Dwight D. Eisenhower. Copyright © 1963 by Dwight D. Eisenhower. Reprinted by permission of Doubleday & Company, Inc.

The Chicago *Daily News* for permission to use quoted material by Peter Lisagor. Washington Bureau Chief, and Keyes Beech, Asian correspondent.

To Larry and Linda Hall

Contents

Prologue   1

1. The Xa Loi Pagoda: Buddha at the Barricades   17

2. Machiavelli with Incense   25

3. The Countryside: American Myths and Vietnamese
   Realities   36

4. Madame Ngo Dinh Nhu: Dragon Lady or Joan of Arc?   59

5. The Buddhist Burnings: Why Do They Do It?   74

6. Hué: How the Buddhist Crisis Began   88

7. The War: Heads You Win, Tails I Lose?   104

8. The Peasants and the Commissars   133

9. Ngo Dinh Diem: The Case of the Misunderstood
   Mandarin   157

10. Plots and Plotters—Vietnamese-American Style   180

11. Coups and Consequences, Human   214

12. Post-Coup Vietnam: Jungle Without Law   230

13. Reprise at the Pagodas   257

14. Our Vietnam Nightmare   287

(vii)

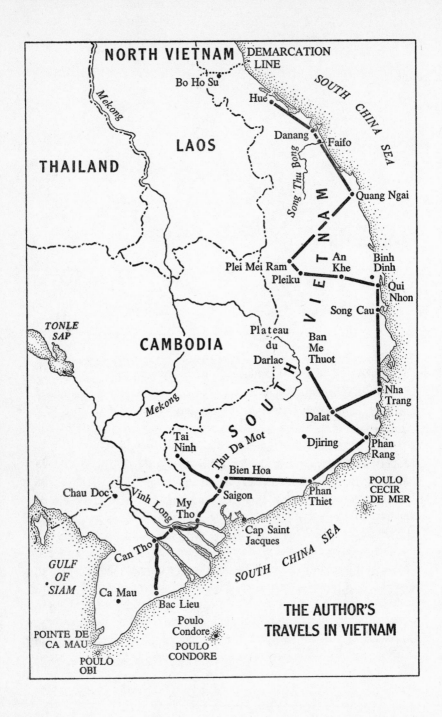

THE AUTHOR'S
TRAVELS IN VIETNAM

Author's Note

Will Rogers said that everyone is ignorant—only on different subjects. Of Vietnam, more than most places, it can be said that there are no experts, only varying degrees of ignorance. This book is written in hopes of contributing a bit to the understanding of that charming, tortured land. Like almost every American in Southeast Asia, I believe Vietnam to be as much a front line of freedom as Hawaii or San Francisco. Perhaps more so. For if we were fighting in Hawaii or San Francisco, it might be too late. In the completion of this book I am indebted to countless journalistic colleagues for help and advice, most especially Peter Lisagor of the Chicago *Daily News* and Michael O'Neill of the New York *Daily News*. The book would have been impossible without the tireless and intelligent help of my research assistant and secretary, Miss Joanne Kent. Vietnamese officials—both in and out of power—have helped immeasurably in the effort to separate fact from fiction, often at political risk to themselves. The same is true of many American government officials. I extend thanks to the thousands of soldiers, sailors, airmen and marines—both American and Vietnamese—who have paused over the years to answer my questions. Finally, I am indebted to the specialist fourth class from Pleasantville, New York, who in a letter home from Vietnam managed to sum up in a few lines much of what this book is about.

"It is maddening," the soldier wrote, "to see clippings from the U.S. newspapers scorning our efforts. Vietnam is a long way from home, but suppose we were in, say Alaska, or Canada, or Mexico maybe. That's pretty close to home. It's easy to sit in front of that old TV and say, 'Aw, to hell with Vietnam.' I don't think anyone here feels that way. It's disheartening to know that many folks back home do. If we do say 'to hell with Vietnam,' we might as well say to hell with Southeast Asia, then, maybe, to hell with Europe, South America, Africa, and then maybe, 'to hell with freedom.' "

M.H.

Saigon
September, 1965

Our Vietnam Nightmare

Prologue

It was shortly before midnight in Washington when the telephone woke me. At the other end was Vic Wilson, who was holding down the night desk of the New York *Herald Tribune*'s Washington Bureau.

He was sorry to call so late, Vic said, but he had a message from New York signed by an imposing array of brass, including Seymour Freidin, the foreign editor, Richard Wald, executive editor, and Jim Bellows, managing editor, and so he presumed that the message was urgent.

"Yes," I said sleepily. "What is it?"

Could I go to Vietnam at the earliest possible moment?

It was mid-July, 1963. I had just returned home from an overseas trip. I had a miserable case of flu. I did not want to go to Vietnam. And I said so in terms just as heated as my 103-degree temperature. I asked Vic to relay my message.

A wise and patient man, Vic suggested that I might want to reconsider the message I had dictated to him. Why not wait until morning?

Three days later I left by jet for Saigon.

It was to be my seventh visit to a country that I had seen for the first time when I was six months old. For as a baby in Hong Kong, where I was born, I had been stricken with malaria, and the family doctor directed that my parents take me to Dalat, a beautiful mountain resort in Central Vietnam, high enough to be therapeutic in a part of the world where the air is not notably salubrious.

In any case, my ties to Vietnam reach deep into that country's tragically long battle for freedom. My grandfather, the Count de Godard, died of a wound received while fighting with the French colonial forces against the Vietnamese in the 1890's.

My first adult encounter with the Far East came in 1950, when I was named chief Asian correspondent for the New York *Herald Tribune*. And during the war in Korea, I had also commuted frequently to the war in Vietnam, which was, so to speak, another front of the same struggle. In 1954 I had been in North Vietnam to write of the last agonies of Dienbienphu. I had been only three jeeps away on the awful day that Robert Capa of Magnum Photos, one of journalism's rare and wonderful characters, had stepped into a rice paddy to take a picture and was blown to instant death by a land mine.

But despite these sad memories, I was enchanted by Vietnam and the Vietnamese people. And enchanted is the precise word. For there is a kind of magic about Vietnam—the magic of that which is exotic, strange, imperfectly understood, and yet deep in the emotions. I remember once in 1953, during a journey out of Hanoi, happening by chance upon a beautiful and apparently forgotten Confucian temple located in a faraway village at the end of an enclosed courtyard, its stones covered by moss and shaded by tall, tall trees which were reflected in a pool filled with water lilies and goldfish. I am not a member of any particular religion, but even as an agnostic I have been drawn to temples and churches and found beauty and an inexplicable sense of rapport to I know not what—but a rapport of magnetic quality that draws me back again and again.

As to Saigon, I knew that lovely city as well as any Westerner can. I counted many a Saigonais as a friend.

So by all odds, I should have felt reasonably sure-footed as a journalist that summer of 1963 on my way back to Saigon.

But I wasn't. I was deeply uneasy. The principal thing on the mind of the *Herald Tribune* editors was, quite rightly, the religious crisis. What was President Ngo Dinh Diem doing to cause these Buddhists to choose such a horrible death as self-immolation? What did the Buddhists want? What was all this headline-making agitation doing to the war effort? The fact that all these questions presumed *a priori* the guilt of Diem bothered me not at all. From everything I had read, it was my presumption too.

What bothered me was that the question about "religious strife" seemed utterly unrelated to what I knew or understood of Vietnam. How strange it was, I kept thinking, that there was no echo, no recollection, no incident in any of my past experience that gave any clue to this Buddhist crisis. Precisely because religious tension had not been part of the political and cultural landscape at any time in the twentieth century, it had never occurred to me to discuss religion or philosophical beliefs in terms of possible conflict and strife within Vietnam. Certainly the newspaper reports of Buddhist monks rampaging through the streets collided with my own memories, for in all my previous contacts with Vietnamese Buddhists they had seemed sincerely to practice the spirit of nonviolence and compassion that was the soul of South Asian Buddhism, as I understood it. (Japanese Buddhism is another matter.)

Predeparture briefings by officials of the Kennedy administration were not much help in sorting out the whys and wherefores of the turbulent picture painted in the daily press.

At the State Department the prevailing tendency was to display a combination of anger and exasperation with the Diem regime. The Department line at the time was that Diem was guilty, at the least, of rigidity and of poor public relations in handling religious grievances created by a riot in Hué, the old imperial capital and university city. This key episode had been provoked by a dispute over the flying of Buddhist flags on Buddha's birthday, May 8. Blood was spilled on the cobbled streets of Hué, and the death toll was eight. Government troops were alleged to have been responsible for the deaths. If Diem would only be more conciliatory and stop repressing demonstrations, according to this dominant Department view, the Buddhists would be robbed of their complaints and the agitation would be brought under control.

As a State Department spokesman put it at the time: "We told

Diem from the very first that if he were not conciliatory, if he did not *admit the army's guilt* and fire those responsible for the killing at once, he would be in for it. But he would not take our advice. And so now we have a full-fledged religious crisis. The United States is getting a black eye all over the world because of Diem's repressions of the Buddhists. Diem's stubbornness has enabled the Buddhists to turn the incident—and their grievances—into a *cause célèbre*. And if you have the Buddhists against you, *you have the majority of the Vietnamese people against you,* and therefore the Buddhist agitation is bound to hurt the war effort."

Even though I knew that both precolonial and colonial Vietnam were overwhelmingly Confucian (which to the simple villager meant ancestor worship), I had no reason at the time to question this official's statement that "the majority of Vietnamese are Buddhists." Perhaps in recent decades the Buddhists had made enormous strides in propagating their faith. Further, in the summer of 1963 almost all news dispatches out of Saigon stated that seventy, even eighty to ninety, percent, of Vietnamese were Buddhists.

Now, if this percentage was correct, and if, as generally assumed, eighty to ninety percent of the Vietnamese army was also Buddhist, then it was potentially a serious situation. It was a crisis of major dimensions indeed if the Buddhist army officers and men were under the discipline of the Buddhist hierarchy, either directly or indirectly, and thus could be influenced by them to turn against their own government.

But even before I left for Vietnam I found that there were articulate persons inside the administration who challenged these assumptions. The discovery was made through a telephone call to Robert Kennedy, who in addition to being Attorney General was a key figure in the committee on counterinsurgency established by his brother President John F. Kennedy and was thus familiar with the situation in Vietnam.

The Attorney General closed our conversation with the injunction, "Don't leave the country without talking to General Krulak. He's just been to Vietnam and has the best perspective on the situation there of anyone I've heard."

General Victor H. Krulak, of the U.S. Marine Corps, who brought a keen, incisive mind to the problems of counterinsurgency, told me that the Buddhist agitation in Vietnam was *not* religious, but political. The Buddhists were *not* a majority of either the population or the army. The agitation in the cities was *not* affecting the war in the countryside, which had started going somewhat better in the spring and summer than at any time since the American operations began in earnest in February, 1962.

General Krulak's views on the Buddhist situation—which I discovered to be shared by many at the Pentagon, Central Intelligence Agency, and White House—were quite opposite to the prevailing State Department line. This was a hint of the struggle of furiously conflicting judgments and furiously conflicting advice that was soon to unfold under both President Kennedy and President Johnson.

Seldom has any drama had such weird, confusing, and spectacular ingredients. In a sense, it was not a single cohesive drama, but separate actions and denouements held together by the tough strands of tragedy. In Vietnam were the political dramas of Saigon and Hué, with overtones of religious conflict—real and bogus—warlordism, conspiracies within conspiracies, Viet Cong penetration, etc.

Back home was the inherent drama of a situation in which President Kennedy was persuaded to do the things that signaled the overthrow and murder of Diem (quite probably he did not realize that his actions led inescapably to these tragic ends) even though his own Vice-President—Lyndon B. Johnson—strenuously opposed the toppling of Diem for fear of political chaos and disintegration of the war effort.

And then, almost three weeks to the day after the murder of Diem, the world shuddered at the assassination of John F. Kennedy. And it was Lyndon Johnson who was left to pick up the already rapidly crumbling pieces resulting from a policy on Vietnam that he had bitterly and vainly opposed.

The core of the drama was, and is, the cause and consequence of the momentous and controversial U.S. decision to flash the green light that would topple an ally in the middle of a war against a common enemy. We had let allies go down the drain before. But we hadn't pushed them.

The central characters of the drama were the Ngo Dinh Diem family.

I had called on President Diem briefly in 1954 before leaving Vietnam, but considered it a journalistic waste of time. After all, everyone had said that Diem couldn't last six months and neither could South Vietnam.

But he had lasted, and now, nine years later, Diem was being portrayed by many as a monster of sorts who caused holy persons to burn themselves alive. As my plane hurtled toward Saigon I tried to reconstruct what had brought us to this pass. Strange, I mused, that two such violent nationalists as Ngo Dinh Diem and Ho Chi Minh, the Communist chieftain in Hanoi, should have been born in the same province and brought up in the same mandarin disciplines—the disciplines of the scholar, philosopher, administrator, and poet. In a way they secretly respected each other. At one point in the 1940's Ho Chi Minh tried unsuccessfully to get Diem to take a job in his government.

Diem's staunch anticolonialism was legendary. He served the French only once without friction. This was in 1923, when he became the youngest province chief in history in the area of Phan Rang. He must have been an extraordinarily good one, for when I went back to the villages near Phan Rang, the older men especially talked of him with esteem and reverence.

Later the French tried to enlist Diem in a higher post in the government by making him Minister of the Interior in 1933. The lure was the promise that he could reform the administrative system and work out a scheme under which Vietnam would break its colonial bonds. Diem resigned when the French promises were exposed as empty ones.

Yet so continuing was his influence among anti-Communist nationalists that Justice William O. Douglas, an authentic liberal, could report in 1953, after a tour of Vietnam: "Ngo Dinh Diem is a hero in Central and North Vietnam with a considerable following in the South too. . . . Ngo Dinh Diem is revered by the Vietnamese because he is honest and independent and stood firm against the French influence. There are few officials in the Vietnamese government who have that reputation."

When Diem finally was handed the reins of government, the time scarcely could have been more inauspicious. He was named Premier by Emperor Bao Dai on June 16, 1954. This followed the shattering war crisis that produced the Geneva conference on Vietnam, which resulted in the country's formal partition at the Seventeenth Parallel and the end of nearly one hundred years of French colonial rule.

The turning point of the crisis was the French defeat at Dienbienphu.

But contrary to myth, Dienbienphu was the *excuse for,* not the *cause of,* the French surrender in Indochina. At Dienbienphu France lost a battle, not a war. That battle involved the loss of only ten thousand men out of an army of two hundred and seventy thousand. As General John "Iron Mike" O'Daniel, chief American adviser in Vietnam, put it at the time: "The French have not been militarily defeated here. The French gave up—not because of Dienbienphu— but because French public opinion was fed up, French domestic politics was in turmoil, and the French economy a mess. The Viet Cong never defeated the French in any decisive way. They broke France's will to continue the struggle."

The distinction between a strictly military defeat and a broken will is an important one for Americans to remember.

During Dienbienphu, the United States made many desperate, eleventh-hour attempts to bolster France's will to fight. On several historic occasions the United States came close to military intervention on France's behalf.

In an interview in 1954, Secretary of State John Foster Dulles told me flatly that "the United States would not fail to consider an appeal for military help from the French if it were made in the proper context." Dulles had reference to several U.S. preconditions for intervening, such as an American demand that France announce unconditional and instant freedom for Vietnam. President Dwight D. Eisenhower and Dulles wanted to be sure that if the United States decided to enter the Vietnamese field of battle we would not be tainted with accusations of colonialism.

Admiral Arthur Radford, then chairman of the Joint Chiefs of Staff, argued in the early days of the battle of Dienbienphu in April, 1954, for a one-shot American aerial-bombardment effort designed to help, or at least ease, the French predicament.

Secret, and ultimately abortive, moves toward American intervention in Indochina were publicly prepared by a speech of March 29, 1954, in which Dulles had sounded the alarm from Washington.

"Under the conditions of today," Dulles said, "the imposition on Southeast Asia of the political system of Communist Russia and its Chinese Communist ally *by whatever means* would be a grave threat to the whole Free World community . . . and should not be passively accepted but should be met by *united action*. This might involve serious risks but these risks are far less than would face us a few years from now if we were not resolute today. . . ."

Behind the scenes President Eisenhower himself was doing his best to achieve the creation of an armed allied coalition that could intervene militarily in Vietnam to snatch the victory that the French had lost the heart to seek on their own. Indeed the persistently repeated statements to the effect that President Eisenhower counseled against ever having American troops involved in Southeast Asia under any conditions are historically false and misleading. The record shows that the opposite is true. What, then, of Eisenhower's public statement that it would be "tragic" to involve American soldiers in ground fighting in Vietnam? The explanation here is that even tragedy is relative. And to Eisenhower, even more tragic than American involvement was the prospect of losing all of Indochina to the Communist empire.

Thus, if Eisenhower had had his way, the United States, together with its allies, would have gone into Vietnam in 1954.

One proof of this is a letter to British Prime Minister Winston Churchill of April 5, 1954, in which President Eisenhower said: "I am sure . . . you are following with the deepest interest and anxiety the reports of the gallant fight being put up by the French at Dienbienphu. . . .

"Regardless of the outcome of this particular battle, I fear that the French cannot alone see the thing through, this despite the very substantial assistance in money and material that we are giving them. It is no solution to simply urge the French to intensify their efforts. And if they do not see it through and Indochina passes into the hands of the Communists, the ultimate effect on our and your global strategic position with the consequent shift in the power ratios throughout Asia and the Pacific could be disastrous, and I know unacceptable to you and me. . . . This has led us urgently to *take serious and far-reaching decisions*. . . . The preliminary lines of our thinking were sketched out by Foster in his speech last Monday night when he said that under the conditions of today the imposition on Southeast Asia of the political system of Communist Russia and its Chinese Communist ally, by whatever means, would be a grave threat to the whole free community, and that in our view this possibility should be met by united action and not passively accepted. . . .

"I believe that the best way to put teeth in this concept and to bring greater moral and material resources to the support of the French effort is through the establishment of a new, *ad hoc* grouping or coalition composed of nations which have a vital concern in the checking of Communist expansion in the area. I have in mind, in addition to our two countries, France, the Associated States, Australia, New Zealand, Thailand, and the Philippines. The United States government would expect to play its full part in such a coalition. . . .

"The important thing is that the coalition must be strong and it must *be ready to join the fight if necessary*. I do not envisage the need of any *appreciable ground forces* on your or our part. . . ." Thus Ike, far from being unwilling to "get bogged down" in Southeast Asia, was ready to commit at least some ground forces if necessary as early as Dienbienphu.

These American efforts to assist the French militarily, either collectively (through Ike's coalition) or unilaterally, came to nothing because the British would have no part of them, and additionally, because Washington and Paris were working at cross purposes.

All American moves were designed to keep France in the war, avoid a Communist triumph at the council tables, and play for time to get allied reinforcements to the scene. Our aim was victory over the Communist-controlled Viet Minh.

The motivations in France were far different. American military intervention in the form of an air strike was wanted, not because France had any intention of staying in the fight, but to enhance her position at the conference table. For by and large, the French were fed up with Vietnam and determined to negotiate their way out. The French had no interest in acceding to the type of U.S. involvement which would have compelled them to stick out that war until victory.

Even so, after the opening of the Geneva conference in April, various plans for American military intervention continued to be intensively discussed with French Premier Joseph Laniel and Foreign Minister Georges Bidault. But the Laniel-Bidault government was swept away on June 20 by the formation of a new government, headed by Pierre Mendès-France, who made it plain publicly that he was determined on peace at any price.

The Geneva agreement that partitioned Vietnam at the Seventeenth Parallel was never signed by either the South Vietnamese or the United States. President Eisenhower and Secretary of State Dulles were massively disappointed at the failure of their effort to keep France fighting and deeply disturbed at the implications of the agreement.

But once partition was an unavoidable prospect, Washington turned to the immediate problem at hand, which was to try and save what was left of Indochina. While the Geneva conference was still on, France was pressured into freeing South Vietnam from its status as a colonial dependency so that the Communists would no longer have that issue on their side. Dismayed at the demoralization of the French military, the United States was disposed to respond quickly to the urgent appeals of Ngo Dinh Diem's fledgling government that Americans take over military training and supply of South Vietnam as soon as possible.

One of the provisions of the Geneva conference stipulated that free internationally supervised elections be held throughout Vietnam in 1956 to reunify the country. These elections never took place because Diem insisted that in order to be meaningful such elections would have to be held in the Communist North as well as in the South. Ho Chi Minh, who in 1956 was already collectivizing and communizing the North, was never prepared to accept anything resembling the free-election concept involving international observers or monitors, as envisaged by the Geneva accord.

When Diem took over, South Vietnam was in chaos. The police were controlled by a bunch of gangsters known as the Binh Xuyen. The Chief of Staff of the Vietnamese army was a French puppet who openly boasted of the day when he would stage a *coup d'état* against Diem. The Hoa Hao and Cao Dai religious sects were run by warlords who constituted states within a state. Vietminh agents were everywhere. Economically the country was a mess, not just because of the war, but because of the exploitative nature of French colonialism, which had begun nearly a century before.

The French conquest of Indochina began with the seizure of Cochin China in 1862 and was complete by 1893. What were these alleged colonial abuses? As one example, when the French took over Vietnam, farmland had not been overabundant. Still, villages had had a unique system of communal fields which the landless peasants were allowed to plant and harvest. But by the time the colonial regime ended, sixty-three percent of the peasants in the North were landless, and in the South, where land had been in far more plentiful supply, seventy-five percent of all peasants were landless.

An equal misfortune was the decline of literacy during the colonial era, particularly in its last phases. For under the enlightened rule (by Asian standards) of Vietnamese emperors and mandarins, learning was revered. Even simple villagers often knew how to read and write. For the mandarins, on retirement, made it a kind of *noblesse oblige* to go back to their own villages to teach their own. But by 1954 only ten percent of the Vietnamese were literate. And these are but part of a long list in the lamentable litany of French colonial wrongs.

It is important to understand that Vietnam was by no means an ordinary underdeveloped country when France imposed itself by force, using as an excuse the persecution and massacres of the Catholics (a persecution that would never have taken place had not the

Vietnam Confucian emperors realized that the Catholic priests were
playing imperialistic politics and were in fact Trojan horses for the
French empire-builders). When the French first seized parts of Vietnam, it had already had two thousand years of recorded history. It
had learned to hate foreign rule. For Vietnam had endured more than
a thousand years (111 B.C. to A.D. 939) under Chinese colonial domination. But the Vietnam emperors and their armies had thrown out
the Chinese in an era when France itself, let it be noted, had not yet
experienced real nationhood. Subsequent Chinese attempts to re-
conquer Vietnam were successfully resisted.

The French triumph over Indochina was not by virtue of superior
civilization, but superior gunpower. The Vietnamese looked upon the
French as barbarians, a label which their behavior as colonialists did
little to disprove.

In writing of the problems facing Diem in July, 1954, historian
Joseph Buttinger has said:

When the Republic of Vietnam was created in July 1954, even friendly
and hopeful observers said that this new nation could not last for more
than two years. So strong was the belief of its early demise that its
existence today is frequently referred to as a political miracle—as if the
survival of this new state were not so much an unexpected as an essentially inexplicable event.

Ngo Dinh Diem was the leader whose record and talents made him
most fit for the task of building a new state out of chaos before anti-
Communist nationalism completely expired. His untainted integrity, his
tenacious refusal to compromise with colonialism, and his profound insight into the political nature of his enemies were topped only by the
courage he displayed toward friend and foe in creating the truly independent and strictly unified administration that his country needed then
more than food and arms.

Next to the survival of his political strength and personal integrity
during the corrupting and debilitating times of pseudo-independence
under Bao Dai, it is this re-establishment of administrative and political
unity that must be regarded as Ngo Dinh Diem's major contribution to
the "miracle of Vietnam." No one disagreed that the task was urgent;
everyone demanded that all unite, lest all should perish, but he alone had
the insight, rare among the contestants in any national crisis, that unity is
an empty word unless the conditions are accepted that can bring it about.
To spell out the terms on which the opposing forces are willing to unite is
bound to bring to light, as it did in Saigon in 1955, that unity can come

about only through the elimination of all elements incompatible with the existence of a healthy state. It is part of Ngo Dinh Diem's political greatness not to have succumbed to the deceptive magic of unity, to have refused to enter into it with elements of national disruption, and to have understood that the sects (Binh Xuyen, Hoa Hao, and Cao Dai), unhealthy products of the colonialist past, could not be appeased. . . .

Ngo Dinh Diem was controversial, of course, almost from the very start, caught in the center of violently conflicting Western judgments.

Historian Buttinger's "strong leader" became a "stern dictator" when viewed by William Henderson, assistant director of the Council of Foreign Relations.

President Diem's use of force to compel the Cao Dai and Hoa Hao politico-religious sects to bow to central authority becomes "a failure of leadership" when judged by David Hotham, former London *Times* correspondent in Vietnam.

The French, of course, intrigued against Diem from first to last. They never forgave him for refusing to collaborate with them.

Still, despite the violence of Diem's supporters and detractors, his rule survived the verbal assaults of the doom sayers. Since 1954 at least a million refugees from Communist North Vietnam had been settled (a miracle in itself), the bureaucratic machine rescued from anarchy, and the army brought under civilian control, rebuilt, and modernized. By 1959 Free Vietnam had *the highest per-capita income in that part of Asia.* No one could minimize these gains or deny that the Diem regime had, from the days of its turbulent birth, confounded the political doctors who had given it only six months to live.

The progress in South Vietnam was naturally anathema to Ho Chi Minh, whose regime was suffering from shortages of everything, especially food. In the early years of Communist rule, per-capita food production dropped ten percent in North Vietnam.

In Ho's Communist dictatorship, the breakneck pace of the land-reform program, plus its many cruelties, provoked a popular explosion on November 2, 1956, that has remained largely unchronicled in the West. For at the same moment, Soviet tanks were crushing the Hungarian rebellion and Western attention was riveted on that European tragedy. According to French officials in Hanoi, the Communist drive to deprive the North Vietnamese peasant of his land and force him on to collective farms was so bitterly resisted that at least fifty thousand were executed and twice that number sent to forced-labor camps.

In the South the Communist cadres that had gone underground since 1954 on Ho Chi Minh's orders never, of course, completely halted their harassment of the Diem regime and of the villages under the government's control. But in the American view, it was in 1959 that Ho Chi Minh decided that political pinpricks, political agitation, and terror by assassination would not be enough to topple Diem. And it was in 1959 that Ho Chi Minh began the substantial infiltration of trained Viet Minh officers and men into the South—an infiltration that by 1965 would place an entire Communist Red Army in the field in South Vietnam.

In mid-1959 Hanoi radio for the first time openly proclaimed that the "destruction of the Diem regime" was its target. In an address to the North Vietnamese Communist Party Congress of 1960, Ho Chi Minh spoke of the need to "step up the national democratic people's revolution of the south." The Congress called for the formation in South Vietnam of a liberation front. And in December, 1960, the so-called National Liberation Front of South Vietnam was duly proclaimed. It is, of course, the creature and creation of the North Vietnam Communist Party. Its propaganda line is dictated from the north and members of the N.L.F. travel abroad on North Vietnamese passports. The National Liberation Front acts as the political arm of the Viet Cong. After Hanoi's public call for "the destruction of the Diem regime," the tempo of assassinations skyrocketed. Between 1957 and 1959 the Viet Cong killed sixty-five village chiefs who had tried to resist Communist pressures. But by 1960 and 1961 village officials, schoolteachers, and health workers were being murdered by the thousands. In 1960, through harassment, plus the murder of teachers and sabotage of buildings, the Viet Cong succeeded in closing two hundred primary schools in South Vietnam, interrupting the education of more than twenty-five thousand students. And this is when the terror was just beginning to explode with full force, warning of horrors to come. At the same time, the Vietnamese Army was also beginning to lose officers and men in steadily rising numbers through deadly Viet Cong ambushes.

The second battle for Indochina was on.

In desperation Diem turned to the United States for emergency aid. He had argued in vain as early as 1958 that the villages ought to be prepared to fight guerrilla attacks, and had even made a trip to Washington to argue for the kind of weapons that could be used in counter-insurgency warfare. Diem feared, with good cause and considerable foresight, that Ho Chi Minh, once defeated politically, would again resort to force. Diem's pleas were initially turned down. But in 1961 President Kennedy sent a team headed by General Maxwell Taylor to survey the Vietnamese scene.

It was the Taylor mission that committed the United States once again to do what was necessary to try to help South Vietnam save itself from the new aggression unleashed by Ho Chi Minh.

The American military-aid mission to Vietnam began to operate in force in February, 1962. It was a mission that was to bring American forces directly into the war in much the same way that President Eisenhower had offered to do in 1954.

But by the summer of 1963 the competence of the American mission, the war against the Viet Cong, the credentials of Diem as a leader of men—all these things were thrown into doubt by the traumatic consequences throughout the world of those shocking Buddhist suicides by fire in the streets of Saigon.

Had Diem suddenly taken leave of his senses? Weren't the Viet Cong enough trouble? Why had he suddenly taken on the Buddhists —or had he? Had the man Justice Douglas described as a "revered Vietnamese hero" a decade earlier suddenly turned into a monster?

As our plane approached the lovely Vietnamese coastline—so jade green against the translucent China Sea—I decided that the first place to start a hunt for the answer was at the Xa Loi Pagoda, the headquarters of the Buddhists.

It would have astonished me to be told that before my articles could appear, some six weeks later, the United States government would have already unleashed the forces that were to achieve Diem's overthrow and murder.

CHAPTER 1

The Xa Loi Pagoda:
Buddha at the Barricades

From inside the ornate, exotic Xa Loi Pagoda, whose peaks thrust three stories high into Saigon's sky, there drifts on ceremonial days the mixed aroma of burning joss sticks and jasmine. In the spacious walled courtyard Buddhist monks and nuns wearing saffron or brown robes mingle with the Buddhist faithful—an extraordinary mixture. There are the beautiful slim Vietnamese girls with their tight-fitting white ao dais, their conical hats, long black hair hanging down to their waists, and often nowadays French pumps with high french heels. There are wizened old women in black pajamas with teeth black from chewing betel nuts, fresh-faced boy scouts, a pedicab driver, a beggar—and, back in 1963, a steady procession of Western newsmen and photographers.

For in the summer of that year, Xa Loi Pagoda, far from offering the soothing harmonies of meditation and mysticism, was a center of political and wholly irreligious excitement in Saigon that produced many grisly scenes. It was the Xa Loi that served as the turbulent command post for the Buddhist campaigns against the Diem regimes. It was here that the unrelenting mimeograph machines ground out the propaganda about alleged persecutions. It was from the small back conference rooms that orders went out to the suicide squads who set the stage for the fiery deaths of their confreres.

It was mid-July when, for the first time, I passed through the Xa Loi's iron-grilled gates and had a close look at the slogans emblazoned on the banners draped over its stucco walls.

With a public-relations focus on the Western press, the banners were for the most part written in English. The slogans that attracted my greatest interest said respectively:

"Youth of Vietnam be ready to sacrifice yourself for Buddhism!"

"Youth of Vietnam follow resolutely in the footsteps of Thich Quang Duc!"

Thich Quang Duc!

That name brought vivid and horrifying headlines to mind. It was his flaming death on June 11 that had riveted world attention on Vietnam. On that day he set the tragic precedent of suicide by fire.

The suicide took place in front of the Cambodian embassy. In the heat of the day, an Austin car drove up, out of which emerged Thich Quang Duc, who seemed to totter slightly and was supported by two fellow monks. Eyewitnesses have said that the aged monk seemed drugged. His appearance coincided with the arrival at the Cambodian embassy of a procession of monks who formed a circle around him. The seventy-eight-year-old Thich Quang Duc then seated himself in the lotus position and gasoline was poured over him. He tried to set himself afire with a small pocket lighter he carried. It failed to work. And so a monk in the circle stepped forward and turned him into a pyre at the stroke of a match. Western photographers were on hand to record the scene.

". . . follow resolutely in the footsteps of Thich Quang Duc," ordered the slogans on the wall.

Turning to Kim, my interpreter, I asked, "Isn't it illegal to incite to suicide?"

"Perhaps," said Kim impassively.

Our voices were instantly drowned by the shouts of a yellow-robed monk who was standing, megaphone in hand, haranguing the crowd from the roof of the pagoda souvenir shop.

Across the courtyard we saw another saffron-garbed monk coming down the steep steps to the side of the pagoda, and he was soon surrounded by Western newsmen.

The name of this monk was Thich Duc Nhiep, and during that turbulent summer this frail-looking twenty-four-year-old was to serve very skillfully as the spokesman for the Xa Loi's militant riot-prone Buddhists. Indeed the public-relations expertise of these Buddhists astonished me from my very first venture into the Xa Loi.

Spokesman Thich Duc Nhiep himself usually manned the busy Xa Loi switchboard, which sent flashes to the Caravelle Hotel (the head-quarters of some correspondents) and elsewhere whenever an "incident" occurred. He held press conferences, sometimes twice a day.

When I introduced myself, Thich Duc Nhiep smiled a big smile and said in somewhat stilted English, "Ah, Miss Higgins, you are from New York; how is the play?"

Not comprehending, I said, "Play—did you have some particular play—drama—in mind?"

"No, no, Miss Higgins," he said, gesturing elaborately to indicate the front page of a newspaper and headlines across it.

It dawned on me that he was using the newspaperman's term for whether a story is "played" well (i.e., given prominence and space) or not "played" well. This was certainly a degree of professionalism which I had not been expecting.

"Oh, you mean are the Buddhists getting headlines?" I said. When he nodded, I responded, "They certainly are. That is the main reason I am here."

A few hours later I had another surprise while I was waiting on an upstairs balcony of the Xa Loi for an interview with Dieu Hue, a Buddhist nun who was threatening to become the first woman to burn herself alive in the same manner as Thich Quang Duc.

On our balcony were several dozen monks leaning on the railing, on which they had propped some kind of mimeographed material in which they were deeply engrossed. I assumed it was some holy tract.

"Kim," I said turning to my interpreter, "I might as well start right now to find out just what this Vietnamese branch of Buddhism stands for. So please, very quietly, very politely, go over and ask one of those Buddhist monks what he is reading."

Those "tracts," it turned out, were digests of the daily crop of American newspaper stories featuring Buddhist agitations in Vietnam as compiled by the United States Information Agency. And it was quite a crop. The world limelight was on these Buddhists, and I could tell by the intensity of their concentration that they were exhilarated by it. And this exhilaration was to prove a very heady brew for some Buddhists for a long time to come.

The newspaper summaries preoccupying the monks were filled that day with stories advertising the publicly declared intentions of Dieu Hue to burn herself, and I was anxious to speak with her to get some insight into the motivations of these suicides by fire.

I had been told that Dieu Hue was an educated woman, the wife of the last minister of rites at the imperial court and the mother of Buu Hoi, an internationally famous scientist. What turn of fortune and life, I wondered to myself, leads an aristocratic Vietnamese woman into such a fantastic situation?

When I put the question that morning, tiny sixty-nine-year-old Dieu Hue took it matter-of-factly. She sat fairly engulfed in an over-stuffed sofa that with its bright chintz slipcovers seemed oddly out of place in the Xa Loi reception room. As she talked in her soft, tiny voice, she fingered amber-colored beads carried by Buddhists in Vietnam. Through the window poured the aroma of incense mixed with that of chopped onions and other highly seasoned foods that the monks use to enliven their vegetarian diet. We could hear the sound of chanting from ceremonies inside the adjacent pagoda.

"It all began," said Dieu Hue, "when Buddha appeared to me in a vision. It was thirty years ago. I was mortally ill. Miraculously, after the first vision of Buddha, I was cured. Ever since, I have felt that the time would come when I would help others by taking their suffering on myself . . . and after the events at Hué, I decided to offer myself."

Dieu Hue was reminded that she had said that she would forego her intended sacrifice by fire if the Diem government's attitude improved.

What about the conciliatory statements made by the government in the last few days?

Before she could answer, Thich Duc Nhiep, who was serving as interpreter, took over. "None of us has political motives," he said, "but under present conditions Diem is not good for South Vietnam."

Dieu Hue nodded vaguely, her mind, it seemed, on her prayer beads rather than on the conversation.

What did her son and husband think of her intentions to commit suicide?

Again Thich Duc Nhiep interrupted. "There is nothing in Buddhism," he said, "that prohibits self-immolation. And such a self-immolation would do a great deal to make the world see President Diem in his true light. In serving the cause of Diem's downfall, Dieu Hue would be serving the cause of Buddhism. . . ."

Wearied of these interruptions, I finally turned to Thich Duc Nhiep and said, "If you are such a great believer in suicides by fire, why don't you offer yourself in this sacrifice?"

"I am not a candidate for self-immolation," said Thich Duc Nhiep stiffly, as if that ended that.

It had been quite a morning. But the drama was only beginning.

At this point Dieu Hue rose to go, saying she was tired. Fortunately this nun never followed through on her threat to take her life in this horrifying way. Her son, Buu Hoi, an eminent scientist, talked her out of it. But her grim trancelike air left me fearing the worst on that momentous first visit to the Xa Loi.

As we were leaving the pagoda, my interpreter and I paused before a bulletin board around which an excited crowd had gathered.

It appeared that newly posted mimeograph sheets thumbtacked to the pagoda bulletin board contained names and places of alleged persecutions. I told my interpreter to take notes of those cases that were situated in areas where I might personally investigate the facts.

Overhearing my instructions, a young French-speaking monk told me that in Saigon the authorities were able to cover up persecutions and that the only way to find out about the "sufferings of the Buddhists" was to go to the countryside, places like Quang Ngai (in Central Vietnam).

Since, as it happened, I was scheduled for an early trip to Quang Ngai, I asked the monk to give me some specific instances of persecutions.

"In Quang Ngai," the monk said, "there have been cases in which the Catholic province chief has had Buddhists burned to death publicly in the streets because they would not convert to Catholicism."

I must have looked at him strangely, for the young man added, "And if you don't believe the Buddhists, go and talk to the Protestants in Quang Ngai City. They can tell you. They know."

To this day, I am sure that the young monk was utterly sincere and believed every word he told me about this and many other "atrocities" he cited for my tour of inquiry. It was some time, however, before I comprehended fully the skill and power of the Xa Loi propaganda machine which took advantage of the credulity, passivity, and respect of lesser monks for the higher-ups. Any accusation, however lurid, was accepted as gospel, especially by monks who had little or no education. For in Vietnam there are no educational qualifications for becoming a Buddhist monk. Anybody can shave his head and join a pagoda whether or not he knows a single Buddhist prayer or can read and write. Once inside the pagoda, all that is required of him is that he follow its rules. And that is why, of course, it was so easy for Communist agents to disguise themselves as monks.

There does exist in Vietnam an elite minority of Buddhist intellectuals such as Dr. Mai Tho Truyen, head of Saigon's Buddhist laymen's association, who eventually had their eyes opened. And it is not without significance that it was precisely such Buddhist intellectuals who were the first to turn against the extremist monks who sent Buddha to the barricades in Vietnam in the summer of 1963. It was the Buddhist intellectuals who, disapproving of such violent political agitation, broke relations with extremist leaders in 1964 and eventually exiled them from the Xa Loi Pagoda, transforming it once again into a place of peace and meditation instead of a haunt for bloody conspiracy and *coup d'états*. The exiled Buddhist extremists built a new pagoda about five miles from the Xa Loi, and this headquarters of political priests was the scene of much turmoil and tragedy in the years to come.

In point of fact, leaders of every faith and race have now admitted publicly and privately that the Communists have managed to infiltrate their ranks in some degree or other. This applies to Catholics as well as Confucianists, Cao Dai, Montagnards, etc. In any case such was the atmosphere in South Vietnam that summer that it was certainly not just the monks and antigovernment agitators who accepted the charges of persecution without attempting to check out the facts.

One midsummer day at the Xa Loi Pagoda, for example, Thich Duc Nhiep told reporters dramatically that 365 persons in a Saigon suburb had been arrested in a midnight sortie by police "because they were Buddhists." But when I went to the suburb in question, I found that a routine check was being made of a neighborhood through which the Viet Cong often infiltrate. With my interpreter, I intercepted them as they came out of the police compound. I talked to twenty persons—ancestor-worshipers, Cao Dai, Taoists, Catholics— before I finally found a Buddhist among them.

When I asked the local police chief why people had been picked up in the middle of the night he said, "This is a district through which the Viet Cong infiltrate into the city. We must make routine checks here, and the Communists do not sit around and wait for us to come and get them in daylight hours."

All those persons interviewed, including the Buddhist, described the incident as an identity check.

So the charge of "365 persons arrested for being Buddhists" was an invention. Nonetheless the next day that figure was headlined around the world. And if the Western press gave credence to such a story, why shouldn't Buddhists—many of them utterly unsophisticated in such matters—do the same?

In Saigon the Buddhist capacity to keep things stirred up—and catch world headlines—was seemingly boundless.

Aside from self-immolations, the most macabre incident occurred on a rainy Monday night when a lovely young eighteen-year-old girl was found on the steps of the Xa Loi Pagoda, her right arm bleeding profusely from what was, fortunately, an amateurish attempt to chop it off at the wrist.

Within ten or twenty minutes of this discovery, American photographers and reporters had converged on the scene. They had been summoned there by spokesman Thich Duc Nhiep in rush calls from the pagoda phones that always kept in close touch with American and other foreign correspondents. But what gave some observers pause was the fact that the Xa Loi monks kept the blood-drenched girl at the pagoda for at least forty minutes to make her available to photographers and the press. She even was asked—and consented—to make a tape-recorded statement. Only after all this was the "emergency case" taken to the hospital.

But there wasn't much reverence for anything at the Xa Loi in those days, possibly because the pagoda was littered with photographers and press people with their minds on how to get tipped off in time to be eyewitnesses at the next burning.

Some photographers—and photographers are not much for reverence anyway—could not pronounce Thich Duc Nheip's name and called him "Tic Tac Toe" for short. This flustered Thich Duc Nhiep not at all. He fielded questions with ease and did not bother to hide the fact that the suicides by fire were prearranged with a view to maximum impact on the American press.

It was commonplace at the Xa Loi Pagoda to hear the photographers say, "Hey, Tic Tac Toe, when's the next barbecue going to be?"

On one occasion he replied smilingly that it would be "very interesting" for the photographers to get to Hué by eight o'clock Wednesday morning.

It is two hours' flying time to Hué, and the Air Vietnam ticket is expensive. And so the photographers were enraged when they got all the way to the imperial city and there was "no eight-o'clock barbecue," to quote one of them exactly.

But Thich Duc Nhiep made it up to them. It appears he had been off about a week in his predictions. Soon thereafter there occurred not one—but two—"barbecues" in Hué.

But Thich Duc Nhiep was a minor actor in the drama that, as I was to find out later, involved such things as suicide squads organized to dispense horrific propaganda, as well as pills to ease pain, suicide letters, and canisters of gasoline.

The mastermind of it all was the enigmatic Thich Tri Quang, whose name I had not even heard until he summoned me on my third evening in town to go to the Xa Loi Pagoda to give me a message for President Kennedy.

CHAPTER 2

Machiavelli with Incense

When Thich Tri Quang sent for me, I went to the interview most reluctantly. His name meant nothing to me. And besides, I was on a different mission that evening when the telephone call came in from the Xa Loi Pagoda. I was rushing out to buy a pair of slacks to meet Air Force regulations on proper attire for combat missions, for I was due to leave at dawn the next morning on a military sortie into the boondocks.

It was the Caravelle Hotel concierge who intercepted me with the message that I had been summoned by a pagoda spokesman to go to the Xa Loi "to see the most important monk of all." The message stipulated that I was to come alone, without my interpreter.

At the Xa Loi, which was reverberating as usual to the hum of its indefatigable mimeograph machines, I passed rows of politely bowing monks in saffron robes and was ushered into the innermost sanctum. It was a small, cozily furnished room in the business wing of the Xa Loi.

There sat a monk in his forties, wearing gray robes. Deep, burning eyes stared out from a gigantic forehead. He had an air of massive intelligence, total self-possession, and brooding suspicion.

Thich Tri Quang was obsequiously introduced by a younger monk acting as interpreter.

"He is our most important leader," said the young monk, "and Thich Tri Quang rarely sees correspondents. But since you represent the White House . . ."

The light dawned.

I had used my White House press card around the pagoda that morning as identification. Perhaps, I thought to myself, that was the cause of the confusion. For the plastic press card carries an impressive picture of the White House. On the front of the card a big inscription in bold letters says "The White House." This is what catches the eye rather than the word "News" placed just above.

So I dug into my purse, got the press card out, showed it to the monks and said, "You don't understand; I don't *represent* the White House. I am *accredited* to the White House."

"Precisely," said the interpreter, triumphantly taking the White House card and showing it to Thich Tri Quang, who nodded sagely.

Obviously, a question of Oriental face was involved, or so I was beginning to conclude. I had been summoned to the pagoda on the representation to Thich Tri Quang that I had some special connection with the White House—and that, by the inscrutable logic of those who had summoned me, was the way it was going to be.

"You are accredited to the White House," repeated the interpreter. "And since you are only here for a short time [six weeks], we have a message for you to take back to President Kennedy."

Did Thich Tri Quang understand my true auspices? I don't know. In the interview I spoke sometimes in English, sometimes in French, always through the interpreter. Thich Tri Quang spoke only in Vietnamese, which I do not understand. I could not therefore gauge how faithfully my words were translated. But I do know that Thich Tri Quang seemed eager to get some ideas across to President Kennedy, and he seemed to think, at the beginning of the conversation anyway, that I was a proper conduit.

It was an extraordinary exchange, long, lasting two and a half hours, always intense, sometimes acrimonious. It began with Thich Tri Quang conducting a virtual interrogation about President Kennedy's views on President Diem, Russia, Buddhism, etc.

Warily I referred Thich Tri Quang to President Kennedy's press conferences, copies of which I said the embassy would surely be glad to furnish.

"But in his last press conference," Thich Tri Quang said, "President Kennedy spoke far too favorably of President Diem. . . . We had reason to believe that President Kennedy was on our side. And so we were puzzled."

While I was digesting this remarkable claim, Thich Tri Quang's voice slid smoothly on, "Besides, it would be most unwise for President Kennedy to appear to be associated with Diem's actions. There will be, for example, many more self-immolations. Not just one or two, but ten, twenty, maybe fifty. President Kennedy should think about these things. For these events will blacken President Kennedy's reputation as well as Diem's. . . ."

"Are you," I asked with some heat, "asking me to blackmail the President of the United States by passing on this threat?"

"Not at all," said Thich Tri Quang. "I am merely telling you what is going to happen."

I began to press him about why some kind of modus vivendi could not be arranged between the Buddhists and President Diem.

The dispute between the Buddhists and the Diem regime had seemingly started out as limited psychological warfare over limited objectives involving mainly protocol and property. The Buddhist demands, later vastly amplified, were at first primarily that the government permit Buddhist flags to be flown at public places (not just pagodas) during special religious observances. They also asked that certain laws (Ordinance No. 10, adopted under the regime of Emperor Bao Dai) be amended to permit the Buddhists to have greater opportunity to buy property. By the time I arrived in Vietnam, President Diem had already yielded to all but one of the original Buddhist demands (that he publicly accept guilt for the May 8 incident). But the ineptness of his police and in some cases their brutality vis-à-vis demonstrators gave the extremists a seeming justification for upping the ante.* For instance, the Buddhists began clamoring in the midsum-

---

*The extent to which professional agitators manipulated the 1963 crowds was not completely comprehended until precisely the same ones again turned up in antigovernment riots in Saigon in 1964–1965.

mer for an investigation of the Hué killings under credible conditions. But when Diem finally offered them an internationally observed joint investigation of this and every other alleged grievance, the Buddhists refused.

As a price for joining the investigation, they demanded that Diem *first* admit guilt for the Hué killings. In other words, the Buddhists demanded that the regime admit—prior to investigation—that it was in the wrong, though the whole point of an inquiry was to establish where the blame lay. At this Diem balked.

"What about the Diem offer to make concessions?" I asked. "And what about his proposal to have every single grievance investigated by an internationally supervised commission?"

"It is too late," said Thich Tri Quang with a shrug.

Who, I wanted to know, was Buddhism's candidate for President of Vietnam if the campaign against Diem should be successful?

Thich Tri Quang replied, "There are many others who could run South Vietnam . . . after all, it is a fact that men close to President Diem have tried to get rid of him before . . . they must have had someone in mind to take his place. . . ."

The next question was whether continued friction between the Buddhists and the government might not soften up the country for a Communist takeover.

"It might help the Communists to victory," conceded Thich Tri Quang.

"But," I interjected, "do you realize what would happen to the Buddhist religion if the Communists took over?"

"If the Communists take over," said Thich Tri Quang, "it will be Diem's fault, not ours. And besides," he added, "we cannot get an arrangement with the North until we get rid of Diem and Nhu."

If I had known more about Thich Tri Quang, I might have been less taken aback by his massive indifference to the fight against the Communists.

Even today Thich Tri Quang's past remains very much a mystery.

When did he emerge as the dominant monk at the Tu Dam Pagoda at Hué? Nobody knows for sure—or will say.

The famous Tu Dam Pagoda remains Thich Tri Quang's headquarters in Central Vietnam and is the political command post from which he launched his anti-Diem drive.

According to records of the French colonial office, Thich Tri Quang was twice arrested for his dealings with Ho Chi Minh. By his own admission he served after 1945 with Communist front groups working with Ho's Viet Minh army.

In a recent report sent to Washington based on conversations with Thich Tri Quang, our embassy in Saigon noted: "Tri Quang himself has said that he acceded to Viet Minh 'invitations' to collaborate with them in the 1940's and that in response to their demands he served 'passively' as chairman of the United Vietnamese Association, which was controlled by the Viet Minh and was located near his home village in Quang Binh province." The U.S. embassy further noted that Thich Tri Quang claimed he was able to leave the Viet Minh-controlled province "by a ruse." Thich Tri Quang also for a time led a Communist-front Buddhist organization collaborating with Ho Chi Minh. But this has to be measured against the fact that many non-Communist Vietnamese worked with the Viet Minh prior to 1954, out of a patriotic desire to rid the country of the French colonialists. In any case, Thich Tri Quang claimed to have fallen out with the Communists since then.

Again, according to the French, who still have representatives at Hanoi, Thich Tri Quang's brother is currently working for Ho Chi Minh in the Communist Vietnam's Ministry of the Interior. The duties of Thich Tri Quang's brother include the direction of subversion in South Vietnam.

Thich Tri Quang is a disciple of Thich Tri Do, who is now in Hanoi as a leader of the Buddhist puppet organization there. Buddhism in North Vietnam operates of course by favor of and for the purposes of the Communist regime.

Also, Thich Tri Quang has made some rather remarkable public statements concerning Communism, having asserted on one occasion that it was in his opinion entirely compatible with Buddhism.

None of this, of course, proved anything in the summer of 1963 about Thich Tri Quang's attitude toward either the Communist Viet

Cong or the so-called National Liberation Front, which in 1960 was formed in the South as the political arm of the Communists.

(Ho Chi Minh's Red army in the North is commonly referred to as the Viet Minh army. The Communist soldiers in the South, even though drawn in part from the Viet Minh, are called Viet Cong, which simply means Communist Vietnamese.)

But in that time of barricade and barbed wire it was clear that Thich Tri Quang has learned a lot from the Communists about organization and propaganda. He ran his emergency headquarters at the Xa Loi Pagoda like a company command post. Orders were barked out directing a demonstration here, a protest meeting there. Messengers scurried in and out carrying banners with their newly painted slogans that were remarkably similar to slogans used by the Communists.

There was something very Machiavellian about this monk—a kind of Machiavelli with incense. And I am by no means the only person to have registered this impression.

Denis Warner, writing in *Reporter* magazine, describes this scene that took place in early August, 1963, in the Xa Loi Pagoda:

"I have rarely met a man so sure of himself. In his drab gray robes, he dominated the strange scene. . . . Thich Tri Quang did not pretend that the Buddhist religious campaign was without political motivations. His plan, it appeared, was to continue forcing the government into rash acts against the Buddhists. . . . When I told him that the Special Forces of the army had been alerted to attack the pagoda, he smiled and answered: *'Don't you think it will help our cause if some of us are killed* [italics mine]?' "

One way to measure Thich Tri Quang's power was to watch him haranguing the mobs. The results were frightening. By the time Thich Tri Quang was through with the mobs, they would cheerfully go drown themselves in the Saigon River, if that were what he wanted. He was, and is, a true demagogue. Hate emanates from the man. Mobs thrive on hate.

Where did he gain his oratorical skill? This question points again to the controversy over his past.

Some highly placed American officers give considerable credence to reports that Thich Tri Quang was trained as a lawyer and that he in fact practiced law in the Communist North.

But when?

There are persistent reports that he went North to Communist Hanoi at some point after the 1954 Geneva partition of Vietnam at the Seventeenth Parallel. This is highly significant, if true. For with few exceptions the only persons in South Vietnam to choose Red rule were the organized Red Viet Minh army under the command of Ho Chi Minh. And they had no "choice"—they were ordered north. Some Vietnamese in Hué claim that Thich Tri Quang did not permanently settle into the Tu Dam Pagoda in Hué, his current headquarters, until 1958.

Thich Tri Quang himself isn't saying.

But those who maintain that he has been a clever Communist agent from the very first base their case in part on the shadow overhanging his movements from 1954–1958. If he was a Communist agent all along, of course, it would have been comparatively easy for him to move back and forth from Hanoi to Hué through clandestine channels. Since he spent much of his youth in Hué, it made good revolutionary sense to concentrate his maneuvers there.

How responsible are the persons who make the charge that Thich Tri Quang is either a Communist agent or cooperates with the Communists when it serves his purposes?

Among them is former Vietnamese Prime Minister Tran Van Huong, a Confucianist and as sane and sensible a person as can be found. He has said that there is evidence that Thich Tri Quang has collaborated with the Communists. He declares that documentary evidence exists that Thich Tri Quang worked to stir up insurrections against his government (November, 1964), which, if successful, "could have put the Communists in power in Saigon."

Major General Do Cao Tri, who commanded the first Vietnamese division at Hué, claims to have captured Viet Cong documents in September, 1963, naming Thich Tri Quang as an agent. He declares that a C.I.A. agent by the suitably anonymous last name of Smith exerted pressure to suppress the documents because they would have proved embarrassing to the Americans.

For by that time Thich Tri Quang had been given political asylum at the American embassy, where he had taken refuge on September 2, 1963, after the Diem regime raided the key pagodas involved in antigovernment agitation. The purpose of the raids was to take the Buddhist out of politics by rounding up key leaders of the revolt. But the most militant of them all—Thich Tri Quang—escaped and was given political asylum by Ambassador Henry Cabot Lodge. Thus the United States saved Thich Tri Quang from Diem even though Diem sought him on charges of seeking to overthrow his government.

And if indeed it turns out that Thich Tri Quang was cooperating with the Communists in any way, it cannot but prove mightily embarrassing to the United States, which sheltered him from the authorities who sought him on precisely these grounds—that he was abetting Communist subversion.

All this may explain why American officials directly involved in the Diem overthrow—and there are some still in government and at this writing in the Saigon embassy—sometimes react so defensively in Thich Tri Quang's behalf. Later (1964–1965), when Thich Tri Quang (as will be described) emerged as Vietnam's ace government toppler, few Americans disputed the fact that the chaos he created served Communist ends. Nonetheless, as late as 1965 Americans, especially younger officers who found Thich Tri Quang a man of great charm and fascination, were debating whether he was conscious that the chaos he created served the Communist Viet Cong or whether he was merely motivated by a desire to advance Buddhism.

It is certain that when Thich Tri Quang erupted on the national scene in May, 1963, he was literally unknown to either Americans or the Vietnamese authorities. And the mystery surrounding his past served him well.

The Americans were not the only ones played for a fool by Thich Tri Quang.

President Diem first began to make inquiries in depth about Thich Tri Quang in midsummer, 1963, when his insurrectionary activities had begun to alarm the government. Diem turned first to his brother, Ngo Dinh Can, who served as a kind of overlord of Central Vietnam, where Thich Tri Quang made his headquarters.

Ngo Dinh Can's initial response to President Diem was to tell him not to worry. As President Diem recounted the episode to me, Ngo Dinh Can expressed complete confidence in his ability to "handle" Thich Tri Quang.

"I have done him many favors," Ngo Dinh Can was reported as saying. "Therefore I feel he will be responsive to my counsel."

As it turned out, Ngo Dinh Can paid with his life for his inability "to handle" Thich Tri Quang. After the *coup d'état* it was Thich Tri Quang who led the pack in demanding Ngo Dinh Can's death by the firing squad.

Gratitude is not one of Thich Tri Qunag's strong suits. The Americans who had granted him asylum were disconcerted, for example, to find him in the forefront of the anti-American campaign. Soon after his departure from his U.S. asylum, his disciples in Central Vietnam even went so far as to accuse Americans of persecuting Buddhism.

His contempt for Americans appears complete. A staff member of the Saigon *Post* reports a conversation in which Thich Tri Quang said: "With the Americans, it is not so interesting any more. They are too easy to outwit . . . some of them persist in thinking they can 'reform' me into agreeing with them. . . . It is useful to smile sometimes and let them think so. . . . We will use the Americans to help us get rid of Americans. . . ."

It seems strangely unreal, looking back on the summer of 1963, that anybody could have still been in doubt about short-term Buddhist aims.

"What do the Buddhists want?" I wrote at the end of my Vietnam tour. "What they want is Diem's head, and not on a silver platter but wrapped in an American flag."

What I most certainly did not foresee was that "Diem's head, wrapped in an American flag," was precisely what the Buddhists would get.

As I emerged from the Xa Loi Pagoda, it was clear to me that Thich Tri Quang was hungry for power, exhilarated by the world's attention, and supremely confident of getting his way.

I remember at one point saying, "But if I repeat some of these things you are telling me, it could hurt you."

"That is not possible," said Thich Tri Quang, "because nobody will believe you."

And he was quite right.

In late August, 1963, I did print the key points of what he said, and few Americans believed me. Thich Tri Quang understood the automatic reflexes of Western opinion very well. The horrors of the self-immolation were such as to put world opinion automatically on the side of those from whose ranks the suicides came.

Any suggestion that a few ambitious Vietnamese in Buddhist monks' clothing might deliberately incite their disciples to suicide for their own political ends and in defiance of the true state of affairs was simply beyond credulity in those days and in that atmosphere.

But Thich Tri Quang was perfectly candid about what he was doing. When I asked him about the ethics of sending people off to fiery deaths for political purposes he merely shrugged his shoulders and said that "in a revolution many things must be done."

Why did I wait six weeks to print the extraordinary story of this monk? It is a good question, because the delay was a mistake if conveying a realistic portrait of the extremist Buddhist to the American people was important. In July the United States had not yet made its decision to dump Diem. Perhaps even a minority report in a paper like the New York *Herald Tribune* would have stirred up a few doubts in those who automatically assumed that the Buddhist politico priests were totally in the right and Diem totally in the wrong.

It was probably unfortunate that the confrontation with Thich Tri Quang took place on the third day of my midsummer visit in 1963. At that point I was still being mentally whipsawed by the confusing and conflicting versions in the U.S. government and the U.S. press about what was going on in Vietnam. And in all my U.S. briefings nobody had ever dropped a word about Thich Tri Quang. Indeed, as I left the Xa Loi Pagoda, I actually had doubts whether to take this monk seriously. Was he really, as his obsequious subordinate had said, the real power behind the Buddhist agitation? And what was to be made of his icily cool manner as he talked of "ten, forty, fifty" horrifying suicides? Wasn't there a quality of madness here? There wasn't time that evening to test my impressions on embassy officials, for I was leaving at dawn for the fighting fronts. But the truth is that I, like many Americans, greatly underestimated Thich Tri Quang for a long, long time.

In any case, by September the message I finally conveyed to President Kennedy about Thich Tri Quang was far different from what the monk intended. Instead of passing on his piece of blackmail concerning self-immolations and the Kennedy image, I tried at the White House to convey some of my own forebodings about these extremist Buddhists that had crystallized, finally, during my fact-finding tour of Vietnam. I think I made another mistake. If I had simply passed on the blackmail, it would have had more effect—if anything could have by that time.

It is clear that Thich Tri Quang understood the forces at play in the world of that time far better than I did. For even when I left Vietnam that summer I did not share Thich Tri Quang's conviction that the United States would take his side in the battle against Diem.

But I was wrong.

CHAPTER 3

The Countryside: American Myths and Vietnamese Realities

The Montagnards, their spears at their sides, stood at rigid attention in the brand-new village whose bamboo fence cut into the vast sweep of jade-green plateau that stretches like a Shangri-la between the shelter of Vietnam's soaring seven thousand peaks in the Northwest highlands.

How do the Montagnards (non-Buddhist mountain people) feel about the Communist Viet Cong guerrillas?

Their chieftain stepped forward to show a badly butchered hand and arm. It was the cruelty of the Viet Cong, he said, that was bringing his people (perhaps a million strong) away from their beloved mountains and nomadic ways to the villages in the lush emerald plateaus.

Now shift the scene south of Saigon, far away from the mountains and deep in the dull, flat, muddy delta, where a wizened Buddhist monk, considered a saint by the local villagers, shook his head disapprovingly at the news of the fiery Buddhist suicide in Saigon. It was a suicide of which he had heard for the first time from this writer.

Standing outside his small pagoda at the side of a charming water-lily-gorged stream, the Buddhist monk said, "I do not understand it at

(36)

all. I would not kill a fly myself. Buddhism does not believe in the taking of life in any form—even by suicide."

The saintly monk's attitude was my first inkling of how wrong were those Americans who assumed that Thich Quang Duc's fiery suicide would produce the same instant horrific impact in a backward, illiterate Oriental country like Vietnam as it had in an advanced, televised, Western nation like America.

But what about persecution or discrimination against Buddhists such as himself or his congregation?

"White people do not understand Vietnamese," said the Buddhist monk in gentle, aggrieved tones; "Vietnamese are very tolerant. There is no discrimination. There are many Cao Dai [a mixture of Western and Eastern religions] in this village, but they are our friends. So are the Catholics. Our village chief [a Buddhist] distributes fertilizer and rice seed without asking anybody his religion. The Catholics don't get more than we do, nor than the Cao Dai do, nor do we get more than the others."

Back to the North again, in the arid coastal plains of Phan Rang province. A Moslem leader of Vietnam's Cham tribesmen (of Indonesian origin) stood outside a village mosque with its blue mosaic dome and looked puzzled at the stranger's question. The villagers who crowded around seemed equally bemused.

"We know nothing of any religious persecution," said the Moslem priest. "President Ngo Dinh Diem was province chief here   [beginning in 1923]. He may be a Catholic, but he helped our people build mosques and did more for us than any other province chief has ever done. Now he sends us rice, seed, and water [a big dam was being built in the area]. And so we are grateful to President Diem."

This is a fragmentary picture of the attitudes that I found everywhere in that summer of 1963 in the deep rural countryside during journeys that took me to all four Vietnamese army corps areas in which the war was being fought. There in the rice paddies and the mountains live eighty-five percent of South Vietnam's estimated fourteen million people. It is there in the countryside that the war will be won or lost. And this remains true even though Saigon, if coup fevers give way to surrender fevers, might of course prevent the war from being won by simply giving up.

The attitudes in the countryside were in forceful contrast to the ferment in Saigon and Hué, where the citified Vietnamese sipped their *apéritifs* in the cafés of the elegant Rue Catinat and gossiped and criticized and squabbled and plotted. When I returned to Saigon for the seventh time in 1963, I found many of the same people plotting against the government—and each other—as were conspiring against the French—and each other—a dozen years earlier in 1951.

And the irresponsibility of the educated elite had, of course, plagued Vietnam long before Diem's rule. In 1945, for example, the Japanese occupiers of Vietnam, seeing the handwriting of defeat on the wall, renounced on March 10 their wartime rule and handed Emperor Bao Dai his country's long-sought independence.

Since the Japanese were in *de facto* control and the return of effective French rule was still many months away, the Emperor, then a young, idealistic, and popular figure, just might have consolidated a free anti-Communist Vietnam under his leadership if his nationalist ministers had had the courage and will to stop quarreling among themselves and set about the business of governing.

But as Donald Lancaster, author of *The Emancipation of French Indochina,* has observed, the young nation's leaders preferred instead to "indulge unchecked their political pretensions and childish vanity in an orgy of demonstrations, processions, and public meetings, which contributed toward the paralysis of the administrative machine." As usual, the free Vietnamese were too busy maneuvering against each other to concentrate on the real enemies and real problems. In the process of the ensuing economic disintegration and famine, more than a million Vietnamese died of hunger. Bao Dai's ministers failed not only him but also the cause of Free Vietnam. For their failures played into the hands of both Ho Chi Minh's Communist forces and the French colonialists. Both vied to move into the vacuum created by the weakness of the Emperor's ministers and in the process collided with each other. Thus began the titanic struggle known as the First Indochinese War (December, 1946).

The trouble is, of course, that plotting in Saigon is a national pastime for the elite, as chess is for the Russians. For a cruel and mocking history has turned the Vietnamese "intellectuals" into full-time "aginners." (I put quotation marks around the word "intellectuals" because the French colonial policy permitted remarkably few Vietnamese to attain scholarly eminence or even a well-rounded education.) In a century of French rule the accent of the elite was on the negative. But even after the French departed, the "intellectuals" of Vietnam, like revolutionaries everywhere, found it easier to revert to plotting than to work constructively for their own nationalist government. Besides, being in the opposition had a lot more *élan*. Part of the trouble with the Vietnamese intellectuals is that they have lost a sense of national identity. They seem uprooted, unsure, alienated, because their French educations, which for so long were the only road to advancement, have also in many cases frayed or severed altogether their deep taproots to their own profoundly Confucian culture. By the end of World War II disobedience had become a virtue, anarchy a way of life. The juices of dissent served both to stimulate and to deceive the worldlings of Saigon.

Not so in the villages.

The French have come and gone, the Viet Cong have come and (sometimes) gone, and yet the Vietnamese village still slumbers, wakes, and works largely as it has for centuries. Behind the great bamboo hedges that so often hide its wooden houses and thatched roofs there is a sense of order and harmony. As through the ages, the village retains a remarkable degree of autonomy. For the most part the village elders are elected or chosen by consensus. The French destroyed the educational framework that under the mandarinal system of the Confucian emperors resulted in a degree of literacy in the villages. But even today, illiterate as they are, most villagers still hand down the wisdom of Confucius, father to son, in such things as the rites and ceremonies connected with the cult of the ancestors.

And in the summer of 1963, as I wandered from village to village, north, south, east, and west, it became perfectly clear to me that so-called "religious persecution" had nothing whatsoever to do with the realities of life as experienced by the overwhelming majority of people in the countryside. Further, most people in the countryside did not have any notion of what was going on in Saigon, or for that matter, ten kilometers beyond the village.

One day in Quang Ngai province, which is north of Saigon, I went to a string of eleven different strategic hamlets before I found anyone who had even heard of the fiery death of Thich Quang Duc. And the person who knew was in effect a city slicker—a Vietnamese from Quang Ngai City, the province capital, who had come to the hamlet to visit his mother and father. And this is typical. In the provinces, Saigon is much farther away than the moon. For the peasant sees the moon and knows its effect. He does not see Saigon or know its effect directly.

For example, I asked a respected village notable in a strategic hamlet near Quang Ngai if he had heard about the troubles in the city.

"I try to keep up on things," he said, "and twice a year a woman who lives in a house six lanes away sends her son by bicycle to the city [province capital] to buy a newspaper, and we get someone to read it to us. But this year the rice crop was very good, so good that the lady could not spare her son, so we did not get any newspapers."

Now, this village notable was intelligent. In our conversation he explained to me clearly and charmingly how the cult of the ancestors helped to keep harmony inside the village. But as for Russia, France, England, or President Kennedy—he had never heard of them. But the old Vietnamese nodded and lit up when I brought up the word Americans.

How did he happen to recognize the word?

"Last year," he explained gravely, "there was only one rice crop. The rice was yellow and people were hungry. But this year some white people called Americans brought some magic poison [*sic*] to kill the rats that ate our rice. And this year we had two rice crops and the rice was very green. Also the Americans brought us tanks that swim. So we have had a big victory over the Viet Cong. Our *district chief* [italics mine] told us that a good man named Ngo Dinh Diem has a government that made it possible for the Americans to bring us the magic poison and the tanks. And so we are in favor of this man."

In the Mekong delta, to the south, Buddhist monks and nuns were politely incredulous when I told them of the suicides by fire in Saigon and elsewhere. When I brought out a worn newspaper clipping (which was usually read out loud in Vietnamese by my interpreter) to prove my point, their incredulity would often shift to disapproval.

Wiser than the West in the ways of their own countrymen, the villagers to whom I showed my newspaper clipping never fell into the trap of equating voluntary self-burnings with a deliberate policy of persecution on anybody's part.

One Buddhist monk, fingering his brown beads, said firmly, "No true Buddhist would commit suicide. It is written in the verses of Buddha that suicide is wrong. Buddha says that a man's responsibility is to mend his own life, not to meddle in politics. So those men who are, according to your newspaper article, marching in the streets are not Buddhists. They betray Buddhism."

"But," I interjected, "these people are believed by the Americans to represent Buddhism."

"White men," said the Buddhist monk sadly, "have brought many things to Vietnam. But white men have not brought much understanding to Vietnam."

It was a remark that was to haunt me.

(Nonetheless, as will be explained later, there are some Buddhists who justify suicide and various forms of self-torture in honor of Buddha. This is a controversial point because the original teachings of Buddha, as for example the Dhammapada, specifically forbid the taking of life in any form.)

In the same village was a whitewashed Cao Dai temple. In it the Cao Dai high priest and half a dozen followers were burning incense before a painting portraying a group of favorite Cao Dai saints. These are chosen not according to religion but according to moral worth and accomplishments. In this particular temple the portraits included Joan of Arc, Jesus Christ, Victor Hugo, Sun Yat-sen, Buddha, and Muhammad, among others.

It was the same story with the Cao Dai. According to the Cao Dai priest, they had heard nothing of the turbulence in the cities. The rice crop had been particularly good in their region and the people of the congregation had been laboring hard. And besides, many villagers were cooperating in the defense of the area. When there is farming in the daytime (and Vietnamese rice growing is backbreaking) and guard duty at night, life is especially burdensome, leaving little time and energy for other pursuits.

Because the Cao Dai priest could not read, I asked the interpreter to tell him the key points of the newspaper article concerning the suicide of Thich Quang Duc and subsequent demonstrations and riots.

Turning to me, the Cao Dai priest asked: "Aren't these demonstrations against the law?"

"Yes," I answered. "They are illegal."

"Disrespect for authority is bad," he said, "especially in time of war. The Viet Cong are very clever. They could get into a mob and make trouble. We would not permit this kind of thing in our village."

Up in the mountainous highland, isolation from world events was even greater among the Montagnards than among the Vietnamese. In contrast to the Vietnamese, the Montagnards are not Mongol in appearance. They seem to be of Polynesian or Indonesian extraction. The Montagnards are of great importance to South Vietnam because geographically they occupy at least half of it. The experts dispute the number of Montagnards in South Vietnam. Some say close to one million. Others say close to two million.

One summer day, after having been "initiated" into the Jirai tribe in ceremonies near Pleiku, I quickly discovered in a conversation with the village chieftain that I was not going to get anywhere trying to probe the question of religious persecution here. I brought the subject up by asking what the attitude there toward Buddhism was. But my interpreter, a French-speaking Montagnard, turned back to me and said, "Our chief does not understand your question. He wants to know if Buddhism is something to eat?"

These tribesmen still carry spears and their women go barebreasted. They are extremely handsome people, although their looks, in a Westerner's eyes, are not enhanced by their habit of filing down their teeth.

Members of the tribe told me that they believed in spirits of soil, water, and trees. If a member of a family feels ill, a sacrifice of chicken or pigs would be made to propitiate the spirits.

Not just with Montagnards, but everywhere among the ordinary people of Vietnam, I found it difficult to talk meaningfully about "religious persecution," because this term, as we Westerners mean it, has no relation to Vietnamese existence. A common dictionary definition of persecution is "to cause to suffer because of religious belief."

But Montagnards were not "made to suffer" because they sacrificed animals to the spirits. Buddhists were not "made to suffer" because they went to pagodas. Confucianists were not "made to suffer" for practicing the cult of the ancestors. Cao Dai were not "made to suffer" because they went to Cao Dai temples.

In modern times no Vietnamese has been socially handicapped or "discriminated against" by the government because of his religion, even to the extent this still happens to some Americans of the Jewish faith in the United States.

Never in history has a Vietnamese paper carried an advertisement saying "No Buddhist need apply." But as the Kennedy family well remembers, ads saying "no Irish need apply" were a fact not so long ago in the civilized city of Boston in advanced America. No Buddhist was barred under Diem from any residential area or school or job because of his beliefs.

More than half of the forty-two different province chiefs in Vietnam were Buddhist, ancestor-worshipers, Confucianists, Cao Dai, etc.— that is, non-Catholic. Turn this around, and the picture is that nearly half of all province chiefs were Catholic. With education left in a lamentable state by the French, it is true that the Catholics, being better organized than other faiths, tended to be better educated. It is also true that the Catholics are probably the most militant anti-Communists, although the Hoa Hao sect is not to be slighted in this respect. But even in a nation at war, perhaps Diem relied too heavily on his coreligionists in his choice of province chiefs. A case can be made for the fact that Diem, being a Catholic, should have bent over backward to make it irrefutably clear that he was not playing favorites.

But in Diem's immediate entourage—his cabinet—there were only *six Catholics out of seventeen men*. The Vice-President of Vietnam,

Nguyen Ngoc Tho, was a Buddhist and was in charge of the efforts to achieve a truce with the Buddhist extremists.

In the military sphere most generals were Confucianists, Buddhists, and Cao Dai. Out of seventeen generals on active duty, three were Catholic and the rest non-Christian.

What of the charge that the Catholics were permitted to have military chaplains while the Buddhists were not? The charge is certainly factually correct. But as usual in Vietnam, things are not as simple as they seem. For one thing, Buddhist monks were exempt (by Diem's order) from the draft, whereas Catholic priests were not. For another, until May, 1963, the Buddhists never asked for chaplains to accompany troops in combat for the reason that Buddhist monks oppose war.

For example, Thich Tinh Khiet, who is the senior monk in Vietnam, told several members of the United Nations investigating mission in the fall of 1963 that "it is not necessary, according to Buddhist belief, to have a chaplain because Buddhist priests do not want to see any battlefield."

But Thich Tinh Khiet is a truly religious monk and his attitude was criticized by the militant politico priests like Thich Tri Quang, who, as his later actions proved, looked to Buddhist chaplains to serve his political aims. When Buddhist chaplains were finally accepted by the Vietnamese army in 1964 by orders of General Khanh, many chaplains began to tell the soldiers that they did not have to obey their leaders. On one occasion an item on the bulletin board at the Buddhist institute boasted that four Vietnamese army regiments had been subverted and in a political crisis would do the bidding of the extremist Buddhists rather than follow orders. In a riot against the U.S. embassy in Saigon in January, 1965, monks, nuns, and other demonstrators were brought to the scene of "battle" in Vietnamese army trucks. Because of these activities, Secretary of Defense McNamara brought pressure to bear on the Vietnamese military council *to abolish Buddhist chaplains or at least confine them to religious duties*. But this was never done.

In mid-1963 there was a host of rumors about favors granted Catholics by President Diem or his brother Archbishop Ngo Dinh

Thuc at Hué in Central Vietnam. There were also rumors of enforced conversions. One example was the rumor passed on by the Xa Loi Buddhists to the effect that Buddhists had been burned in the streets of Quang Ngai City because they refused to convert. This last, of course, proved to be nonsense. Even the Buddhists of Quang Ngai Pagoda acted as if they thought I had lost my mind when I inquired about the rumor.

Eric Wulff, the German doctor of Hué, has written articles giving credence to stories of forcible conversions by overzealous Catholic officials seeking to curry favor. He cites the account given by a cook of one of his German colleagues, but gives no name. Such a lack of specifics makes verification difficult. This does not mean that some of this proselytizing may not have gone on. It probably did, but the evidence indicates that if enforced conversions occurred, this was *in spite of* Diem's wishes, not because of them. In the long view, his deeds were not those of a man trying to stamp out Buddhism.

For example, in the Diem years at least 1,275 new Buddhist pagodas were built and 1,295 were restored, more than at any time in modern Vietnamese history. Would a man intent on "forced conversions" have permitted, and indeed in many cases partially financed, building of new Buddhist pagodas? I have always thought it significant that Buddhist leaders of Vietnam in their writings of the Diem period* boasted that a "renaissance of Buddhism" was taking place. By 1963 there were 4,776 active pagodas, as compared with 2,206 in 1954, the year of Diem's takeover.

Further, the records show that the Vietnamese government contributed nine million Vietnamese piastres to various Buddhist organizations to help in construction and reconstruction of pagodas.

Efforts of Diem's critics to "prove" religious persecution have taken many forms.

Professor Bernard Fall, a Frenchman who has always shared his countrymen's historic aversion to Diem, attempts in his book *The Two Vietnams* to "lay to rest once and for all the *myth that Diem never persecuted the Buddhists.*"

*"Buddhism in Vietnam," by Dr. Mai Tho Truyen.

How is the myth of religious tolerance laid aside? Professor Fall tries to prove the existence of religious persecution by citing the following quotation from Australian journalist Denis Warner:

"In July 1961, I went from Saigon to Vinh Binh province to watch six army and newly trained civil guard battalions with artillery and naval support launch a major drive. . . . But the Viet Cong slipped away as the artillery blazed fruitlessly into the line of advance. No one saw anything wrong in this. . . .

"The following month, after the army had retired . . . Buddhist bonzes petitioned the province chief in Tra Vinh against the shelling of hamlets and pagodas. . . . Some months later Superior Bonze Son Vuong appeared on the lists of the central committee of the Viet Cong's National Liberation Front. . . ."

Now, if, as Professor Fall alleges, being hit by your own artillery—or any artillery—is "religious persecution," there are a lot of water buffalo, ducks, geese, elephants, American advisers, and American war correspondents in Vietnam who have, and are, being "persecuted." But badly aimed and badly used artillery surely cannot be equated in fairness and reason with religious persecution, Professor Fall notwithstanding.

Certainly after my 1963 journeys through Montagnard country, to Cao Dai temples, Confucian temples, Muslim mosques, and other havens of worship, it seemed unreasonable to believe that such a wondrously diverse country could be "seventy to ninety percent Buddhist" or seventy to ninety percent anything at all.

And the General Buddhist Association, which was dominated by the extremist rabble-rouser Thich Tri Quang, clearly did not represent most Buddhists. Innumerable pagodas I had visited in the Mekong delta (the most heavily populated part of the country) were not affiliated with the General Buddhist Association and were hostile to the idea of getting Buddhism mixed up in politics.

As to the Buddhist numbers game, one good source is Dr. Mai Tho Truyen, who is director of Buddhist laymen in Saigon. In his authoritative booklet "Buddhism in Vietnam" he states that the General Buddhist Association totals a million members plus three thousand monks and three hundred nuns. Additionally, there are three million

Buddhists who are *spiritually* linked to the association even if they are not *formally* attached to any of its pagodas. So by this account, Buddhists would still represent less than thirty percent of Vietnam's fourteen million people.

The Defense Department, in its "Pocket Guide to Vietnam," gives a generally sound breakdown between the various religious and ethnic groups which, as amplified by various Vietnamese authorities and other experts, produces the following picture: Out of the fourteen million people in South Vietnam there are 1,500,000 Catholics; 500,-000 other Christians, including Baptists, Mennonites, Seventh-Day Adventists, and converts of the Christian and Missionary Alliance; 1,000,000 animists (these include mainly the Montagnards who worship the gods of the soil, river, etc.); 1,500,000 Cao Dai (believers in a mixture of Eastern and Western religions and worshiping as saints diverse figures such as Victor Hugo, Joan of Arc, and Sun Yat-sen); 1,000,000 Hoa Hao (a new religion, founded in 1939, containing elements of magic and Buddhism—its founder, Huynh Phu So, was famous as a teacher and miracle healer and preached that pagodas were not necessary to the worship of the Enlightened One); 4,000,000 Confucianists, who at the peasant level are simple ancestor-worshipers (these include the nearly one million Chinese who were left over from the one thousand years in which China ruled Vietnam); 500,000 Taoists (again a heritage of the many years of Chinese rule); 500,000 Hindus and Muslims (these include the Cham tribesmen, the human relics of the once-proud Champa Empire that was conquered by the Vietnamese).

Add up all these figures and the result is that 10.5 million people of Vietnam are *not* Hinayana or Mahayana Buddhists. This leaves 3.5 million such Buddhists at most, *eliminating* those who have no beliefs at all.

Buddhism is, will be, and has been a deep influence in Vietnam. Its impact on architecture, poetry, literature, and custom has been vast. The high point of Mahayana Buddhism in Vietnam was in the Ly dynasty (1009–1225), when some of the emperors themselves became monks. But there is a crucial difference between saying that Buddhism is *important* and claiming that it is *all-important*. This distinction is vital because so many American policies have been based on errors of judgment in the matter.

For example, the Washington moves leading to Diem's death were based in important part on this argument that Vietnam was overwhelmingly Buddhist, that the agitation of the Buddhist Association extremists represented Vietnamese Buddhism as a whole, that resentment against Diem's repression of this agitation was bound to spill over into the countryside, that the morale of the army and the peasants would therefore be undermined and the war effort hurt.

But this analysis was wrong, as experiences and evidence cited in this chapter are designed to show.

Since this error is basic to the developing drama and tragedy of Vietnam in 1963, I think it is important to recapitulate here the reason this judgment was mistaken:

Buddhists, far from composing the "overwhelming majority," comprised at most about thirty percent of the population, with maybe fifteen percent being pagoda-going Buddhists.

The extremists of the Buddhist Association, far from speaking for Vietnamese Buddhism as a whole, represented but one small faction or one out of *fourteen* rival Buddhist sects and therefore spoke for a minority of the Buddhist movement.

Orthodox, or pure, Buddhists, far from sympathizing with the turmoil instigated by this faction of Buddhists, disapproved of politicking by violence.

The demonstrations engineered by this Buddhist faction involved in any case only a fraction of Vietnam's urban population (the *New York Times*, which was highly sympathetic to the Buddhists, estimated that only a total of sixty thousand persons in four cities turned out on July 31, which was the day set by the Xa Loi headquarters for a general strike and demonstrations).

Most peasants, with their village-bound horizons, knew nothing and cared less about events in Saigon. They knew only about the things immediately affecting them, such as the supply of rice seed, insecticides, and protection from the Viet Cong. These things were in more plentiful supply in South Vietnam in the summer of 1963 than at any time since Hanoi renewed its campaign of killing and terror in South Vietnam in late 1959.

Most soldiers (as anyone who has been under fire with troops in war knows) are motivated by their training, by their immediate chances, and by their regard and/or fear of their commander and buddies. Despite what was going on in some cities, the Vietnamese army was doing better than ever before in the summer of 1963. According to U.S.-government figures, the summer tempo of attacks by the Viet Cong had sunk to a new low—an average of about two hundred to three hundred incidents a week as compared with five hundred a week in the previous summer, 1962. More of Vietnam was clear and free from Viet Cong control than at any time before—or since—the renewed fighting turned into a real war (1961).

But Americans are not the only ones to have had problems grasping the realities of Vietnam.

Jean Pleyber, an authority on Vietnam by virtue of thirty years spent in the country as a high French official, wrote in 1963 in the Paris weekly *Rivarol* concerning the "origin of the mistake so widespread in the white world that the yellow races are all Buddhists":

The sources of the error may go as far back as the navigators of the eighteenth century, who made only brief stops in Indochina and whose short stays did not permit them to penetrate to the interior of the country and know its people. The Catholic missionaries made no such error. They realized very well the distinction between the *Buddhists, who had no power at all* [italics mine], and the Confucianist leaders, who represented the royal authority and the mandarins.

Where did this absurd confusion arise between Buddhist and Confucian doctrines? One reason, of course, is the massive ignorance of the West on the subject of religion. Also, at the time of the French conquest, colonial soldiers made no distinction between the Buddhist pagodas [Chua in Vietnamese] and the Confucian temples [Dinh in Vietnamese]. These soldiers called any religious-looking building they saw a pagoda. The confusion went so far that in Hanoi today there is a "pagoda" of the Great Buddha which is in fact a Confucian temple built in honor of the spirit of the North Wind and containing a giant statue of this spirit. . . . There are many such examples. The Vietnamese are of Chinese and Confucian culture. . . . On several occasions in the course of the centuries

Buddhism was persecuted in Vietnam [italics mine] but not for reasons of religion but because (Confucian) mandarins considered Buddhist doctrines of renunciation of the world to be against the interest of the family and the state. The same Confucian emperors also persecuted the Christians. *It was never the Buddhists* [italics mine] who persecuted the Christians or anybody else, as they had no power to do so. This point is made to answer ignoramuses who imagine that President Diem as a Catholic was taking vengeance on the monks for some persecutions once endured by his coreligionists. . . .

It was in the fifteenth century that a Vietnamese form of Confucianism became the state religion. The Emperor of Vietnam was the high priest of the religion and the mandarins were the guardians of Confucianism in the provinces.

The imperial decision in favor of making Confucianism the state religion naturally inhibited the institutional growth of Mahayana Buddhism, which, like Confucianism itself, had been imported from China.

Some American reporters in Saigon have stated repeatedly that "most Vietnamese feel themselves to be Buddhist." I have never understood this formulation.

Cao Dai do not "feel themselves to be Buddhists." Muslim Chams do not "feel themselves to be Buddhists." Educated Confucianists such as former Prime Minister Tran Van Huong most certainly do not "feel themselves to be Buddhists." Peasant ancestor-worshipers that I interviewed did not "feel themselves to be Buddhists." In the case of these peasants, I always began the conversation by saying, "Are you a Buddhist?" The easiest answer could have been yes. But the peasants said instead, "No, I practice the cult of ancestors," or made other responses indicating they knew the difference between their own religious practices and Buddhism.

There is a Vietnamese saying that "all Buddhists are ancestor-worshipers but not all ancestor-worshipers are Buddhists." And this statement is closer to the truth.

Vietnamese Confucianists practicing the cult of the ancestor believe that the souls of the departed are immortal: These souls wander in the air around us; and it is the duty of the descendants to keep these souls content by ceremonial offerings of food, wine, gold, silver, and other material objects that might contribute to ancestral happiness. These rites are performed according to regional, village, and family custom in ceremonies in which the eldest male presides.

Both Buddhists and Catholics often participate in rites honoring their ancestors, even though as true believers in their own doctrine they must obviously have reservations about the accompanying dogma.

For the Buddhist believes in rebirth, which is in doctrinal contradiction to the cult of the ancestors, as is the Catholic concept of one god.

Buddha teaches that man is destined to be reborn many times and that this process stops only after he has perfected himself to the point where he may travel the path of enlightenment to Nirvana—the perfect bliss that is reached when human desires and cravings have been extinguished. In the endless cycle of life and rebirth that precedes Nirvana, a man might be reincarnated into anything from a great king to a lowly mosquito, depending on the virtue of his previous existence.

Born a Hindu, the son of a Himalayan prince, Gautama Buddha discovered the path to enlightenment after he deserted his aristocratic life to wander as a holy man. His mystic rapture lasted forty-nine days, and at the end of his meditation he had become the Buddha, or the Enlightened One.

In contrast to Christianity, Buddhism, in its original form, did not recognize anything resembling a personal god or a supreme being.

The Buddhist ethic preaches the middle way based on moderation and compassion. It springs from the four noble truths: existence is suffering; suffering springs from desire or craving; the cure for suffering is extinction of desires; and to attain the absence of craving one must travel the eightfold path of right views, right effort, right mindfulness, right intentions, right speech, right conduct, right livelihood, and right concentration.

Buddhist laymen as well as monks are also expected to observe Buddha's five moral rules of conduct: let no one kill any living being; take not anything that is not given to you; speak not falsely; do not drink intoxicating beverages; be chaste.

In Vietnam there are two main schools of Buddhism: Hinayana, or "little raft," which is the most orthodox in that it relies heavily on the actual sayings of Buddha; and Mahayana, or "greater raft," which is a form of Buddhism that has been greatly diluted by superstition. Some Mahayana interpretations of Buddhism authorize worship of the Enlightened One as a god (which, of course, he himself never claimed to be).

Mahayana Buddhists claim the largest following in Vietnam, but some Hinayana Buddhists dispute this. They point out that Hinayana Buddhism is dominant in neighboring Cambodia. Since there are at least half a million Khmers (the race that inhabits Cambodia) in South Vietnam, Hinayana Buddhism is certainly very influential in the part of the southern Mekong delta that they occupy.

As to the Catholics, there is no dispute about their numbers because they are all registered in each parish and the figures turned in to the government.

To return to the importance of ancestor-worship in Vietnamese custom and psychology, even the popes of Rome have in recent decades made concessions on this score. Earlier prohibitions against Catholic Vietnamese participating in ceremonies associated with this cult were lifted in 1939. And President Diem himself had an altar devoted to his ancestors in his family home at Hué.

In the Defense Department pocketbook of Vietnam, it states, "It is not unusual for Vietnamese to believe in several religions at one time." This is correct mainly in the sense already described, the sense in which Catholics, Buddhists, and others join in traditional family rites honoring their ancestors.

In the front lines of the war, I saw Buddhists and Catholics fighting side by side without either knowing or caring about the alleged "religious" dispute in Saigon.

I remember asking Major Olen O'Connor, adviser to the province chief at Mytho, in the Mekong delta, whether there was any sign of religious-inspired dissidence among the Vietnamese troops that he regularly accompanied into combat.

"Good heavens no," replied Major O'Connor; "I have never even thought to ask who is Catholic or Buddhist or whatever, and I bet the major here"—pointing to his Vietnamese counterpart—"has no idea who practices what religion." The Vietnamese officer didn't.

As a Vietnamese lieutenant puts it: "Saigon is not real to us. What is important to my men is how we are doing against the enemy sitting across the river in those palm trees. And lately we have been doing better. We would be very bitter if the disorders were to reach the point where supplies to our troops were held up. But I cannot imagine that happening."

Or as a Buddhist colonel in Mytho put it: "Everybody knows that the students are spoiled little draft-dodgers who ought to be sent back to the books they are lucky enough to possess. I have not risked my life all these years to have our situation undermined from within. President Diem must act to stop these disorders. A mandarin must be just. But a mandarin must act."

Mandarin?

As I had learned, it is impossible to comprehend anything whatsoever about Vietnam, past or present, without understanding the mandarin system. For centuries in Vietnam authority has been synonymous with rule by the mandarins. It has become the fashion in the West to sneer at the mandarin system. In my view the mandarins of Vietnam deserved the esteem in which their people held them.

In precolonial Vietnam the flowering of the mandarin system was the finest in Asia. The Vietnamese mandarins showed more responsiveness to the people, for example, than was ever the case in China, where the system often became synonymous with abuse of power.

As previously stated, Confucianism was the state religion of Vietnam until the ouster of the last of the Vietnamese emperors, Bao Dai, in 1955. The mandarins were the Emperor's deputies in both spiritual and temporal affairs. Despite the assaults on the mandarin system by the French colonialists, the mandarins continued even during the upheavals of a disintegrating empire to prevent what might otherwise have been a total fragmentation of the nation by the terrible ordeals of the twentieth century.

Defenders of the mandarin system are given a hearing in this passage of Joseph Buttinger's *The Smaller Dragon**:

. . . In Vietnam the mandarinal system of government allowed for maximum democracy in a pre-capitalist society and was free of the universal evils that go with all class and caste rule. The mandarins were recruited from the whole people and recruited only in one manner, to which every aspirant for office was compelled to submit. In order to become a mandarin, a young Vietnamese had to go through the required studies and pass the prescribed number of official tests. No other road to public office existed in Vietnam, and no dispensation from the labor of study and the trials of examination was granted either to the wealthy and noble or to a mandarin's own sons. The office of mandarin was neither hereditary nor for sale, and since education was always free in Vietnam (prior to colonial days) *the mandarinate was accessible to the poor and the rich* [italics mine]. Such a selection of the country's officials was based on democratic principles before anyone in the West could ever dream of such a governmental process. Only the very brilliant were able to get to the summit as young men, after absorbing no less than all the knowledge that existed, or was recognized as existing under the prevailing Confucianist views. . . . Vietnam was administered and ruled by its intellectuals. . . . Indeed a closer examination of Vietnamese society during the first half of the nineteenth century reveals a surprising historical phenomenon: a state had come into being in which the ancient dream of government by philosophers was literally fulfilled. The training of the mandarins was philosophical in the fullest sense of the word.

In the villages, the respect of the people for authority reflects to this day the Confucian doctrines of the virtue of obedience, of an ordered mandarin-regulated world, in which each has his place and whose status in life was achieved on merit. The respect and courtesy with which the peasants defer to their council of notables or village chiefs has never failed to impress me. Perhaps this accounts for my instinctive distrust of the great American myth that the back-slapping, press-the-flesh, hi-ya-Charlie, so-called "democratic" approach of the West was the great "quality" that Diem lacked.

*This book, published in 1958, was the *first* comprehensive history of Vietnam to appear in English in the United States. This alone indicates the newness of our interest in Southeast Asia and helps to explain the widespread ignorance that still prevails in the U.S. about Vietnam.

Among the Vietnamese peasants there is a delicacy and perfection of manners plus deep attachment to custom that I have seldom witnessed in worldwide travels. And by custom, the peasant demanded of the mandarin a certain aloofness fitting his superior moral and philosphical training, a reputation of justice, and a capacity to act.

None of this is to say that there were no frictions inside Vietnamese society in the summer of 1963. There were very serious frictions. There was, for example, friction between the Montagnards and the Vietnamese. It was friction based not on differing religions but on resentment that Vietnamese settlers in the highlands were taking over hunting grounds traditionally belonging to the Montagnards.

There was resentment among the South Vietnamese of the refugees who flooded into the land from Communist Vietnam. It happens that a majority—but by no means all—of these refugees were Catholics. Many anti-Communist intellectuals including Buddhists and Confucianists came south also. These refugees were resented because they were suspected of taking away jobs or land or anything else. Not because of their religion.

In talking to the United Nations mission to Vietnam in October, 1963, Counselor Ngo Dinh Nhu touched very frankly on the refugee situation:

The important thing is that some Buddhists may have regarded the refugee movement as evidence of government encouragement of Catholics rather than Buddhists for the reason that there were seven hundred thousand Catholics out of the total of a million refugees [a controversial figure, with some observers putting total refugees much higher and others much lower]. The Buddhists did not realize that this was a matter of organization. Because Catholics were better organized in secular matters, whole parishes could be mobilized to leave the country, while the Buddhists were dispersed and disorganized. At that time the Diem government was weak. It had just come into power and the previous government had carried off all the money. President Diem asked the French how many refugees to expect. The French said twenty-five thousand. Instead, there were a million. The French were overwhelmed. People waited months to embark [from North Vietnam]. We had to appeal to the Americans. This [huge exodus] may have given the Buddhists the idea that the government favored the Catholics.

In any case, my first journey to the countryside in the summer of 1963 produced no evidence whatever to bear out the wild Saigon rumors of rampant religious hostility between Catholics and Buddhists.

Indeed, in light of my predeparture briefings, I was amazed at the degree of cooperation between men of different beliefs. Quang Ngai province, for example, offered an impressive example of how a Buddhist army commander had worked closely with a Catholic province chief in handling a most awkward situation.

The situation arose when the main Quang Ngai Pagoda sent word to the Quang Ngai province chief, Nguyen Van Tat, that the nuns and monks had been ordered on a seventy-two-hour hunger strike.

The province chief, who had felt on best terms with the Buddhists, inquired politely if he had unwittingly done anything to offend them.

"No," replied the Buddhist messenger sadly. "It is the decision of the Buddhist leaders of the Xa Loi in Saigon. And we dare not disobey their orders."

Further, the Buddhist messenger added, the monks and nuns had been ordered to stage their hunger strike at Mr. Tat's own city hall.

At this point the province chief sent forthwith for his Buddhist ally, Colonel Luu Lan. Together they evolved a plan and enlisted the material assistance of Major John Kelly, the American adviser to the province chief.

The Catholic and the Buddhist compiled a message to the Quang Ngai Pagoda that went like this:

"The province authorities are distressed that you have been ordered to stage a hunger strike. But if you have no alternative but to obey orders of your Buddhist headquarters in Saigon, we will attempt to make the experience as harmless as possible. We will welcome you at city hall. We will provide medicine, first-aid experts, water, and blankets. We will cooperate in making your hunger strike as painless and comfortable as possible."

And the Buddhist colonel made a personal contribution. He went privately to Buddhist leaders and expressed his concern that the Catholic province chief's conciliatory attitude be matched by an equally conciliatory—that is, nonprovocative—attitude on the part of the Buddhists.

And so the Buddhist "hunger strike" went off without incident at the city hall, with the Catholic province chief benevolently presiding and Major Kelly and Colonel Luu watchfully in the wings.

And as Major Kelly summed up, "The Buddhists were happy as clams. They followed orders, pleasing the Buddhist hierarchy in Saigon, without displeasing their friend the province chief. It was the best public relations on the part of a province chief that I know of."

I arrived in Quang Ngai on July 30, 1963. It was an important day because the Xa Loi leaders had called for a nationwide shutdown of work and business. But in Quang Ngai, the shutdown order brought scarcely a ripple of response.

No stores were closed. No soldier, civil-defense fighter, or youth-brigade member failed to show up for duty. Not a single bureaucrat refused to work. And no peasant was absent from the backbreaking task of tending the shimmering emerald-green fields of new rice. And as I learned later, there was a similar lack of response throughout the nation.

My dispatch on the harmony between the Buddhist and Catholics of Quang Ngai caused a furor at the Xa Loi headquarters of the General Buddhist Association. Instead of being gratified at news of good relations between Catholics and Buddhists, the Xa Loi was infuriated.

A Xa Loi spokesman even called a press conference to contradict as "lies" my reports of harmony. During the conference, a Xa Loi monk showed a telegram purporting to come from the Quang Ngai Pagoda declaring that "reports of female journalist Marguerite Higgins published in the New York *Herald Tribune* dated July 31, 1963, are entirely untrue."

This was pretty bold. For in my dispatch I had quoted Major Kelly. If I was a liar, so was he. At this point in the Buddhist campaign Xa Loi had not yet attacked any Americans. But the Buddhists were in a bold mood. Within days the Xa Loi was to come out and denounce the American ambassador himself for saying that in two years he had seen no evidence of religious persecution.

And so it became clear to me that anybody who did not toe the Xa Loi propaganda line about alleged persecution and hostility would have a fight on his hands.

All these judgments on Buddhism, persecution, and the war were of course based on a great deal more than my own experience and fact-finding. They reflected, and in great part coincided with, the views of Ambassador Frederick Nolting; John Richardson, head of the Central Intelligence Agency in Vietnam; and American military advisers in the field. It was also a view largely shared (and to me this had great importance) by Robert Thompson, head of the British advisory mission, who had a reputation for objectivity and an admirable basis of judgment because he had been instrumental in Malaya in quelling the Communist guerrilla action there. It was a view supported at the grass roots by reports of the six Vietnamese-speaking Americans who had been assigned in the summer of 1963 to do nothing but circle the countryside so as to take the pulse of Vietnamese opinion.

It is also true that in Washington certain of President Kennedy's advisers distrusted and ultimately rejected this view of Vietnamese realities and persuaded J.F.K. to initiate actions based on contrary judgments. This, of course, is one of the most acutely controversial points of the developing drama of Vietnam and will be fully discussed in a later chapter.

CHAPTER 4

Madame Ngo Dinh Nhu:
Dragon Lady or Joan of Arc?

The war in the countryside seemed in many ways tame compared to the emotionally charged war of words that was rending Saigon when I returned from the boondocks to the dubious luxuries of the famed Caravelle Hotel.

This time Madame Nhu had really done it.

In my hotel box was a copy of the *Stars and Stripes,* proclaiming the incredible. The first lady of Vietnam had used the word "barbecue" in talking of the Buddhist suicides. Her exact words were that the Buddhist leaders were without a program and had done nothing except to "barbecue a monk and, at that, not even with self-sufficient means, since they had to import gasoline. . . ."

"How," I gasped, "could anyone be so barbaric?" The hotel concierge, who had been studying my reaction with interest, wordlessly handed me an official-looking message. It had been in my box a week. It stated that in line with my request for an interview, Madame Nhu would be pleased to receive me at the Presidential Palace at eleven A.M. the next morning. I received the message with mixed feelings. Journalistically, I was pleased. Personally, I was repelled.

Madame Nhu's atrocious verbal *gaffe* had been swiftly seized upon by most of the resident press of Saigon, who had long been at war with her. To them it justified their appraisal of her wickedness. And indeed it is easy to understand their reaction: anyone capable of so insensitive and callous a remark surely qualified as the villainess in a scenario of torture, persecution, and worse. All this in turn lent new ammunition to the war against Diem by those correspondents, who no doubt, out of the most idealistic motives, believed that his regime had to go because he didn't correspond to their occidental views of how an Oriental leader getting one million dollars a day from the United States ought to govern.

But the wars within wars did not stop there. There was a war on between many American reporters in Saigon and Ambassador Frederick Nolting and General Harkins, head of the military advisory mission, and vice versa. In this hostile environment the press had as allies many members of the U.S. embassy, most of whom were junior-grade, with one astonishing exception, William Trueheart, deputy to Ambassador Nolting.

But the "war" conducted by the Vietnamese intellectuals and the press against Madam Nhu was the hottest Saigon conflict going at this moment. It was one of the few certainties of Vietnam that intellectuals of Saigon enjoyed cutting up Madame Nhu second only to plotting against her brother-in-law, the President. Diem may have been authoritarian, but he never imposed controls on his people's right to criticize him and his family orally—at least no controls that worked.

Among the self-centered, socially important upper tier in Saigon society, almost everybody knew Madame Nhu personally and had his storehouse of tales that both titillated and terrified the *apéritif* set.

One day at breakfast I was told that Madame Nhu had a new lover among the generals. At noon the general, according to the latest hot rumor, had been sent to prison, which, I reflected, was pretty fast work even for a dragon lady. But such unverified drivel was the stuff on which Saigon feasted.

There are very few elite families in Saigon—families of education and status—because the French put stringent limits on the opportunities for Vietnamese to attain positions of power, responsibility, or even wealth. As a consequence, this small inbred clique of Saigon's elite usually knew all about each other's affairs. Much of the serious criticism of Madam Nhu was in the aggrieved vein of people who felt betrayed by one of their own.

I remember vividly a lunch at the wonderfully handsome and tasteful German embassy in Vietnam at which Madame Nhu, inevitably, was the centerpiece of conversation. Among the guests was the Brazilian ambassador to Vietnam—Ambassador Antonio Roberto de Arruba-Botecho—one of the most cultivated and charming men I have ever encountered anywhere. And he had just emerged from a long interview with Madame Nhu, openly and unabashedly enchanted.

He had been astonished at Madame Nhu's knowledge of Brazil, her acquaintance with the magnificent antique Vietnamese art, and her informed account of Vietnam's attempt at industrial and agricultural progress.

"Why don't the Vietnamese appreciate Madame Nhu?" innocently asked the Brazilian ambassador.

The Vietnamese Education Minister, a Confucian member of Diem's cabinet, had been sitting in stony silence until now. But at this point he fairly spat out his words: "The Vietnamese do not appreciate Madame Nhu because she is an evil sorceress, a scheming shrew, an inhuman woman."

Then the Vietnamese official went on bitterly to denounce Madame Nhu's sponsorship of the famous morality, or family, laws that had been pushed through the Vietnamese legislature by the energetic lady. These laws, the Vietnamese said, were in conflict with Confucian ethics and the centuries-old customs of Vietnam. They represented Madame Nhu's attempts to impose an alien puritanism on Vietnam. How, he asked, would the Americans (by now talking for my benefit) feel if suddenly Confucian laws and customs or Muslim laws and customs were imposed on a primarily Christian nation? The unrest and resentment in Vietnam at these actions of Madame Nhu were profound, he said, and had done more than anything else to alienate the Vietnamese "Establishment," which otherwise might have given crucial support to President Diem. Everybody knew the President to be an honest and admirable man. But why the honorable President tolerated "that woman," nobody in Vietnam understood. As Education Minister, the official said his task had been complicated by the resentments "spread like poison" among the people by Madame Nhu's arrogant and indeed downright unladylike actions. Now this hated woman was becoming the power behind the throne. . . . His peroration over, the Vietnamese lapsed into silence.

The next morning, when the hour came for me to meet "that woman," my feelings were a queer mixture of curiosity, excitement, and anticipated revulsion. Promptly at eleven o'clock I began climbing up the broad flight of stairs leading to the giant main hall of the Presidential Palace, with its enormously high ceilings and whirring fans.

There at the top stood Madame Nhu, tiny (5'2"), smiling, and looking not a bit fierce. She was, I noted, truly lovely, although the eyebrow pencil had been applied too lavishly for my taste and the powder was too thick. Her beautifully coifed head was piled high with black hair, and wispy bangs covered her forehead. Her white silk ao dai, the traditional dress of Vietnam, hugged her well-proportioned figure closely in a way that suggested a womanly pride in it. She wore black pumps with high French heels. Her long mandarin-type nails were decorated with pink polish.

Madame Nhu plainly intended to disarm me.

"I read everything you wrote during the Korean War," said Madame Nhu. "I never thought I would be fortunate enough to meet you."

But I was not to be put off. As we settled in two big overstuffed chairs in the middle of the hall, I asked her why she had used the word "barbecue" to describe the Buddhist suicides.

"If I had it all to do over again, I would say the same thing," she said defiantly. "I used those terms because they have shock value. It is necessary to somehow shock the world out of this trance in which it looks at Vietnam with false vision about religious persecution that does not exist. If the President keeps bowing to the unreasonable demands of the Buddhists, they will keep right on taking advantage of this weakness to make new impossible demands. They are hypocrites, that's all. A handful of 'Buddhists' [here her contempt flared] who know perfectly well there is no religious persecution in this country are willing to tarnish the image of Vietnam and of every Vietnamese citizen. Why? Because they hope to build up pressures that will serve their true aim—to overthrow the government. And they are doing this in the middle of a war. These illegal demonstrations give aid and comfort to the Viet Cong, and opportunity to create trouble."

Then, her voice subsiding from tones of anger to tones of ice, Madame Nhu went on: "I would welcome a condemnation of Vietnam by the United Nations. I will tell you why. Sometimes things have to go to the deepest depths before they rise to the top. Let the United Nations condemn us on these ridiculous grounds of religious persecution. Then they will send a team in here to investigate and they will discover the truth—and what fools they made of themselves."

At the time neither of us had any way of knowing how prophetic she would be proved. For a United Nations investigation of alleged religious persecution did take place in the autumn of 1963. And just as she had predicted, it failed to find any convincing evidence that religious persecution of Buddhists was in fact Diem's policy. But by the time the United Nations commission was on the point of completing its report, President Diem and Ngo Dinh Nhu were dead, so the committee merely published all the data collected (234 pages) in December, 1963, without pointing this up with hard and fast conclusions that would have caught the headlines.

At the palace, my first few minutes with Madame Nhu made it difficult to remember that this fragile beauty was the powerful, highly controversial personality so feared by her compatriots. It is only when she speaks that an almost visible, tangible force of character breaks through the brittle facade. She should have been a warrior. As the conversation wore on I found it impossible to keep from admiring her personal courage and total commitment to her country's cause of winning against the Communists. And yet it was easy to see how this fiery, totally engaged, brutally frank woman could shock American opinion. Indeed, I wondered how America and Madame Nhu could ever learn to understand each other. And, of course, they never did. They were totally incompatible. How could a bland, aloof, uncaring, don't-involve-me society understand a fierce, totally involved Oriental Valkyrie? And vice versa.

Madame Nhu's attitude toward me was puzzling. My questions were sharply pointed. Yet she obviously conducted the conversation on the assumption that as a woman I must automatically be an ally in her favorite field of battle, which, as she so dramatically described it, is "the struggle to wrest decent treatment of woman from the reluctant, devious, and often hypocritical men of Vietnam."

To achieve this objective Madame Nhu had, among other things, formed the Paramilitary Women of Vietnam. She proudly told me her "troops" had trounced the men in a publicly staged shooting contest. The Paramilitary Women village-defense forces were widely sneered at in the Dragon Lady's heyday. After the November 1 *coup d'état*, one of the first acts of the military junta headed by General Duong Van Minh was to disband them. After the *coup d'état* against Minh, one of the first acts of General Khanh was to reconstitute Paramilitary Women. And nowadays the Vietnamese WACS (a Paramilitary Woman by any other name, etc.) flourish.

"If the women have their own army," Madame Nhu explained, "they have a better chance to obtain their own rights."

Madame Nhu admitted with a shrug that the creation of the Paramilitary Women and the passage of the family laws "made many people hate me." But she was unrepentant. She went into enormous detail about the cruel and inhuman exploitation of Vietnamese women by men in the period prior to the family laws.

Until the passage of the 1958 family law Vietnamese women had no legal rights, she said, and could be discarded at will (which technically was more or less true). So the Vietnamese woman was reduced to being "an eternal minor, an unpaid servant, a doll without a soul."

Madame Nhu's family law made adultery a prison offense and outlawed polygamy and concubinage. Divorce could be obtained only by special presidential dispensation. And Vietnamese café society instantly deduced that the divorce provisions in the law were Madame Nhu's way of gaining vengeance on her more beautiful sister, who at the time wished to leave her husband.

This was malicious nonsense. There is no doubt in my own mind that Madame Nhu was acting out of a genuine feminist zeal. But it was premature zeal. Vietnam, in this time of travail, could ill afford to have centuries-old social customs (and abuses) assaulted head-on by such controversial reforms, however desirable in the abstract they might be. Madame Nhu's reforms created hatreds that brushed off on President Diem when he needed every drop of sympathy he could wring out of that dry, cynical, citified elite. They were, by and large, a squabbling, destructive, no-good lot. But it was a fact of political life that their criticisms and ill will were reflected in the Western press, which does not always distinguish between articulation and representation. Therefore such criticisms and ill will hurt Vietnam abroad, and domestically the reforms alienated many tradition-minded Vietnamese. As with so many things in life, politics—and especially reform politics—is a matter of timing. Madame Nhu's zeal was genuine, but her timing was terrible.

Madame Nhu had often been quoted as saying that "I made many people unhappy with my family bill—people who were in illegitimate liaisons but who are strongly in love. But society cannot sacrifice morality and legality for a few wild couples. I have chosen to defend the legitimate family."

Such pompous righteousness was absent from the attitude struck by Madame Nhu in her talk with me.

The various bills sponsored by Madame Nhu included bans on prostitution, contraceptives, abortion, organized animal fights, and taxi dancing. This last had been punctuated by her famous quotation that "Dancing with death is enough." But when I asked her if she didn't think there was something unhealthy about banning an outlet like dancing, she denied that it had ever been her intention to see the law carried so far.

"I am not a fanatic," she said. "I like to dance. I am one of the few Vietnamese women who know how to."

She added, "The family law that I originally introduced was aimed only at abolishing taxi girls. It seemed to me that tourists and others should be given the right to follow their own customs. But when the bill reached the committee, the men amended it to apply the dancing ban to everybody."

And the reason the Vietnamese men did it? "Because the Vietnamese are very jealous and they do not like to see Vietnamese women dancing with American men."

At the time of my interview Madame Nhu was at the peak of her turbulent quarrel with her father, Tran Van Chuong, who was on the point of resigning as ambassador to Washington. He had already publicly rebuked her for making the statement—on a U.S. television interview—about "barbecuing" the monks.

Madame Nhu made no secret of her fury with her father, a Confucianist, or of her low opinion of her mother, an ardent Buddhist, insofar as scholarly knowledge was concerned.

"My mother is a fanatic Buddhist," said Madame Nhu, "but she does not know any more about Buddhism than a five-year-old child. Go ask her and see."

On this occasion Madame Nhu was demonstrably inaccurate. I have talked with her mother, Madame Tran Van Chuong, in Washington many times, and she is an extremely intelligent woman who knows a great deal about Buddhism. She is also an extremely strong-willed woman who clearly did not need any reforms to give her a sense of equality. At a dinner party, it is not unusual for Madame Chuong to outtalk her husband, former Ambassador Tran Van Chuong, on political subjects. While the conversation is always stimulating, such forthrightness is unusual for Vietnamese women, who are customarily somewhat reticent in these matters. Madame Chuong does not hide her hostility toward her daughter, which, unfortunately, makes it mutual.

During the interview Madame Nhu emphasized her own Buddhist heritage in order, of course, to reject the accusations that she had any personal reason to be against Buddhism. She was converted to her husband's Catholicism at the time of her marriage.

"In my eighteen years as a Buddhist," said Madame Nhu, "I often went to the pagodas. And I still have a lasting interest in Buddhist philosophy. I know that the violence that those monks perpetrate out there in the streets is contrary to Buddhist philosophy, which is one of compassion, and nonviolence, and kindness to all living things."

When we got to the subject of whether she was the power behind the throne, she was again full of denials, shaking her beautifully coifed head to emphasize her points.

She painted an opposite picture. "The trouble is," she said, "that nobody listens to me. In every major crisis in our country, I told them [the President and his ministers] what would happen and what would have to be done. They did not listen to me. But afterwards they realized that I had been right."

In rebutting "the exaggerations about my power," Madame Nhu pointed out that she and her family lived in a separate wing of the palace and ate their meals totally apart from President Diem.

"I have not spoken to my brother-in-law for three months," she tossed out at one point.

And she was probably right in the sense that she did not, as many Vietnamese imagined, order the appointment of generals or the removal of cabinet officers. But on main lines of policy her powerful personality clearly had enormous potential influence because she discussed all national issues with her husband, who was, after all, the second most powerful man in the country. However, there was no question but that Ngo Dinh Nhu—not his wife—was the intellectual powerhouse of the family, as became plain to me later in a lengthy interview I had with him. And probably one of the reasons that Madame Nhu caused such antagonism is that the Vietnamese suspected that she was expressing what Nhu really felt but was too careful, most of the time, to say out loud.

"Nobody can shut me up—not even my husband," she said at one point. And this is entirely believable. For she is a combatant for her beliefs and it is hard to believe that she will ever be *hors de combat* until she is with her ancestors.

During our conversation Madame Nhu several times used the two buzzers installed in her chair, pressing on them with her delicate fingers with their long nails. One buzzer apparently was for a secretary, the other for a servant. Frequently servants bearing documents and messages on silver platters emerged from the Nhus' private apartments to approach us. Once her little girl, the youngest of her four children, appeared and ran over to be patted and given a bonbon.

What made Madame Nhu into such a fierce and fiery woman? And fierce is the right word. She is fiercely proud, fiercely energetic, fiercely intelligent, and fiercely honest. Moderation was never Madame Nhu's style.

What had forged this Oriental Valkyrie? One thing is certain: Without precisely such a forceful, defiant personality, Madame Nhu would never have survived.

She needed every drop of her fierce courage, for example, when she was captured by Ho Chi Minh's Viet Minh guerrillas near Hué in December, 1946.

This was the era in which Ho Chi Minh launched his bloody drive to murder any prominent anti-Communist nationalist that might be a rival to him personally or an impediment to his plans.

The Viet Minh (full title: Viet Nam Doc-Lap Dong Minh Hoi— Revolutionary League for the Independence of Vietnam) was in theory a grouping including non-Communists, but in fact was run ruthlessly by Ho and his Communist comrades, who, in the spirit of "the end justifies the means," practiced political assassination to a degree rare in modern annals.

Provincial mandarins (whose guilt in Communist eyes was their prestige and intelligence) were murdered by the score. Among the dead was Diem's older brother, Ngo Dinh Khoi, governor of Quang Nam province, who was eliminated along with his son by being buried alive. The Communists also went after the religious sects such as the Cao Dai and Hoa Hao, which controlled two thirds of the population of Cochin China (the southernmost third of Vietnam, centered on the Mekong delta). Huynh Phu So, the founder of the Hoa Hao and a famous miracle healer, was among those murdered.

Ngo Dinh Diem was also captured at this time and taken to the Tonkinese mountains but released after four grim months in which he nearly died of hunger and disease.

In the meantime, the Communists had destroyed one of Diem's most prized possessions, his library of ten thousand books, at Hué.

By the time Madame Nhu was taken prisoner by the Viet Minh the second war for Indochina was on. For on December 19, 1946, the Viet Minh had launched surprise attacks against French garrisons throughout the country, in reprisal, they claimed, for "bloody provocations."

Captured along with Madame Nhu were her infant daughter and her mother-in-law, the matriarch of the clan. During her captivity Madame Nhu lived on two bowls of rice a day, somehow saved her baby, and kept her mother-in-law from dying. Her outfit for four months consisted of one pair of pants, one blouse, and one wasp-waisted coat that also served as a blanket.

If she had been less resilient, this cruel experience could have left her in a deep sense of shock. This imprisonment and rough handling were in poignant contrast to the luxury she had known as a child.

Madame Nhu had been born into one of the wealthiest families in Vietnam. Her maiden name—Tran Le Xuan—means "beautiful spring." As a young girl Tran Le Xuan was waited on by twenty servants. It did not make up for what she considered a lack of loving attention from her mother, and perhaps her unhappy childhood prepared her for the later hardships.

Her mother, a local beauty in Hanoi, ran a kind of intellectual salon, and one of its frequenters was Ngo Dinh Nhu, then chief archivist at the Indochina Library. "Beautiful Spring" wanted to escape from her mother, and marriage seemed the only way. "So," she explained, "I asked myself, 'why not my friend Ngo Dinh Nhu?' "

Although Madame Nhu said that her love for her husband was not "a sweeping passion," there was a deep bond of affection and respect between them. When many months later I talked to her at midnight within hours of her husband's murder, she was a very frail and broken Valkyrie—so frail and broken that it was hard to remember that she had ever been a Valkyrie at all.

When the French army began to spread out to the countryside, Madame Nhu finally regained her freedom. "The Communists," Madame Nhu recalls, "did not seem to consider me much of a prize."

In any case, before the Communists moved higher into the mountains, they gave Madame Nhu a *laisser-passez* into the nearest village, where she, along with her mother-in-law and infant child, found refuge in a convent.

Ngo Dinh Nhu evaded capture because while on a trip to Saigon he was tipped off about the Communist assassination plans for the family. He sent a message of warning but it arrived too late.

For the Ngo Dinh Nhus, the happiest times were the days in Dalat from 1946 to 1954, when she and her husband were defying the French, the Communists, and at the same time preparing the ground for Diem's return from self-imposed political exile in the United States and Belgium. During this period Ngo Dinh Nhu ran a newspaper and recruited support for Diem from among the poor and middle classes. Madame Nhu turned down offers of a big allowance from her wealthy family. The woman who had once had twenty servants pedaled a bicycle to the store and cooked the family dinners.

When finally, in 1954, the French conceded the total independence which Diem had always demanded, the country he took over was not much of a bargain. Anarchy was the rule. Diem did not control his own police. It was in the hands of the Binh Xuyen sect, which was a band of adventurers who through control of the police exploited gambling, prostitution, and other rackets. Hoa Hao and Cao Dai warlords feuded and obstructed. France never forgave Diem for his defiance in the long years he resisted their offers to collaborate with the colonial regime and insisted on total independence. And the French really only surrendered to him on the surface. From the instant he took power, the French connived to unseat him and blacken his name. They even left behind, as army commander, General Nguyen Van Hinh, who was widely regarded as a French agent and who boasted publicly that he would make a *coup d'état* against Diem when the mood seized him.

"I shall exile all the Ngo Dinh Diem family," boasted General Hinh, "except Madame Nhu, whom I shall keep as my concubine."

When the general and the lady finally met at a Saigon party, Madame Nhu marched across a crowded room to beard him.

"You are never going to overthrow this government," she said, "because you don't have the guts. And you are never going to have me because I would claw your throat out first."

General Hinh, of course, had been named commander of Vietnam's army when the French were still in charge. It was not easy for

Diem to get rid of him, not only because of the chaotic situation but because the French, in the early days of South Vietnam's independence, still exercised considerable power. This was by virtue of the fact that the French still trained the Vietnamese army and controlled much of the economy.

Diem only got rid of General Hinh by appealing urgently for his ouster to Emperor Bao Dai, who for once sided with his Prime Minister. In 1955 the Emperor himself got the gate when Diem asked the people to choose in a plebiscite between a republic with himself as leader and a monarchy with Bao Dai. As the Diem regime consolidated its power, tales of corruption began to swirl about Madame Nhu. She was supposed to own several Paris cinemas, have gold in Swiss banks, etc. But after the *coup d'état,* no evidence was ever produced to show that any of the Ngo Dinh Nhus had in fact collected masses of personal wealth. Madame Nhu for some time lived a financially spare existence in Paris, even finding it necessary to try to sell interviews to Paris newspapers. In 1965 she moved to a small whitewashed villa south of Rome, where the climate is more congenial to a Vietnamese accustomed to tropical heat.

None of the Ngo Dinh Nhus struck me as interested in luxury or wealth for its own sake. They were interested in power.

"Power is wonderful," Madame Nhu once said. And as usual, she meant every word of it.

I wonder how many hours the President of the United States, the Secretary of State, and the American ambassador to Vietnam have spent trying to silence the biting tongue of Madame Nhu. Collectively, many hundreds surely. The fury of great men everywhere over what a slip of a woman was saying would have been comic had it not been so tragically typical of the atmosphere of the times.

Indeed, Madame Nhu was infuriated when Ambassador Frederick Nolting made urgent representations to get her barbed tongue silenced. These representations were so urgent that at one point President Diem publicly disavowed Madame Nhu. It did not silence her for long, unfortunately.

"Don't you realize," I asked Madame Nhu insistently, "that your use of the word 'barbecue' has hurt your country's image terribly and damaged Vietnam's relations with Washington at a terribly critical time?"

"But look," she said, pressing the buzzer and sending for her secretary. "Here is a telegram from a Buddhist leader in Thailand. The telegram commends me for stating the truth about these Buddhist barbecues."

"That is *one* telegram, Madame Nhu," I said stonily. "The rest of the world is outraged. Ambassador Nolting is an objective man. He would not be raising such a rumpus if there were not a reason."

"And besides," I hurried on, taking advantage of her silence, "you complain that the American press is making war on your government out of ignorant and arrogant judgments. But then, why do you give them verbal ammunition to make you out a monster and blacken your image and that of your government?"

"But," Madame Nhu retorted, "I never would have thought of the word 'barbecue' if it had not been used first by the Americans."

"The Americans?"

"My daughter," Madame Nhu explained, "was at the post exchange the other day. And she heard some American photographers talking about some new 'barbecues' that the Xa Loi monks were predicting."

"But, Madame Nhu!" I exploded. "Don't you see the difference between a photographer using such a term in a private conversation and the first lady of Vietnam using such a term in a television interview that will be carried into the living rooms of Americans and onto the headlines of the whole world?"

Madame Nhu shook her head wordlessly. She did not seem angry at my bluntness. Just uncomprehending.

And I don't think she ever really did comprehend.

Madame Nhu often met her Waterloo with Anglo-American audiences because her English was so atrocious. She should never have spoken anything but French, in which she was fluent. Her mistake was to assume that English words derived from the French have the same connotation in both languages. She once declared that Buddhist monks were "intoxicated," which some American journalists took as a charge that they had been imbibing too much alcohol. But the French word "intoxiquer" means to poison. Madame Nhu was trying to say that the minds of the Buddhists had been poisoned against the Diem regime. But with her misuse of English Madame Nhu made it look, in some eyes, as though she was crudely slandering the monks, who, as everyone knows, are not allowed by their religion to touch a drop of alcohol.

Another reason for Madame Nhu's difficulties was the evident fact that occidental psychology remained forever inscrutable to her. Her direct knowledge of the world outside Vietnam was very limited. She might be able to spout off statistics about Brazil to its ambassador or about the United States to its ambassador, but she had no real clue in terms of personal experience as to what made Western nations tick. She had made a few quick trips to the West but had never lived outside the Orient.

All this helped to explain why in her soon-to-be-undertaken travels Madame Nhu often said precisely the things most calculated to succor the forces leading inexorably to murder and treachery.

And in her bitterness and desperation she only sharpened the worldwide condemnation of herself and her government that helped to precipitate the moment that would leave her a widow.

CHAPTER 5

The Buddhist Burnings: Why Do They Do It?

The dirt landing strip at Phan Thiet is carved out of the top of a small hill overlooking the translucent and sunflecked South China Sea. I might have enjoyed the view had it not been for the fact that the German pilot of our plane was an ex-Luftwaffe type who obviously got his kicks by scaring helpless passengers to death. On a perfectly clear, cloudless day our pilot sent the small one-engine plane into steep banks, dives, and fast turns that tossed us mercilessly about. Infuriatingly, he kept turning around to grin broadly at our discomfiture. But after buzzing the town itself, making an aerial pass at some junks offshore, and a few more assorted antics, he finally brought the plane down, and we were still alive.

The other passenger was a U.S. embassy specialist in the Vietnamese language. Whenever I could join forces with one of these linguists in their tours of the countryside I counted myself lucky. I profited from their knowledge of the language and the security of knowing that their interpretations would not be motivated by the attempt to grind an ax for the Diem regime.

At Phan Thiet the U.S. embassy reporter-diplomat had precisely the same mission as I. We wanted to know the whys and wherefores

behind the suicide by fire that had taken place the preceding day—a
Sunday—in a public square.

The story was a haunting one.

Bells in the picturesque, whitewashed town had been tolling the
hour of noon when the civil-guard commander, riding by a hibiscus-
filled memorial square, noticed smoke.

"Someone is taking a chance burning leaves in dry, dusty weather,"
he remarked to his driver as they left their vehicle and headed
through the palm trees to put out the fire.

But what they found that Sunday noon on the white slab of granite
before a blue-tinted memorial to the war dead was the toppled, already unrecognizable body of a young Buddhist who had decided on
a flaming death to protest the "suffering of Buddhists."

The civil guards quenched the flames, still burning in the monk's
brown robes, and somehow got him into the car and to a hospital.
But Duc Phong, the Buddhist, was already on his way to his next re-
incarnation. Such spiritual considerations, alas, had little to do with
the disposal of Duc Phong's charred corpse.

We learned from several Buddhist witnesses of an appalling scene
that had taken place in the morgue of the two-story stucco hospital at
Phan Thiet. Buddhist monks had arrived at the hospital in the night
to demand that they be given the young monk's body so that they
could "carry out mourning befitting the sacrifice." They were blocked
by the gnarled and weeping parents of the immolated boy, who
wanted to take his body back for burial in their own village pagoda
many miles south. The province chief had personally notified them of
the tragedy and had made transportation available to bring the parents to Phan Thiet. Many un-Buddhist shouts and curses were hurled
back and forth across the morgue room. At one point it looked as if
the monks were going to rush physically forward to prevent the
charred remains from being put in the burial casket. The aged parents won the battle, as we discovered upon arriving at the hospital.
We got there just after the casket, accompanied by the elderly couple,
had been put on a truck provided by the province chief.

But the place to find out what had really motivated the young suicide was clearly his pagoda, which was one of several hundred (out of 4,776) associated with the General Buddhist Association. So in a jeep borrowed from the local military adviser we started in that direction.

En route we passed a main intersection where several hundred Vietnamese, mostly women in ao dais and conical hats, were sitting in the burning sun in the middle of the street. They applauded when they saw us, for they assumed we were reporters. And the American press, as I have noted, was considered by the Buddhists to be championing their cause. The Xa Loi distributed mimeograph copies of U.S. press stories to member pagodas in the provinces. A yellow-robed monk was haranguing the seated demonstrators and denouncing province officials for "stealing the body" of Duc Phong in order "to bury it secretly in a military cemetery."

By now an English-speaking Buddhist layman had attached himself to us. Since he claimed to know the monk making these accusations, I asked him to help translate a question I wished to put to him.

"Reverend," I said, "isn't there some mistake? The body of the young member of your pagoda was given to his parents. We have just returned from the hospital and were witness to this."

"The only mistake," said the monk, "is that you have been tricked."

And he went on haranguing the people and repeating the accusations against the province chief—accusations which of course were totally untrue.

At the Phan Thiet Pagoda big rolls of barbed wire made an arc around most of the entrance, but a pathway was left open along the sidewalk. The barbed wire had been placed there by the civil-guard commander (a Buddhist) after the fracas in the hospital and the hostile appeals by Buddhist leaders for a march on the city hall.

No one tried to hinder our entrance into the pagoda. And inside we were warmly welcomed by monks and nuns with grave, gaunt faces. Soon, in their swift, silent way, they had fetched the senior Buddhist monk of the pagoda. He was a tense, middle-aged man of infinite courtesy. He motioned us to a rough-hewn wooden table. Almost instantly, delicate, tiny porcelain cups filled with green tea were proffered. I personally find the tea delicious, although I cannot say the same for the orange soda pop which Vietnamese appear determined to serve Americans. Luscious tangerines were also hospitably handed around. And with the formalities over, we could begin.

Explaining that I was an American journalist, I asked the Buddhist leader if he could give me his views about why young Duc Phong had chosen to take his life by fire. Had the Diem regime harassed Duc Phong or his associates in any way?

"It came as a complete surprise to us," said the Buddhist monk. "We did not even know that he had gone from the pagoda until we discovered the letters he left behind."

I asked the Buddhist monk if we could have a look at the letters, and he motioned for someone to fulfill my request.

In the interim he told us what he could about Duc Phong. It appears that the boy's family had brought him to the pagoda when he was nine years old because they could not support him. Since then the pagoda had been father, mother, and school.

Duc Phong's identity card showed him to be a clear-eyed, pleasant-looking youngster. The identity card had been left behind in a neat pile on his sleeping mat, along with a letter written in strong blue script explaining that he was taking his life "to help humanity and peace."

The Buddhist superior also handed me a neatly typed poem about Buddhist suffering and said he had an extra carbon available.

"Was this young monk a typist?"

"No," said the Buddhist leader, "but we have had a telegram from the Buddhist Association headquarters in Saigon asking for copies of all the things he left behind, and we typed up several copies."

In the poem the young would-be suicide had written that "I am offering my soul to Buddha to end discrimination that is growing daily more serious. . . . I cannot hope to attain the status of the venerable Quang Duc [the first monk to burn himself alive in the summer of 1963], but I aspire to become his disciple. Sacrifice for the Buddhist way is higher than the highest of all ways. He is the most sacred who brings his body to burn in public places. Suffering is the way of Buddhism."

But what specific form, I wanted to know, had this suffering taken in the case of young Duc Phong?

"We cannot hold demonstrations unless we get permission in advance from the authorities," said the monk.

"But," I inquired, "don't all Vietnamese oganizations—Catholics, Cao Dai, etc.—also have to get permission?"

"Perhaps," said the monk, "but it is wrong to make the Buddhists do it."

Anything else?

Finally, after a round of consultation with other monks and kibitzing from a growing throng of curious onlookers, the Buddhist monk said that on the occasion of the celebration of Buddha's birthday (May 8) it had been necessary to fly the national Vietnamese flag several notches higher than the Buddhist flag was flown.

"But surely," I said with incredulity in my voice, "you aren't trying to tell me that this young monk burned himself alive because the Vietnamese national flag was flown a notch higher than the Buddhist flag? Is this what you mean by religious persecution?"

At length, after many such go-rounds, the Buddhist monk observed that "Even if there is no persecution in Phan Thiet we know that discrimination exists elsewhere because the Buddhist Association bulletins say so. We know that the Buddhists are suffering terribly . . . and if we know this, Duc Phong did too. That is why he took his life."

And the Buddhist monk was probably right. Duc Phong's suicide had probably been completely "voluntary" in the sense that he had implicitly believed the propaganda line put out by the Buddhist Association, as did his fellow monks at the pagoda.

It was plain that in a small provincial pagoda like Phan Thiet, the effort to sort out the facts in the maze of charges and denials between the Buddhist Association and the government was beyond the desire of the monks. Indeed, it never occurred to them that they might be the victims of false propaganda. If the venerable elder monks of the association said Buddhism was being persecuted, then it must be so.

Did young Duc Phong really write the letters and long poem left behind? Possibly. It did not occur to me to doubt this until many months later, when I discovered that inducement to suicide was a formalized activity of the General Buddhist Association.

I have reproached myself as a journalist for not having pinned down the details of this earlier. It was clear to me that the Buddhist spokesman, Thich Duc Nhiep, knew in many cases precisely when, where, and at what hour a "volunteer" was to burn himself for the cause. In most instances the suicides were carefully selected for maximum impact on world opinion. And *selectees* implied *selectors*. Therefore, many of these tragic self-immolations were prearranged. But how? The first time I learned the precise details of such prearranged suicides was when I read the report on Vietnam issued on December 7, 1963, by the United Nations team which was in fact investigating charges of religious persecution in Saigon at the time that the November coup occurred. The UN team, which had been given wide leeway by the Diem regime to interview Buddhists in hospitals and internment camps as well as pagodas, came upon the subject of Buddhist suicide squads during a fateful interview with a Buddhist monk described in the United Nations report as "witness number eight."

The key points of the testimony given by this young nineteen-year-old monk follows:

During this period [October, 1963] I heard about the atrocities perpetrated by the government against the Buddhists. I heard for example that Buddhist monks and nuns were beaten, that their hands were broken, that they were drowned, and that they had their stomachs ripped open. . . . I was very upset at the news. . . . One day a student claiming to belong to a student association met me and asked me to join the Buddhist movement. I accepted because I believed that it was for the Buddhist cause. . . . On October 22 the student came to see me again and at that time he told me his name was Linh. He told me that the *Buddhist Association worked for the Communists* [italics mine]. On October 23 I was taken to a school by this Linh to meet two men. They told me that they needed ten volunteers [for death by fire] and asked me if I would accept to be one of the ten. I accepted because I felt so upset about the news I had heard earlier about the government's treatment of monks. . . . I was told that a monk named Phanh My would commit suicide by burning in front of the Redemptionist Church and another in front of Tan Dinh Church on Hai-Batrang Road. . . . They said I should do so at the National Day celebration because many people would be there, including the representatives of the United Nations mission. . . . I asked him how I would get into the area, because it had been cordoned off. I was told not to worry, that the *suicide-promotion group* [italics mine] would make all the arrangements. I asked what kind of arrangements, and they answered on the twenty-sixth of October I would be given a white suit and a yellow robe soaked with gasoline. They would provide me with a car bearing a sticker enabling the car to go into the area. When the car got there, I was to get out in a normal manner. The car would be driven away. I was then to sit down, put on the yellow robe, and strike a match and set myself on fire. Also before this, they would give me some pills so that I would not feel the pain. On October 24 the student came again to the Tu Van Pagoda to give me three letters, one of which was addressed to the President of the Republic. This letter demanded freedom of religion, release of the arrested students, monks, and nuns. The second letter was addressed to the chief monk, Thich Thien Hoa, at An Quang Pagoda. In this letter there were accusations against Thich Thien Hoa for betraying monks, nuns, Buddhists [this venerable monk had publicly denounced the politicking of Thich Tri Quang and others and called on Buddhists to get out of the streets and go back to their religion]. The third letter was addressed to the United Nations mission telling them the reason why I committed suicide. These letters had been prepared ahead of time and they asked me to sign them. I did not hesitate. I signed them immediately.

Fortunately for this young monk he saw a fellow Buddhist, a Mr. Hai, on the street several days before his "voluntary" suicide was due to take place. He told his acquaintance that he would not be seeing him again after October 26. Alarmed, Mr. Hai took immediate steps to see that the young man's suicide was averted and that he be told the truth—that stories of atrocities had been inventions.

During the interrogation of witness number eight Ambassador Amor of Morocco, who served as rapporteur of the UN mission, asked, "Are you repentant of the idea of offering yourself for religious sacrifice and are you happy that you did not commit suicide?"

"I am happy that I did not kill myself," replied the witness.

There were, fortunately, additional instances in which would-be suicides were intercepted—or discovered the truth themselves—in time. In an article in *Il Borghese* magazine Ivan Matteo Lombardo, former Italian Minister of Production, tells such a story, the details of which came to his attention during a visit to Vietnam in the fall of 1963.

The Vietnamese involved was an obscure monk named Pham Ngoc Cam, who lived in a province remote from Saigon. He was approached by Buddhist suicide-promotion groups and told horror stories of burning pagodas and tortured monks. He was told that if he would sacrifice by fire he would have a good chance to be reincarnated as a high-ranking monk, possibly even a Buddha. Only a Buddha, as previously noted, can tread the path of enlightenment and reach the eternal state of Nirvana, which is supreme bliss and absence of suffering. The young monk consented and was taken to Saigon. In this case, he was provided with a plastic pan of gasoline that was to be placed under his robe and pierced with a knife at the moment before the match was lit. The instructions about the route to be followed were extraordinarily precise. It was a roundabout way leading to the place of sacrifice, the boulevard Thon San Nhut, behind Saigon's big cathedral. The young monk's route was chosen, it became apparent, in order to make sure that he would not pass by any pagodas, since he had been told that the pagodas had been burned and left in ruins. But the Buddhist suicide-promotion group had not foreseen that because of the celebration of National Day some of the prescribed streets would be blocked. Pham Ngoc Cam, in deviating from orders, happened to pass an important pagoda, which, far from being burned to the ground, was being visited by the faithful. As he described it later on a radio broadcast of October 30, Pham Ngoc Cam was standing in front of the pagoda, mouth agape at seeing it open, when he was challenged by two security policemen who were on the alert for the mass spate of suicides reportedly planned for that day. When the police found the gasoline pan, they took the would-be suicide in for questioning.

The macabre fillip to the story involves the two pinkish pills which Pham Ngoc Cam had been given "to kill the pain." But as a policeman showed him by calmly chewing one pill, the chemicals were without effect. A laboratory test had already shown the pills to be less effective than aspirin. In other words, the poor monk had been duped even in this. The pills which he believed would kill the pain would have done no such thing. The suicide promoters did not want any drug detected in the event of a post mortem. Had Cam gone through with his promised death, he would have suffered atrociously.

What about the situation in the provinces?

Could the young monk in Phan Thiet have been saved if he had been told the truth in time? Or would this idealistic young man's confidence in the horror stories told by the venerable Buddhist superiors in Saigon have made him oblivious to facts?

It is certain that the propaganda of the extremists in the Buddhist Association was ruthlessly skillful and ruthlessly dishonest. It is certain that in Vietnam, with its low level of education among the masses and low level of moral responsibility among the café-society elite, people were capable of believing almost anything.

Ambassador Frederick Nolting tells how for a whole month the Saigon cocktail circuit was convinced that Nguyen Ngoc Tho, the Buddhist Vice-President of Vietnam, had disemboweled himself on the ambassador's doorstep. Despite persistent U.S. embassy denials, Mrs. Nolting for example, kept finding herself laden with whispered commiserations from Vietnamese ladies who cornered her at teas to say, "My dear, it must have been dreadful for you—the incident with the Vice-President."

The only way the American ambassador could lay this rumor to rest was by persuading a local newspaper to print a photograph of himself in company with the Vice-President.

The Vietnamese were not the only ones to accept rumor as fact. For example, the State Department spokesman, in discussing the Diem raids on seven key Saigon pagodas (out of one hundred or more), stated that two persons had been killed. But this was not true. No monks or nuns were fatally hurt in the closing of the Saigon pagodas on August 19 or subsequently.

In Saigon the injured Buddhists taken to the hospital totaled five monks and four nuns. Most injuries were to ankles and legs, suggesting that they might have been caused by tear gas and concussion grenades and flying wood and glass. And in the Xa Loi Pagoda the

Buddhist monks must have put up a rousing good fight, because twenty policemen were injured. The monks attacked them with everything from gongs to sticks and stones.

In the atmosphere of the time it was the fashion to take anything scurrilous said about the Diem regime as fact and any contrary information as fiction.

In the summer of 1963 American newspapers certainly tended, at first anyway, to give credence to charges of religious persecution.

Nowadays some of the most ardent anti-Diem writers, such as David Halberstam, former Saigon correspondent of the *New York Times*, contend that the Buddhist agitation of the summer and fall of 1963 was politically motivated. In an admiring magazine article written by his close friend George J. W. Goodman, Mr. Halberstam is quoted as saying: "I always said it. The Buddhist campaign was political. . . . I thought I always emphasized that this was a political dispute under a religious banner—the only place an opposition had found to gather in an authoritarian regime. . . ."

Whatever Mr. Halberstam's intentions, his and other press dispatches of the time did create the impression in the outside world that some kind of religious crisis was going on in Vietnam.

It seems probable that the American public would have been less hostile to Diem if it had realized that he was not repressing anybody because of their religion but trying to put down a political rebellion led by some extremist Buddhists aimed at overthrowing his government. Nobody in the State Department at that time had the courage or sense of fair play to correct what they knew to be a distorted image of Vietnam.

One of the few correspondents in Saigon to diagnose the situation correctly was Patrick O'Connor—an Irishman, not an American—who wrote at the time for the Catholic News Service. He had had more than a decade of experience in Southeast Asia.

"The Buddhists in South Vietnam," wrote O'Connor, "have been selling the American public a bill of goods. They sold it first to some foreign correspondents in Saigon. . . . The militant intersect committee of Buddhism has listed five demands. . . . For these five demands the Buddhist Association is prepared to throw the country into disorder and defy the government in the middle of its life-and-death struggle with Communism. . . .

"For these it is prepared to let bonzes [monks] burn to death—if the foreign press can be present. As one bonze had admitted to a correspondent, the five demands no longer represent their aim.

"No matter what the government may do, the leaders will find new cause for complaint. Only the political overthrow of the government will satisfy them."

O'Connor had two strikes against him. He was Catholic, which, in a kind of reverse prejudice, made his word suspect. And his dispatches had a small audience compared with that commanded by the anti-Diem correspondents, who dominated the news out of Saigon. Indeed O'Connor was quite controversial among some so-called liberal Catholics, who were, it seemed to me, in a great hurry to condemn Diem in order to demonstrate their purity and their immunity from the political and social diseases he was accused of spreading.

During this period Ambassador Nolting, whom history will give high marks for courage, intelligence, and perseverance in carrying out the Washington policies of his time, made his categorical statement that in two years in Vietnam he had seen no religious persecution. But nobody in Washington supported him, most of the press attacked him, and he was left psychologically high and dry.

Nonetheless, as of this writing no evidence has ever been produced to show that any Buddhist was arrested for practicing his religion. Buddhists, Catholics, Cao Dai, Montagnards—all these different faiths and races on occasion tangled with the police when they staged riots and rebellions, although for many weeks in the summer of 1963 President Diem, at American urging, often overlooked the breaking of the law by street mobs.

Diem's police in those days were not exactly gentle. There were occasions when tempers flared and the police lit into the mobs, with bloody—though never fatal—results.

To the observant riot watcher the demonstrations were obviously stage-managed with a view to provoking violence. The professional touch is always apparent when the "riot" managers put women and children in front, then use them as a shield. Standing behind this human shield, the demonstrators start throwing things—rocks, bits of metal, etc.—at the police. So when the police start to retaliate they have to wade first through the women and children. This provides a dramatic shot for the photographers—this picture of uniformed police plowing through innocent-looking women and children to get at the rock-throwing. I was to see the same stage-managed riots over and over again in the next two years in Vietnam, often with the same veteran riot leaders in command as in the Diem days.

By mid-August, 1963, when the total number of suicides by fire had reached five, it was hard to remember that only two months earlier—June 16—the Buddhist leaders and Diem had reached a formal written agreement that both sides had hailed as a solution. The agreement had covered everything from the matter of flying of the flags to property rights.

Thich Tri Quang managed to renege on the agreement by asserting that the government was "not sincere" in carrying it out, though when pressed he could never show verifiable proof of this. It is almost certain that the extremist Buddhist faction he led never regarded the joint Buddhist-government agreement of June 16 as anything more than a tactical maneuver to lower Diem's guard and make the Americans think they held a "reasonable posture."

Washington kept insisting that if Diem would stick to his policy of concession and conciliation, regardless of the provocation, the Buddhists would be induced to desert the political barricades. The assumption was that if Diem were reasonable, the Buddhists would have to respond in kind.

These American assumptions only serve to show how little Washington understood what was going on in Vietnam at the time. Perhaps if the Buddhists had been convinced that we would remain loyal to our commitments to Diem, things might have turned out differently. But by August, 1963, the Buddhists had persuaded themselves—with some justice, as it turned out—that Henry Cabot Lodge, the announced successor to Nolting, would take a hard line toward Diem. One of the Xa Loi monks openly asked me, "How many suicides will it take to get rid of Diem?" The mounting number of suicides was intended to give the new American ambassador the ammunition with which to get rid of the Vietnamese President.

In retrospect there is no doubt that these suicides by fire were what did the most to turn United States opinion against Diem. Americans, who quite naturally have a hard time avoiding the temptation of applying Western logic to Oriental situations, tended that summer to assume that the suicides were proof in themselves of religious persecution. Why should anyone, a Westerner reasons, choose such a horrible death unless he or she had irrefutable proof that Diem was doing terrible things to Buddhists?

Few Americans knew anything about Buddhism and therefore did not realize that the suicides by fire, the violence in the streets, the vituperative slogans painted on banners draped over pagoda walls—all were contrary to what Buddha himself had taught.

The Dhammapada (path of virtue), which is a collection of Buddha's original teachings, is categorical in forbidding all the violent actions and words of the so-called Buddhist monks.

For example, Verse 270: "A man is not one of the Noble because he injures living creatures; he is so called because he refrains from injuring all living creatures."

Verse 170: "Look upon the world as a bubble, look upon it as a mirage: The King of Death does not see him who thus looks down upon the world."

Verse 133: "Do not speak harshly to anybody; those who are spoken to will answer thee in the same way. Angry speech breeds trouble; thou wilt receive blow for blow."

Does this philosophy square with the vitriolic, bitter propaganda tirades ground out by the Buddhist Association? Or with the incitement to suicide and exploitation of these deaths? Or with the involvement in politics? It doesn't.

Is it naïve to expect Buddhist monks to live by their religion? But the fact is that the overwhelming majority of Buddhist monks in Vietnam *do* forgo the world of violence and politics, practicing gentleness and compassion and seeking not to injure or kill any living thing.

If Catholic priests suddenly were to start a campaign of suicides by fire, it would be just as foreign to Christianity as these same acts are to Buddha's own teachings. But Americans know more about Christianity than about Oriental religions. And so in Eastern matters we are more easily taken in.

Even though original Buddhism strongly condemns the taking of life in any form, there are some Buddhists, particularly those of the Mahayan (greater raft) persuasion, who believe that certain sacred Buddhist books (sutras) give precedents of sacrifice for the sake of Buddha in the form of self-mutilation, including such things as burnings and the chopping off of a hand or leg. But practices of self-mutilation are very controversial among Buddhists. And according to Thich Ne An, a Vietnamese monk who has a Ph.D. in Buddhist studies, there were no burnings in sacrifice to Buddha in Vietnam before June, 1963 (although there were instances of suicide by fire for other reasons).

Certainly events after Diem's murder demonstrated dramatically how false was this Western assumption that suicides by fire per se meant persecution.

There were, for example, six self-immolations in Vietnam in the five weeks *following* the *coup d'état* of November 1, 1963.

Thus it came to pass that under the post-Diem military junta, which was dominated by Buddhists and which had seized power in the name of an end to "persecution," *there were more suicides by fire in a short period than had ever been the case in a similar interval under President Diem and his brother Ngo Dinh Nhu.*

CHAPTER 6

Hué: How the Buddhist
Crisis Began

The city of Hué is a historic, aesthetic, and philosophical adornment to South Vietnam. It is the imperial citadel where the Confucian emperors reigned. The site is protected on all sides by the great mountains of the Annamite chain. Its palaces, tombs, parks, and above all its temples tell of the time of the mandarins, when poetry and art and literature and philosophy and the study of the ancients were the only things that mattered in a simpler and surer world. On a hill overlooking Hué is Nam Giao, the Confucian Temple of the Heavens. Here for centuries the Emperor of Vietnam walked ceremonially every third year thrice around the crest of the hill, driving before him two white bullocks that had never before worn a yoke; to complete the ritual, they were duly sacrificed to the ancestors and the gods. The present fortifications of Hué were built in the day of the enlightened Vietnamese Emperor Gia Long and bear a French imprint. Hué is intersected by the clear and inviting waters of the River of Perfumes, which contributes enchantingly to its charm and grace. Like many things in Hué, the river is sheer ornamentation. It is not navigable. It turns into shallow rapids as it flows out past the city to the South China Sea. And so the coarse ways of commerce never threatened Hué's gentility or cluttered the River of Perfumes with oil slicks and industrial waste.

But on the 2507th* birthday of Buddha, May 8, 1963, the River of Perfumes was witness to bloody tragedy—the tragedy that began the so-called Buddhist crisis. The site of the tragedy was the Hué radio station, which is situated on the south bank of the River of Perfumes.

The Hué radio station is a most unlikely-looking place for violence and sudden death. It is housed in a small stucco building with bougainvillaea, hibiscus, and other tropical flowers planted in abundance around its foundations. On ordinary days, pathetically skinny cows graze in its grassy courtyard. A small, low cement wall encloses the station and its grounds. The main entrance is gained by walking up three long, low steps to a paved rectangular veranda. French doors open into the station itself.

On the day that I visited the Hué station it was cloudy and gray and all the French doors were shut. But when the caretaker saw a stranger prowling about the veranda, he hurried out. He was a small, genial Vietnamese who obviously drew some sense of importance out of retelling the story of the tragedy.

The caretaker first pointed to two holes in the veranda pavement which nobody had bothered to repair.

"It happened right there," he said. "All the windows and doors—everything near this veranda was shattered."

The journey to Hué was the last stop on a long investigation of the causes of the Buddhist crisis. The investigation in depth was undertaken because I quickly learned in the summer of 1963 that there was wide disagreement about what had happened.

For example, on June 30, 1963, a dispatch from Saigon to the *New York Times* said, "The Buddhists said that they would not join a commission to investigate the alleged Buddhist grievances unless the government accepted responsibility for the incident on May 8,

---

* The exact birth date of Buddha is in controversy. Some authorities insist he was born about 563 B.C. Elsewhere in Asia, Buddha's birthday of May 8, 1963, was considered his 2525th.

1963, that set off the crisis. *Troops fired* then on Buddhists demonstrating *against a ban on displaying their religious flag. Nine Buddhists were killed* [italics mine]."

But these three sentences do not reflect the true situation. And yet the account given in the *New York Times* news dispatch represents what many Americans, even some in official positions, still believe to be the truth about Hué. I find this appalling, because crucial national policy was, it now appears, based on "facts" of highly doubtful authenticity.

Certainly the truth about the outbreak of the crisis is essential to any verdict on the rights and wrongs of the actions of the Diem regime. Indeed the truth about Hué has a bearing on what is going on right now in Vietnam and vitally bears on judgments about the current aims of Thich Tri Quang and his band of Buddhist extremists.

My account is based on three sources: the stories of eyewitnesses and participants as told to me; testimony taken by the United Nations team investigating the alleged religious persecution in Vietnam in the fall of 1963; and the allegations and testimony of witnesses as contained in the indictment of Major Dang Sy, the Catholic assistant province chief at Hué, who was accused of being responsible for the incident. His trial was staged by a revolutionary military court in the spring of 1964. The trial was authorized by the regime of General Khanh, a Buddhist who in January, 1964, deposed the military junta that overthrew Diem.

According to the Khanh regime's own indictment of Dang Sy, eight persons (not nine) were killed at Hué, and not all were Buddhists. At least one was a Catholic and two were children.

A minor point?

Not at all. For if a Catholic and children were also victims, this helps dispel the widespread impression that the incident was directed solely by a Catholic against Buddhists.

Nor were the deaths the result of gunfire.

Dr. Le Khac Quyen, the medical director of the hospital at Hué, said in a statement incorporated in the Khanh regime's indictment that "the death of the people was caused by *an explosion* which took place in midair, and the *effet de souffle* and *éclatement* caused the decapitation and mutilation of the bodies." Dr. Quyen further said that he could not identify the nature of the explosion.

Dr. Quyen was a leader of the anti-Diem campaign in Hué. He is a physician and a disciple of Thich Tri Quang. In 1964 Dr. Quyen formed the National Salvation Council, which conducted a particularly savage anti-American and anti-Catholic campaign. It was a notable campaign because never in modern times in Vietnam had there been such attacks by one religion on another. Dr. Quyen thus would scarcely have gone out of his way to say something favorable about the Catholic Dang Sy.

As to the *Times* dispatch's assertion that there was a *ban* on Buddhist flags, no such thing existed. This dispatch implied also that there was some ruling applying *solely to Buddhists*. Again, this is not true. There was a Vietnamese government regulation against giving any religious flag—either the Buddhist or Catholic—precedence over the national flag in public places or in public view. *Inside* pagodas and *inside* churches, flags could be flown at will. The regulation applied to *all religions*.

There is no doubt, however, that the Vietnamese government's decision to revive these flag regulations on May 6, 1963, made possible the Hué tragedy.

Ironically, Diem's May 6 circular was provoked a few days earlier in Danang by excessive use by *Catholics* of Vatican flags, which were flown in profusion, whereas the national Vietnamese flags on view were few in number and sometimes tattered and torn.

It is clear that Diem's emphasis on precedence for the flag of Vietnam was part of his uphill struggle to give some sense of nationhood to Vietnamese of all faiths and superstitions. But the issuance of the circular on May 6 could not have been more ill-timed.

For of course the celebration of Buddha's birthday fell only two days later. At Hué, as was the custom, the city had been bedecked with Buddhist flags for many days prior to the receipt of the circular, which, owing to the slowness of communications, reached the city only on May 7. Therefore, since the flags were already hoisted on the main streets, in front of shops, on private homes, etc., considerable consternation was created by the May 6 circular amongst the Buddhist hierarchy at the Tu Dam Pagoda, which is the most important Buddhist center in Hué.

Fortunately the Vietnamese Minister of Interior, Bui Van Luong, arrived in Hué on the same date as the circular and was able to see for himself that a profusion of Buddhist flags were already in place. At once he recognized the bad impression that would be created if suddenly the government attempted to force a major change of plans, even to the point of insisting that a national flag be found to fly alongside every Buddhist emblem already hoisted.

"Therefore," explained the Interior Minister (as quoted in the United Nations report of December, 1963), "I told the administrative authorities in Hué provisionally not to apply the circular. . . ."

The Minister also took the precaution of visiting the Buddhist leaders at the Tu Dam Pagoda to explain the flag regulations and to assure them that under the circumstances the regulations would not be enforced.

"The leaders of the monks were very pleased," said Minister Bui Van Luong. "They listened to me and told me that I had given complete satisfaction to their desires." Thich Tri Quang was present during this exchange and joined in expressing satisfaction with arrangements.

Unfortunately, some Hué police did take down a number of flags before the province chief could get word to them that the orders had been changed.

And Thich Tri Quang got into the act. As soon as the Minister of the Interior had left the Tu Dam Pagoda, Thich Tri Quang sent a few monks around to tell the people to haul down flags, even though he knew this was no longer required, thanks to the Interior Minister's actions. The monks were told to tell the population that this was being done as a result of Diem's orders to "ban the Buddhist flag." The case being built against the government was blatantly phony, inasmuch as no such *ban* had been promulgated.

As it turned out, Thich Tri Quang had many strange tricks up his saffron sleeves on Buddha's birthday. For example, when Hué city and province officials arrived at the Tu Dam Pagoda for the birthday ceremonies, they found themselves staring at big banners bearing strident slogans directed against the government.

Such antigovernment propaganda at a religious ceremony of course flouted every regulation in the book. Under the rules of a government at war, slogans, speeches, and objectives of a large meeting had to be approved in advance. Indeed, the proposed "religious" program at the Tu Dam Pagoda had been scrutinized with special care, since under Hué custom the religious ceremonies of Buddha's birthday were always rebroadcast the same evening by the radio station.

The unprecedented appearance of a raft of antigovernment political slogans at a supposedly religious ceremony was the least of the surprises in store at the Tu Dam Pagoda on that day. For suddenly, right in the middle of the supposedly religious ceremony at the pagoda, Thich Tri Quang strode forward to seize the microphone. He began slowly and clearly to read anti-Diem slogans into it, thus ensuring that his bitter accusations would be recorded on tape. Then he followed with a vitriolic antigovernment speech on the subject of the nonexistent *ban* on Buddhist flags.

All this caused great commotion and excitement, because it was highly illegal as well as unprecedented to use a pagoda ceremony as a launching platform for antigovernment tirades.

The scene now shifted to the banks of the River of Perfumes. In early evening Thich Tri Quang and some of his disciples began telling the crowds still thronging the pagodas to "Go to the radio station— something very interesting will happen there."

About eight P.M., after the crowd had gathered at the station, Thich Tri Quang arrived carrying in his own hands the tape recording which contained his antigovernment outburst recorded that morning at the Tu Dam Pagoda. By now all Hué knew what had happened. So when Thich Tri Quang made the impossible demand that the director of the station play his tape of antigovernment outpourings, he was refused.

Thich Tri Quang proceeded to stage an oratorical spectacular. Angrily he turned to the crowd pressing into the grassy courtyard of the station and encouraged them to shout abuse at the station director for his refusal to play the propagandistic tape. In the middle of all this shouting and cursing some of the mob started to press forward onto the cement veranda.

"So the director of the radio station became very frightened and locked himself inside," the Interior Minister related. "The first thing he did was to telephone the province chief [Nguyen Van Dang] and the military authorities. The chief of province is a practicing Buddhist and a recognized spiritual son of the venerable monk Thich Tinh Khiet. . . . Soon the province chief arrived on the scene and saw what was happening. He tried to appease Thich Tri Quang, but the latter would not listen. So he had to ask for . . . armored cars to come to the rescue, because he hoped that their mere presence would frighten the crowd and prevent it from breaking the doors and windows of the radio station. The director . . . was afraid for his machines. . . . Thich Tri Quang repeatedly demanded that the province chief broadcast his antigovernment tape. He told some faithful followers, who were already very excited, to climb on the veranda to break the windows, force the doors, and enter the radio station. . . ."

According to the indictment presented at his trial, it was at this point that Major Dang Sy, the assistant province chief, arrived with some armored cars. His orders were to disperse the crowd. The orders, as Province Chief Nguyen Van Dang acknowledged at the major's trial, were general in nature. Dang Sy was told what to do but not how to do it.

The scene in front of the station was a shambles when Major Dang Sy arrived. Motorbikes, bicycles, and closely packed people were blocking the attempts of the armored cars to get close. At the station's entrance on the veranda, excited Thich Tri Quang followers were throwing stones at policemen and firemen. The latter were aiming giant hoses at the crowd, seeking to drive them away from the entrance of the radio station.

But the jet streams from the fire hoses only provoked the mob into greater frenzy. Seeing this, Province Chief Nguyen Van Dang went inside the station, taking Thich Tri Quang with him. From inside the station the province chief began broadcasting appeals to the firemen to shut off the water.

"While we were inside," said the province chief at the Dang Sy trial, "two loud explosions suddenly reverberated on the veranda. Then came the sounds of broken glass, gun shots, and exploding hand grenades."

The two explosions were also heard by Major Dang Sy. The awesome sound reached him just as his armored car was entering the gate in the low wall surrounding the station's courtyard. In the darkness and confusion Major Dang Sy was unable to see what was going on and he feared the worst, a Viet Cong attack. Therefore he pulled out his gun and fired three shots in the air. This was a prearranged signal authorizing his troops to use grenades if necessary to disperse the crowds. The grenades in question were American-supplied MK III concussion grenades. At least fifteen of these were thrown. As a result of all this, the crowd fled.

When the province chief and station officials burst out onto the veranda, they saw pools of blood, seven dead, and one child dying. All the dead were lying on the concrete veranda, but the explosion had been of such force that bits and pieces of flesh and human hair were widely scattered and found on the wheels of at least one armored car.

The most precise and detailed account of the state of the bodies has come from Interior Minister Bui Van Luong:

I went to see the bodies of the dead. I found most of them had the top of their heads blown off, but there were no wounds below the chest. There were no metal splinters in the bodies, but only holes. No metal was found on the concrete veranda. All the bodies were found on the veranda, none of them in the courtyard. I asked the legal doctor to make a post-mortem and send me the results. He made a very careful examination and took out the organs for examination and sent his findings to me in Saigon.

Afterward there were rumors that tanks had driven into the crowd and crushed the people. But the fact is that tanks were not used. Only lightly armored cars. The dead had not been crushed but had had their heads blown off and had been wounded only from the chest up.

I have now in hand the findings of the legal doctor, who says they were killed by an explosion and a violent blast.

When I came back from Hué to Saigon, I attended a meeting between Buddhist leaders and the President. Among the Buddhists was Dr. Mai Tho Truyen (head of the Saigon Buddhist Association). Dr. Truyen asked me the reason for the explosion and deaths. I told him that the experts in weaponry whom we had consulted in both Hué and Saigon were of the opinion that it was probably bombs made of plastic [explaining why no metal splinters were found]. I also told Dr. Truyen that we had many bullets because the United States had given us many bullets free. But we had no plastic. Plastic is the arm of the Viet Cong guerrilla.

Immediately after May 8 President Diem ordered a formal investigation of the Hué affairs. For this purpose he appointed a three-man technical commission led by Major General Tran Van Don, the acting head of the army. (General Don was considered a man of integrity by the Americans.) The commission also included the surgeon general of the Vietnamese army and its chief of ordnance. After extensive interrogation of witnesses General Don's mission cited plastic charges as the cause of the deaths on May 8.

At the time, nonetheless, the Diem regime's claim that plastic bombs caused the deaths was widely ridiculed.

Unfortunately, no American officials were witness to the incident. The American consul had been out of town, but he tended to disbelieve the government efforts to place the blame on Viet Cong plastics. He felt that the American-supplied grenades were responsible for the killings.

At the trial of Dang Sy the Khanh regime's prosecutor also insisted that the deaths had been caused by MK III American-supplied grenades whose use had been ordered by the young Vietnamese major.

Khanh's military court, incidentally, did not even consider the sensational accusation of a German doctor at Hué that the eight deaths had been caused by *artillery* shells. For there was in fact no artillery around. The armored cars were equipped with thirty-caliber machine guns, BAR automatic rifles, and submachine guns—that is, small arms. Even the prosecution witnesses at the Dang Sy trial were agreed that these automatic weapons on the armored cars were never brought into use.

The conviction of Major Dang Sy by the Saigon military court was based on the argument that the eight deaths were caused by the American-supplied MK III concussion grenades thrown by the troops at the signal from Major Dang Sy.

The argument is in contradiction to the Pentagon's assessment of the explosive power of the MK III grenade.

For example, the "U.S. Department of the Army Field Manual Number 23-30 on Grenades and Pyrotechnics" states that "the maximum capabilities of the MK III grenades are concussion, burst eardrums, and shock." In other words, even the maximum effects are nonfatal.

Additionally, various weapons experts were cited at the Dang Sy trial to the effect that the MK III grenade does not have sufficient force to decapitate and mutilate eight persons, let alone bring down the ceilings, doors, and windows that were adjacent to the concrete veranda.

Even though the relevant technical evidence certainly would seem to rule out the MK III as responsible for the May 8 deaths, nobody can *prove* that plastic bombs did it. But circumstantial evidence would certainly point to plastic bombs as the most likely suspects. The lack of *any* metal splinters in bodies or on the veranda suggests it. Also, the effects, such as decapitation, were the same as the results of the bomb detonated by the Viet Cong outside the U.S. embassy in Saigon in the spring of 1965. In Saigon, as in Hué, many Vietnamese on the street near the embassy simply had their heads blown off.

The conviction of Major Dang Sy certainly throws no light on the matter one way or another. The trial was clearly rigged from the start. During the trial Major Dang Sy, who was seven times decorated for heroic action against the Viet Cong and who is the father of eight children, told journalists, "I am guilty of two mistakes. I am a Catholic. I obeyed orders."

Major Dang Sy also told at his trial of efforts made by Vietnamese police to force him to shift the blame for the Hué killings onto Archbishop Ngo Dinh Thuc, the elder brother of Diem.

"They kept me for months in a darkened underground cell," said Major Dang Sy. "They promised me I could go free if I would put the blame on the Ngo family. I refused."

This, taken together with the conduct of the entire Dang Sy trial, is a vivid commentary on the quality of "justice" that came into being in a post-Diem era. It is also a sharp reminder of the strange double standard with which the West deals with Vietnam. If President Diem had offered such mock "justice" he would have been reviled ad infinitum.

But the Dang Sy case was taken at face value in the West and dismissed with only a few paragraphs in our most prominent American newspapers. The U.S. embassy, so quick with its condemnations of Diem, had nothing at all to say of the Dang Sy trial.

The trial was to have its effects inside Vietnam. Observing the penalty paid by Dang Sy for following orders, Vietnamese army officers were subsequently to stand tragically aside in many instances. For example, paratroopers permitted Vietnamese to hack each other to death during a bloody "Buddhist" attack on a Catholic refugee village at Danang. Questioned on this *laissez faire* attitude, a paratroop officer said he would not risk becoming "another Dang Sy" without specific written orders. That is why he had refused to act. So nine people died and a village was burned down.

Honest men have subsequently stated that Dang Sy's condemnation was a politically motivated act. Major General Tran Van Khiem, who was Minister of National Defense under General Khanh, states, "Dang Sy was condemned in order to appease Thich Tri Quang. It was a price General Khanh felt he had to pay in order to win Thich Tri Quang's favor."

With the benefit of hindsight, it is certainly clear that President Diem showed incredible political insensitivity in reactivating regulations controlling the public display of religious flags two days before Buddha's birthday. But as the situation in fact developed at Hué, Interior Minister Bui Van Luong under normal circumstances surely should have saved the situation by his wise instructions to suspend application of the flag regulations until the celebration was over.

However, it is also clear, with the benefit of hindsight, that Thich Tri Quang was determined to find an excuse for launching a campaign against the government with Buddhism as the issue. Otherwise why would he have pretended to be satisfied with Minister Bui Van Luong's assurance on the flag issue but then proceed to foment antigovernment propaganda on the basis that no such assurances existed?

On this point Minister Bui Van Luong states:

I was very surprised when I heard about the bloody incidents of May 8. So I went back to Hué [May 9]. I asked myself why the leaders of the monks had given me assurance that they were satisfied and now they had had the incidents. I could not understand at the time, but later I obtained a handwritten statement* from a close collaborator of the Thich Tri Quang, Dang Ngoc Luu. I read it and then I understood. . . . In his declaration he said that this incident, which is part of a Communist conspiracy, dates back to 1960, when agreement was reached on the form of incidents to be created.

I can only conclude that the circular of May 6 was used only as a plausible reason for creating incidents, since the conspiracy had already been decided as early as 1960. When I arrived in Hué [May 9] the city was still very excited. There were demonstrations of certain groups and individuals in the streets still going on. I again saw the leaders of the monks, especially Thich Tri Quang. I did not realize at the time that he was the leader, because, according to the prevailing customs of the Buddhist hierarchy, he is younger and therefore subordinate to the old reverend, Thich Tinh Khiet. I did not suspect at that moment the true role that Thich Tri Quang played in the incidents. I discovered of course from my investigations that it was Thich Tri Quang who changed everything in the program of Buddha's feast—a program agreed with the local authorities. He changed it unilaterally, without consulting the administrative authorities. I thought it would be best to speak to him and ask him the why and the how of things, and I did.

When I met him, I reproached him. Only two days before I had seen him, I had respected him and he had given me assurance that the explanation I had given him and the instructions not to do anything to implement the circular of May 6 for the time being were satisfactory. In spite of these assurances, he proceeded to create incidents. I told him that as Minister of the Interior I did not wish to see incidents in the streets of Hué which had been instigated by him.

I may add that when I drove into Hué, I had found him among the demonstrators. I had him immediately summoned to my office, where I told him that I did not want any more trouble. I put a jeep and microphone at his disposal and told him to go with the chief of the province into the streets to calm the demonstrators. Thich Tri Quang agreed to do it. And in fact he kept that promise. Again he assured me that no more

*The statement was lost in the shambles of the *coup d'état*. But other Vietnamese Buddhists, including a prominent member of the laymen's association in Hué, have said that Thich Tri Quang had been planning a revolt against the regime since 1960 but had been waiting for the right time and right issue.

incidents would occur. But it was only a strategem to appease me. As soon as I returned to Saigon, new incidents broke out.

Is there any way that President Diem could have defused this crisis deliberately created by Thich Tri Quang and nurtured not only by his propaganda but also by the horrifying suicides by fire arranged by the Buddhist "suicide-promotion groups"?

The American position at the time, according to John Mecklin, director of the U.S.I.A., was to "urge Diem to repair all Buddhist grievances forthwith, to *accept responsibility* for the May 8 killings, and to indemnify the victims and *apologize*, perhaps by visiting Hué himself to do so." (Ambassador Nolting was on a Mediterranean vacation at the time.)

According to Mecklin, William Trueheart, the chargé d'affaires, applied, on orders from Washington, *"direct, relentless, table-hammering pressure on Diem such as the United States had seldom before attempted with a sovereign friendly government* [italics mine]. . . . In despair Trueheart in June resorted to a formal warning to Diem that if he continued repressive measures [police effort to prevent and disperse *illegal* demonstrations] the United States would be forced to disassociate itself publicly from such actions, as indeed we did two months later. The warning was a momentous step. It amounted to a direct official command from the United States. Public disassociation could have disastrous results, encouraging the Buddhists, heartening the Viet Cong, strengthening the regime's foreign critics, *perhaps even stimulating the Vietnamese army to try another coup* [italics mine]."

Mecklin accurately reflected the view I heard from every American in Vietnam that summer when he said, "If Diem had immediately heeded American advice, he probably *could have stopped the upheaval before it got started* [italics mine]."

But *could he*?

How was this possible if, as the facts show, Thich Tri Quang deliberately provoked the crisis in order to promote disorder? It stands to reason that if Thich Tri Quang at Hué indulged in so much trouble and trickery to provoke upheaval, he had well-laid plans to turn it to his advantage. We know that by July Thich Tri Quang was openly talking of toppling Diem. And during the summer of 1963 Thich Tri Quang saw to it that no matter what concessions Diem made the crisis was kept at boiling point. It all showed careful, clever planning.

The Washington-generated pressure on Diem for concilation was based on the assumption that Thich Tri Quang's grievances concerning flags and such were what motivated his Buddhist protest movement. But it is evident that what Thich Tri Quang wanted was a pretext to seize on. His objective was not a solution, but no less than Diem's head.

Perhaps Diem might have had a better image in the United States if he had personally shown greater immediate public concern for the victims of the Hué tragedy. He did instantly order generous indemnification of the families who suffered losses, but this was never publicized. Perhaps he was too prideful. So inwardly sure of his innocence was Diem that he did not deign to go to the trouble of proving it. He would certainly have pleased the Madison Avenue boys at the embassy by visiting a pagoda or two.

But such stratagems would scarcely have appeased Thich Tri Quang, whose target was not Diem's image but his jugular.

Indeed, two days after the Hué incident Thich Tri Quang confidently assured an American official in that city that his anti-Diem campaign would not be halted till the regime had been overthrown. Neither the embassy nor Washington, it appears, took this threat at all seriously, and indeed one of Thich Tri Quang's great strengths was the degree to which the Americans underestimated his guile and his ability to manipulate public opinion.

In fact, the only concession to the Buddhists that Diem refused to make in the summer of 1963 was to admit the Vietnamese army's guilt for the eight deaths in advance of the joint and internationally supervised investigation of the affair. Such an investigation was first demanded by Thich Tri Quang, then rejected when offered.

And, as we have seen, a cool look at the facts shows that there is no *proof* whatever of the Vietnamese army's guilt. In fact, if the American army manual on pyrotechnics is to be believed concerning the MK III grenade, all the evidence is in the other direction—plastic bombs.

From the point of view of an Oriental ruler dependent on army morale, should Diem really have accepted responsibility for the tragic incident which he—and his entire government—deeply believed was not of the army's making? Should he have blamed his troops when he believed them innocent?

All during the summer of 1963 officials in Washington and Saigon called Diem a bungler precisely because he wouldn't publicly go to the confessional, apologize to Thich Tri Quang, and do it with a demeaning abasement that was wholly alien to a prideful man, not to say a mandarin.

What is the other side of the coin? Could it be that Diem did not act against the Buddhist revolt soon enough?

This view has been precisely expressed to me by a Vietnamese professor who, at this writing, is prominent in Saigon political life:

President Diem's greatest mistake during the spring and summer of 1963 was to listen to the Americans. Washington forced Diem to dig his own political grave when it urged him in the summer of 1963 to be conciliatory and allow that extremist wing of Buddhists and students to create turmoil in the streets, and so to parade their false charges in the gullible American press and powerful television media. During this period of "conciliation" the Buddhists cleverly used to the maximum the time of supposed negotiation with the government as a cover to slander it and weaken it. Pretty soon the whole world began to believe the accusations against Diem. The Americans were tying Diem's hands behind his back and telling the manipulators of the mob, "Hit him again." Thich Tri Quang can hardly be blamed for being smart enough to aim his blows for the moment when CBS News and the *New York Times* were ready.

Diem knew that Thich Tri Quang was using the Xa Loi Pagoda as a propaganda and subversion command post to topple his regime. Diem knew that Thich Tri Quang had served with the Communists and that the tumult was serving Communist ends. He knew all about those horrible Buddhist suicide squads in which monks brainwashed likely recruits and furnished them with gasoline and antipain pills. Diem had every sound reason to end the mobocracy, arrest its leaders, disband its suicide squads, and get on with the war. Instead, to please the Americans, Diem allowed the turbulence to go on, in the name of conciliation, for three whole months, and in the process permitted the Buddhists to poison world opinion to the extent that Washington decided to get rid of him. It was a perfect vicious circle and served Diem right for ever having trusted the Americans in the first place.

Perhaps Diem would get some satisfaction from a wry remark made in the spring of 1965 by Secretary of Defense McNamara: "Thich Tri Quang has made serious trouble for us before and he will again. . . . Perhaps the greatest mistake we made was when we gave Thich Tri Quang asylum at the U.S. embassy" (from September through November, 1963).

But the fact is that in 1963 we were trying to force Diem to act on policies which we now concede to be mistakes.

CHAPTER 7

The War: Heads You Win, Tails I Lose?

During the bitter intra-administration argument on the war in Vietnam in September, 1963, President Kennedy dispatched Major General Victor H. Krulak, head of Counterinsurgency, and Joseph Mendenhall, a State Department expert on Vietnam, to make one more tour of the country to determine the effect, if any, of the Buddhist crisis on the war against the Communist Viet Cong.

After they had returned to Washington and had each delivered a formal report to the National Security Council, President Kennedy asked wryly, "Have you two fellows been in the same country?" For General Krulak and Mr. Mendenhall brought back from Vietnam entirely opposite conclusions about what they had seen.

In a sense, Krulak and Mendenhall had *not* been in the same country. Mr. Mendenhall gave the President a metropolitan reaction. He had visited only Saigon and Hué, those havens of Vietnam's chronically critical and bickering intellectuals. General Krulak gave the President a rural reaction, having visited all four corps areas and six divisional and some twenty-five regimental and battalion headquarters.

Indeed, President Kennedy's question to Krulak and Mendenhall summed up in capsule form much of our trouble in Vietnam.

Many of our policy failures resulted from far too many authorities, in much too high places, being misguided in the view that there was only one Vietnam—the slightly effete, volatile society built around Hué and Saigon. This was the only Vietnam most high-level visitors ever saw. Events in these two cities—the suicides, student protests, demonstrations, terror—dominated the American headlines. But the war is not, and never was, in the metropolitan centers. It is, and was, in the countryside, where the food and shelter and intelligence needed by the Viet Cong are to be found. The country that General Krulak saw was the theater of war. The country that Mr. Mendenhall saw was the theater of political intrigue. So the controversy between them was inevitable.

The war in Vietnam has a way of producing such controversies because it has been a dichotomous, decentralized, sprawling series of engagements, without fixed lines and a clearly identifiable enemy. It has the mobility of a ballet and a cast of characters as variegated as the arrivals in New York harbor at the floodtide of immigration. It mocks the conventional rules of warfare and defies the standard yard-sticks for measuring progress and prospects of battle. To the Ameri-cans it is a new combat experience. The language, customs, and mentality of the ally often form incomprehensible patterns. They are the despair of military-manual writers. And the Communist enemy is a master of deception. In any given tactical situation the elementary facts are as elusive as the guerrilla. The war in all its aspects—politi-cal, military, psychological—has a prismatic quality. The angle of vision and the standpoint of the viewer must be gauged with care lest the illusions be mistaken for reality.

The difficulty of a clear view is compounded by the fact that the war in Vietnam has passed through at least three different phases.

In its first phase, beginning in 1959 (some claim 1957) and ex-tending roughly into 1960, the Communists staged mainly a war of *terror*. In night and in stealth they would enter a village and murder the schoolteacher or the village elders or the district chief. At first only a few thousand officers and noncommissioned officers, plus political commissars of Ho Chi Minh's Red "Viet Minh" army, were sent south via Laos or other clandestine routes to join agents left behind after the Geneva agreements partition of Vietnam in 1954. These hard-core Communist infiltrators used a combination of terrorism and persuasion to "recruit" villagers into their ranks. These "converts" remained peasants by day but became practitioners of ambush and terror by night. Weapons were largely primitive.

In phase two, starting sometime in 1961, the war became two-pronged: terrorism and guerrilla warfare. The pace of infiltration increased, although the scope of the fighting was limited to squad-, company-, and battalion-size attacks, almost all of a hit-and-run character. But in addition to irregulars, Ho Chi Minh's army officers and noncommissioned infiltrators were at this point forming up regular Viet Cong (as they were called in the South) battalions in which soldiering was a full-time occupation. The hard core of these battalions were Red army infiltrators from the North, but the ranks were filled out by kidnapping young men and other methods of Viet Cong "recruitment." In this phase somewhat antique rifles and Molotov cocktails and bamboo daggers were supplemented by light machine guns and other automatic weapons. A few elite Viet Cong battalions were supplied with hand-carried mortars. In this period the capability of the Viet Cong vis-à-vis the Vietnamese National army was roughly equivalent to the strength of the Communist Hukbalahaps in the Philippines vis-à-vis the Philippine National army at the height of the Red attempt to subvert the Filipinos.

In phase three the war became three-pronged: terrorist, guerrilla, *and* conventional. At this point, which followed the overthrow of Diem in November, 1963, Ho Chi Minh enormously escalated the infiltration into the South, hoping to move swiftly enough to take advantage of the turmoil and chaos that he felt sure would prevail as *coup d'états* and bloody riots became the disorder of the day. By mid-1965 Ho Chi Minh had fielded a whole new Red army in South Vietnam, which included crack battalions and regiments that had once won victories over the French. These Red Viet units were capable of conventional warfare, that is, sustained offensive operations, rather than mere hit-and-run raids. They were equipped with the heaviest weapons ever to reach the Viet Cong: recoilless rifles, mortars, artillery, flame-throwers. Many of the weapons were the best that Czechoslovakia, the Soviet Union, and China had to offer.

Thus by 1965 the Americans and the Vietnamese were fighting three different kinds of war at once. These three phases of the Vietnamese war in the countryside have to be kept in mind for any clearheaded judgment of what we did right and what we did wrong at any given period of the war.

It is obvious, for example, that a strategic hamlet, with all its barbed wire and internal defenses, planned in the period between 1961 and 1963 for protection against a Viet Cong enemy capable of hit-and-run attacks in company or battalion strength would be inadequate to withstand pressure in 1965 from an enemy capable of staging regimental-size raids supported by artillery.

But does that mean that the strategic hamlet was a bad idea?

Of course not. To so contend would be like saying that aspirin was not good because it did not cure a patient afflicted with pneumonia!

The most celebrated clash of views on whether the United States was losing or winning the war took place in the summer of 1963 in Saigon between the resident American correspondents in Vietnam and the American mission. The resident American journalists felt that the word "losing" properly described the United States effort almost from its very inception in early 1962, and that the American mission was covering up when it said that by midsummer, 1963, the war had taken a turn for the better. In its corner of the ring the American mission was not flatly predicting that victory was at hand. But Ambassador Frederick Nolting had said that the war was "*beginning* to be won." General Paul Harkins, head of the military advisory group, had stated flatly that "the Viet Cong are going to lose."

No great prescience is needed to see that if the United States effort in Vietnam was a losing one from the start, it would make nigh irrefutable the argument that the United States has no business getting mixed up in wars of liberation because we are doomed to fail. This contention has become, in fact, the main prop of the "can't-win" school. And the corollary of the "can't-win" argument is that in the case of subversive wars the United States should either stay out or get out, regardless of America's strategic interests.

But if at some point in the war in Vietnam the tide was turning in our favor, then the argument crumbles under its own weight. For if we could turn the tide once, why can't we do it again in Vietnam or any other place where the Communists start their wars of subversion?

Not the least unusual feature of the Vietnamese struggle has been the matter of newspaper coverage. In most wars correspondents cover the battle situations by going with the troops to more or less discernible front lines—lines of advance, retreat, or stalemate. But in Vietnam the front lines were everywhere and nowhere. Even in the countryside, where the war begins, a community thought to be clear of Viet Cong might be the scene of a sudden hit-and-run terrorist action.

The face of war in Vietnam varied enormously from province to province, a complicating factor in accurately picturing the true situation. In the tip of the delta south of Saigon, for example, the countryside belonged mostly to the Viet Cong. Only a few enclaves were held by the free Vietnamese. In the coastal strip north of Saigon—from Phan Rang to Hué—the area in 1963 was largely under Vietnamese government control, or so the American mission claimed.

To check out these claims, I traveled to all four main areas of the fighting and talked to dozens of American and Vietnamese soldiers, peasants and—the most fascinating of all—many deserters from the Viet Cong.

One priority mission on my itinerary was to visit storied Quang Ngai province. In Washington officials had described progress there as "a miraculous success story." They had also complained with justice that the Saigon resident press corps had ignored it.

And yet Quang Ngai was of pivotal importance, both militarily and psychologically. In the time of the French, Quang Ngai had been known as the Red province. Many of its people had been sympathetic to Ho Chi Minh when he led the fight against French colonial rule. Indeed after the Geneva agreement of 1954 many of the Viet Minh regiments formed from those who came out of South Vietnam consisted of young soldiers born and raised in the area around Quang Ngai. They went north because as regular Viet Minh soldiers they were subject to the orders and discipline of the Hanoi command, irrespective of where they were born. And when Ho Chi Minh began to send soldier-infiltrators into the South, he gave soldiers from Quang Ngai province priority in assignments to fight in the area. His reasoning was soundly practical since a soldier born in Quang Ngai would be acquainted with the terrain and the dialect.

It has been argued—inexplicably to me—that Ho Chi Minh's dispatch of Red army officers and men into South Vietnam was not really an invasion because some (but by no means all) of these men were southerners by birth. What kind of logic is this? Let's turn it around. Supposing the United States and Diem had organized Hanoi-born Vietnamese into military units and sent them into North Vietnam to "liberate" it from Ho Chi Minh? Would the Communists have considered it any less an invasion because the places of birth of those who had come to overthrow them happened to be located north of the Seventeenth Parallel?

In Quang Ngai at least two crack Communist battalions—the Sixtieth and Eightieth—had made their way down the Ho Chi Minh trail during 1961 and 1962 into the foothills in the western part of the province and settled there. The foothills were the headquarters for their harassing raids against the villages and towns. The villages were totally unprotected when the Viet Cong first arrived and many mothers and fathers had personally seen their sons kidnapped and carried off at gunpoint to serve these Viet Cong units.

When Major Roger J. John Kelly, of Allegan, Michigan, arrived in Quang Ngai in late 1962, its people were sullen, sickly, terrified, and hungry.

The American major, the holder of combat ribbons for Korea, New Guinea, and Luzon campaigns, had the uncharted post of being adviser to the Vietnamese province chief at Quang Ngai. As such, he was to become an outstanding example of the versatile new breed of Americans developed by training and circumstance to cope with that strange war. Major Kelly could not rest on mere expertise as a soldier. He had to know all about firepower and the capabilities of weapons, but equally important, he had to be able to apply basic common sense in such fields as the construction of pig sties, eradication of rats, and fighting psychological and political war.

Major Kelly met me upon my arrival at Quang Ngai's dusty airport with its dirt runway, and as we drove into the provincial capital he talked eagerly and intensely about his assignment, which he characterized as "the most rewarding, exciting, eye-opening experience that I have ever had":

The reason the job gets a hold on you is that you can see the things getting better before your very eyes. You can feel the Vietnamese trusting you more each day. And you know you are really doing all right when they start begging you to extend. . . . [The ordinary tour of duty is twelve months, and the word "extend" means volunteering for a second tour.]

When I first came here things were really at rock bottom. There was scarcely any attempt to protect the villages. I asked the province chief why he didn't at least put barbed wire around the villages and make it a little less comfortable for the Viet Cong to sneak into them at night and get food and kidnap youngsters. The province chief just looked at me and asked me where would I suggest that barbed wire be procured and how would it be paid for. Do you know there was no barbed wire to be had in South Vietnam? Do you know that barbed wire is damned expensive? Well, I got some money allotted out of the economic-aid budget and we worked with the villagers and got them to put up fortifications. We didn't move the villagers—their homes were grouped together to begin with. We just put fortifications, barbed wire, around them. In this way they were turned into strategic hamlets. We also worked to build up the strength of a new Vietnamese army division being formed up here—the Twenty-fifth. Well, in mid-April the test of all we had done was at hand. The Viet Cong Sixtieth decided to attack the string of eleven strategic hamlets to which we had given priority.

Here Major Kelly paused to show on a map that this string of hamlets forms a giant semicircle around a series of low-lying rice fields. The Viet Cong sneaked into the rice fields in the dark and attacked from there. He said:

And that was the battle that bloodied the Twenty-fifth Division and made soldiers out of 'em. It was the first time that armored personnel-carriers had been used in this area and the Viet Cong did not know what they were tangling with. That battle raged for four days and when it was over the Viet Cong had been torn to pieces. We picked up two hundred and twenty-six bodies out of those rice fields. I counted them myself. I didn't want any back talk from Saigon. The effect of that victory on morale around here was sensational. Quang Ngai City gradually turned from a terror-stricken town to a town enjoying a building boom.

And that's not all. When I first came here the rice was yellow and sickly. There was only one crop a year. The rats were so fierce that they ate up eighty percent of the rice before it could be harvested. Quite apart from being terrified of the Viet Cong, the people were half starving. We had to import rice from the delta. So we went to work to turn things around. We started a rat-eradication program and a fertilizer program. The U.S. operational mission came in and showed the peasants how to use fertilizer. We built pig sties and brought in pigs and lent them out for breeding. We showed them how to make compost out of pig manure so that they could make their own fertilizer. Pretty soon the Vietnamese of Quang Ngai will be close to self-sufficient in fertilizer and will be exporting pigs. And just take a look at those beautiful green, thick, high stalks of rice.

The major's arm pointed toward the jade-green fields, where fragile Vietnamese girls in their straw bonnets were carrying buckets of precious water from the canal to the crops. And those shimmering green fields were indeed beautiful.

In short, the story of Quang Ngai was, for a change, one to gladden the hearts of the American taxpayer. Here was an instance where our aid was getting down to the little people and with spectacular success. In Quang Ngai, and indeed in several other places in Vietnam, what impressed me was how drastically a peasant's life could be changed for the better in a short time by the effective application of American aid. Here had been semistarvation. Now there were two rice crops a year!

But in Quang Ngai, as elsewhere in Vietnam, the peasants' improved lot could be maintained only so long as the strategic hamlets could be kept out of the villainous reach of the Viet Cong. Nothing is more naïve than the belief in some circles in America that if you give a peasant a well or some medicine or some "democracy" he will suddenly have the strength of ten in coping with the Viet Cong. The Vietnamese, being prone to live, consider water important but more important is avoiding death. And if a Viet Cong squad sneaks into a village at night, puts a gun at the back of a peasant's neck, and orders him to throw a grenade into the well and destroy it—or be destroyed —the well is destroyed, and no questions are asked. That is why physical security—freedom from marauding Viet Cong—is even more important than economic aid in the war in Vietnam. That also is why it is blather to say the problem is more political than military. The problem is both—and a lot more.

According to Major Kelly, there was a striking difference in peasant attitudes after the mid-April victory over the Viet Cong.

"The most important thing," he said, "was that after that battle the villagers, instead of being neutral, started coming to us with information about the Communists. And that is a real turning point."

I was anxious to see the scene of the "victory" and talk to the hamlet's defenders. It was twenty miles distant from Quang Ngai City, the province capital, and a lovely drive on a hard-surface road through the countryside, whose glistening green rice was the pride and joy of Major Kelly's life.

Strategic hamlets are, roughly speaking, Far Eastern versions of the stockades that American pioneers built to protect themselves from marauding Indians. The Vietnamese use bamboo instead of logs. Most peasants have not been physically moved from their old huts, although at the beginning of the program there were some unfortunate instances in which the Vietnamese army forced entire families to pick up their belongings and go against their will to places three to four miles distant from their ancestral rice fields.

The strategic-hamlet idea was first successfully applied in Malaya in its war against Communist guerrillas. It proved to be an effective way of separating the peasants and their rice from the marauding Communists. And the Communist who cannot get rice from the peasant often suffers from hunger in a comparatively barren province like Quang Ngai, especially when he makes his headquarters in the foothills.

In the strategic-hamlet system the peasants are backed by a village militia. Under the hamlet concept the village militia can swiftly invoke the help of regular Vietnamese army units if a large-scale Viet Cong attack develops. And on April 15 the Twenty-fifth Vietnamese Division had responded swiftly to the cries for help—flares and radio appeals—from the hamlets.

The eleven victorious hamlets obviously took pride in keeping their fortification in good shape. Outside the hamlet were deep, wide trenches filled with bamboo stakes. In some cases the trenches were filled with water. Then came the fences wrapped in barbed wire. Then, on the inside, still another bamboo-filled trench. Even though all the hamlets were contiguous, like links in a chain, a gate and a guard separated one hamlet from another.

Wandering around the hamlets with my interpreter (Major Kelly, who was dispensing candies to the children in the vicinity of the jeep), I clearly sensed that morale was high. By contrast, in a frightened Viet Cong-penetrated village, the peasants quite logically keep their distance. They don't want the Viet Cong to see them talking to an American; Communist retaliation for such fraternization is notorious, not infrequently a bullet in the back of the head.

As we walked through our hamlet of the April 15 victory, children, teen-agers, and even old ladies followed us as if we were pied pipers. Almost nobody had heard about the so-called Buddhist crisis and their lack of interest was polite but plain. The young teen-agers were, for example, far more anxious to show us exactly how their victory over the Viet Cong had been won and to describe their own roles in the fighting.

It was a heartening day, and I was sorry to leave.

When we had dinner that evening at the American compound in Quang Ngai City, it was the same optimistic story. Admiration for the Twenty-fifth Vietnamese Division, Commander Colonel Luu Lan, and the Vietnamese province chief Colonel Nguyen Van Tat was considerable among the American advisers. Some gripes could be heard, but remarkably few.

But how typical was Quang Ngai?

Progress here was no doubt exceptional. The Quang Ngai peasants had been considered possibly sympathetic to the Viet Cong, since many of their sons or relatives had been fighting the French as units of Ho Chi Minh's army and had been ordered north at the time of the Geneva partition. And yet, when the chips were down, the peasants had helped to give the Viet Cong one of their worst setbacks of the war. It had been a deep fear of the Vietnamese military that the Communists might try to concentrate on Quang Ngai province and use it as the spearpoint of an effort to cut Vietnam in two. If Quang

Ngai province were seized by the Communists, they could then turn north and try to annex the area between Quang Ngai and the Seventeenth Parallel—the dividing line between Free Vietnam and Communist Vietnam. This would accomplish a *de facto* second annexation. Now, for the time being, these fears were stilled, though as we shall see, the Viet Cong were in 1965 to try this tactic of cutting South Vietnam in two by seizing Quang Ngai and nearby northern provinces.

Quang Ngai's success story was unmatched anywhere I visited, except possibly in the areas surrounding the coastal city of Phan Rang, where many Muslim Chams live.

But even if the accomplishments elsewhere in the North were less dramatic and inspiring it was nonetheless agreed by the U.S. advisers that progress had been made in other key areas, such as Hué, Danang, and Qui Nhon. American soldiers and civilians were eager to document their contentions that there had been improvement in the security and well-being of the Vietnamese in their area as compared with the situation when the American effort began in 1962. And this, of course, was the only fair comparison to be made.

In other words, my travels convinced me that in the past twelve months—between the summer of 1962 and the summer of 1963—things had been looking up in the coastal areas of Central Vietnam. The improvement was genuine and documentable. Granted, improvement is not the same as winning. But it isn't losing either.

Farther west, in the lushly beautiful mountains and valleys occupied by the Montagnard tribesmen of the northwestern highlands, Americans in charge of coaxing the mountain folk away from their nomadic ways and into strategic hamlets had hilarious but heartening stories to tell. Along with a few Montagnard leaders already in the valleys, the Americans had managed in the short space of a year and a half to persuade two hundred thousand of the tribesmen to try their luck in government-protected hamlets.

But it had not been easy.

Spinning out the yarn over coffee in the mess hall at the Pleiku compound (the site of the Viet Cong attack that triggered the bombings of the North in 1965), a veteran colonel told of his trials and tribulations in the "taming " of the Montagnards. He had tried to get through to them by relying on agents, leaflets (relying on drawings rather than text), and messages delivered by phonographs broadcasting from low-flying small planes that would dip low over the Montagnard villages.

It was Montagnard custom to find a propitious place in the mountains, slash it, burn it, and then farm it for two or three years until it became infertile. Then they would move on and repeat the process elsewhere. But up in the mountains the settlements of the tribesmen had become a source of food supply for the Viet Cong. And the Viet Cong would also impress them into service as guides, and on occasion, kidnap their young.

Even so, according to the colonel, "the program got nowhere in the first couple of months. Then, when we were just about ready to give up, about a dozen Montagnards, mostly old women, old men, and children, came to us carrying the leaflets. We treated them as if they were royalty—or rather as if we were rushing them for the best fraternity in the land. There wasn't anything we didn't give them: food, blankets, soap, medicine, ice cream! Then suddenly, despite all the attention we lavished on them, our Montagnards disappeared. We were sunk in gloom. What had we done wrong?

"Then all of a sudden it happened. One of our propaganda planes buzzed the compound so close I thought he was going to land here in this patio. We dashed to the field. The pilot was so excited he was hopping up and down. The pilot was shouting, 'Those Montagnards are coming out of the mountains now . . . they're coming by the thousands. It's a regular avalanche. . . .'

"And it was, too."

With a little investigation, the colonel and his staff finally figured out what had happened. The first Montagnards that had come down —the old folks and the children—had been on a trial run. The American promises were being tested. When the Americans lived up to their billing, the old folks went back into the mountains and made the report that the promises were genuine.

"And that," concluded the colonel, "was how a trickle turned into an avalanche. It was hectic. But we managed."

My last stop on that summer's journey to the war was far, far south of the spectacular mountains, in a world very different from the Montagnards and their primitive ways.

Around and south of Saigon is the fertile Mekong delta, which is agriculturally the richest area of Vietnam and the most densely populated.

Before going to the delta I had a long talk on the state of the war with Robert Thompson, the head of the British advisory mission to Vietnam. Thompson had been in Vietnam nearly three years and had a reputation for being in almost constant motion, going from province to province, village to village, hamlet to hamlet. He was therefore considered exceptionally well informed.

Inasmuch as the resident correspondents regarded the American brass as liars, and the American brass largely returned the compliment, it seemed to me that Thompson, being British, might have a greater claim on objectivity. He more than lived up to my hopes, and I was to impose a great deal on Thompson's time that summer in attempting to get some kind of "neutral" evaluation of conflicting points of view.

Thompson did not agree with General Harkins' flat statement that "the Viet Cong are losing" because he felt it was premature. (In fairness to Harkins, it ought to be pointed out that Thompson did not have to worry about the state of American morale, and the General did.) Thompson's experience with Communist insurgency in Malaya had impressed him with the volatility of a situation involving guerrilla war; the progress of one July could easily be reversed by the next— especially if Hanoi decided to increase dramatically the number of hard-core units sent south (and it so developed in 1964 and 1965). But Thompson certainly did not feel that the war in Vietnam was being lost. Indeed, the head of the British advisory mission said that the improvement in 1962 and 1963 was far greater than he had anticipated.

"The way I would put it," said Thompson, "is that at last I can see light at the end of the tunnel."

In the delta, Thompson's principal concern was that the strategic-hamlet program was overextended; too many had been established without prospect of adequate defense in the case of attack. In order to get statistical credit, some province chiefs had simply thrown barbed wire around a village, given the village militia some weapons, and forthwith proclaimed the birth of another strategic hamlet. The proliferation of hamlets was a drain on the regular Vietnamese army which was already spread thin, for most hamlet defenders were not well enough trained and disciplined to hold out against a serious Viet Cong attack. On such desperate occasions they needed reinforcement by the regular army. The spectacle of too many hamlets vulnerable to attack and too few troops to defend them finally persuaded the most ardent supporters of the hamlet plan that Thompson was right. Diem and Nhu also accepted the criticism of overextension. In September, 1963, the two brothers agreed to slow the program so that no strategic hamlet would be created unless it was reasonably sure of being able to resist attack, in the context, of course, of the known Viet Cong strength of that era. In those days there were between thirty thousand and forty thousand regular hard-core Viet Cong soldiers and between eighty thousand and one hundred thousand irregulars —farmers by day, guerrillas by night.

In the summer of 1963 the American-Vietnamese war strategy was to sweep the Viet Cong out of the highlands and coastal plains and push them progressively deeper into the boot of Mekong delta. The strategy of course was predicated on the prevailing balance of strength between the Viet Cong and Vietnamese. The planners assumed a stability that Diem had managed to preserve in the previous nine years. A glance at a map shows that the boot of the delta is a peninsula that juts into the South China Sea and hence is not subject, like the rest of Vietnam, to Viet Cong forays across the borders from Cambodia and Laos. It was the only possible place to isolate the Viet Cong from their outside sources of military supply. And since much of North Vietnam had been cleared by the summer of 1963, the strategy made sense, even though it has been derided as "military idiocy" by Bernard Fall, the Frenchman who teaches international relations at Howard University, in Washington, D.C. It is true, as Professor Fall states, that food is abundant in the delta and sparse in the highlands. But short lines of military supply and the use of nearby privileged sanctuaries such as Laos and Cambodia are more important to the Communist warriors than the yield of the local rice harvest. Even in the delta the Communists in great part rely on caches of food hidden long in advance and imported often from Cambodia. It is significant that in 1965, during the monsoon offensive, the Communist military concentrated the fury of their attacks precisely on the highland and other northern provinces closest to their privileged sanctuaries. Thus —Professor Fall notwithstanding—the Red military professionals and the American professionals were in agreement about the most advantageous place to fight (from a Communist point of view).

The most famous provincial capital in the delta is Mytho, which is forty miles south of Saigon and the headquarters of the Vietnamese army's Seventh Division, sometimes known as the "coup division" because it has been pivotal in many of the coups and coupettes with which South Vietnam has been afflicted.

A trip to this part of the delta provided vivid documentation of the fact that strategic hamlets were far from invulnerable. A few days before I arrived in the Delta a tiny hamlet called Van Vien, about fifteen miles (as the crow flies) from Mytho, had been hit by the Viet Cong and held for eighteen hours. Major Olen O'Connor, U.S. adviser to the province chief at Mytho, wanted to check upon the situation, and so did I.

After our jeep turned off the main paved highway onto the narrow dirt road leading to Van Vien, our apprehensions mounted on a parallel scale with the hazards of the road. It appeared that the day before a truckload of fifteen Vietnamese soldiers had been blown up on a Viet Cong mine.

"If there was a mine incident yesterday," said Major O'Connor in his casual, reassuring way, "we have a better than even chance today of getting through. It usually takes a couple of days for them to get around to mining it again.

Halfway to Van Vien we stopped to talk to an old farmer whose thatched house looked particularly clean and well built. We were soon surrounded by dozens and dozens of doll-like Vietnamese children, who, as so often happened, followed us right into the farmer's front yard.

Our conversation was scarcely begun when my attention was distracted by the intermittent bursts of machine-gun fire from a rice paddy nearby. It seemed, from the sound, as if the Viet Cong were moving in closer to get us in range. I noticed that neither the children nor the farmer paid the slightest attention.

The farmer, who had apparently been drinking some rice wine, was unusually voluble.

"You ask about the Viet Cong," he said. "We hate the Viet Cong. But we must be very polite to them. I do not like them because they tax me two hundred piastres (roughly three dollars) a year and a bag of rice. I cannot afford it. But I pay. The lady three doors away did not want to let her son go with the Viet Cong and they shot her in the head and in the stomach. Now the government officials have good intentions. The district chief arranged for me to get some pigs and a bag of fertilizer last year. In the daytime government troops go up and down this road and the Viet Cong stay in the rice paddies. But at night the soldiers go to the barracks and the Viet Cong come to the villages. If we do not do what the Viet Cong say, they kill. . . ."

In a nutshell, this was the sadly familiar story of the peasant caught in an area controlled by the government in the day and by the Communists at night.

When we reached the hamlet of Van Vien, it looked deceptively little the worse for wear. The Viet Cong had burned the information booth, and the barracks of the self-defense corps was in ruins, but much of the rest of the place seemed to intact.

The real tragedy, however, was the kidnapping of fourteen young men. It was heart-wrenching to talk to their mothers and fathers, especially one old woman who was absolutely convinced that "the white people can get my son back" if only we would try to.

During the Viet Cong attack, we learned, the self-defense corps had put up a gallant fight before being overrun. But the hamlet chief told us, looking accusingly at Major O'Connor, that "all the appeals to Mytho for help went unanswered."

"It's true," said O'Connor uneasily. "It just so happens that the Vietnamese Seventh Division was engaged in an offensive operation in the Go Cong area (a hundred-kilometer distant) when this attack came. It was bad luck. Ordinarily we could have responded almost immediately."

Despite some weaknesses, though, the strategic-hamlet idea was universally endorsed by our military even though there was criticism about the carelessness with which some were constructed.

Said an adviser at Can Tho: "Sure the hamlets do not guarantee absolute safety from a Viet Cong attack. But it is better to have some protection than none. It is better to have two hundred hamlets and have a couple overrun than have none. That means one hundred and ninety-eight hamlets have helped safeguard the security of the people. When there was no protection, the Viet Cong could move in and out of villages at will. The strategic-hamlet concept at least makes them work at it—and very many times they don't succeed. But our successes are not what interest the press. Just our mistakes."

"After all, we are still taking real estate away from them," said Major O'Connor. "In some places [Long An province] they are taking real estate from us. But overall, our gains are greater than theirs." (Alas, a state of affairs that was not to endure after the *coup d'état* against Diem.)

The attitude that I found in the delta was reflected, more or less, in a dispatch that summer written by Keyes Beech, Pulitzer Prize-winning correspondent of the Chicago *Daily News* and a veteran of more than one war. I read his dispatch after my own articles had appeared in the New York *Herald Tribune*, but I clipped it because I had come to value Beech's judgment as an old Vietnamese hand.

Datelined Can Tho, Beech's 1963 dispatch said:

South Vietnam is composed of two worlds. One is Saigon, a sophisticated snake pit of intrigue and rumor where American and Vietnamese officials are currently spending most of their waking hours figuring out ways to slit one another's throat. The other world is the rest of South Vietnam where fortunately most of the people live. The most important part of this other world is the Mekong Delta, South Vietnam's rice bowl.

Never more than ten feet above sea level, criss-crossed by 1,500 miles of canals and 300 miles of river, the Delta is 26,000 square miles of some of the richest land in Asia.

Through this vast expanse, the Mekong, one of Asia's great rivers, winds its five-fingered way to the sea after a 2,800 mile journey from the high plateau in Tibet.

Contrary to the Saigon rumor mill, the war in the countryside has not ground to a halt. Just the opposite is true. It has intensified. This morning while shaving, a red-eyed American military adviser muttered through his lather:

"I was sure surprised to hear the war had ground to a halt. I judge this war by one yardstick. How much sleep I get. . . . This month has been rough. Night before last I got three hours in. Last night I got no sleep at all."

How much effect if any has the Diem regime's crackdown on the Buddhist in Saigon had on the peasant population? A good guess is little, if any, mainly because the peasants don't know about political developments in Saigon. One thing is certain. The Saigon crisis *has had no visible effect on the morale of the average Vietnamese soldier*, although it may in the long run [italics mine].

On more than one occasion in the last few days Vietnamese soldiers have fought and fought well. . . .

I've watched the Vietnamese army develop over the last few years, especially since the United States began its massive buildup here. . . . Watching them in action in the Delta today, I can report they are a vastly improved lot. They handle themselves like pros.

A Vietnamese corps commander still has to get permission from President Diem to fire a District Chief who goofed, and this drives U.S. advisers to the brink of madness, but it's something they learn to live with before their tour is up.

Casualty reporting by the army has undergone a revolutionary change. Instead of exaggerating enemy losses and minimizing their own, now they are under-playing Communist casualties.

At least that is what U.S. advisers tell me, and being good Americans, they cannot all be lying. One adviser told how he went out to investigate a report government troops had killed ten Viet Cong.

I counted only nine bodies and asked where the tenth was. The Vietnamese company commander apologized and said there had been a mistake. They had the hand of the tenth but couldn't find the body, so they decided not to count him.

To me these judgments by reporter Beech carried special weight. He and I had covered many of the same battles in Korea and I had learned to respect his evaluations of wars and soldiering.

But I too had personally seen these Vietnamese soldiers fight bravely in difficult circumstances. Luckily my opportunity to see the

Vietnamese soldier grow and develop as an efficient fighting man dated back to the period 1951–1954, when I had often joined these troops (under French command) on a variety of "clear-and-search operations" of villages in the Red River delta near Hanoi.

In South Vietnam, where the swiftest way to the battlefront nowadays is by helicopter, I rode along on missions transporting the attacking forces. In some instances the Vietnamese officers and men were so keyed up and eager for the battle that they would fairly leap from the helicopter before it even touched the ground. In other instances, "sluggish" would have been a kind word for the Vietnamese performance. The difference, as with every army, was a matter of leadership training and morale. It is true that American advisers had plenty of gripes about this Vietnamese colonel's lack of aggressiveness or that Vietnamese major's sheer lack of guts. But on balance, even in the delta, the American advisers felt that their Vietnamese counterparts were gradually gaining more confidence and more aggressiveness. Paradoxically, in August, 1963—the peak of the Buddhist crisis—the number of attacks initiated by the Vietnamese army against the Viet Cong reached an all-time high in the war up to that point.

Most informed witnesses, including the Vietnamese, admitted that things in the delta were going much less satisfactorily than in the North. But despite the frustrations and the griping, the phrase that I heard the most often from the American advisers was that "we are inching ahead."

Therefore, I was amazed upon returning to Saigon to find the town buzzing with news of recent newspaper dispatches proclaiming that the Buddhist crisis was "spreading to the countryside," that it was "deep and smoldering" in the army, that the war in the delta had "deteriorated," and that the situation was "ominous."

One dispatch reported that Buddhist and Catholic officers had suddenly begun to eat at separate tables in Vietnamese army messes.

This was in direct contradiction to everything I had observed and had been told by the military advisers, aid officials, and Vietnamese officers and enlisted men out in the boondocks, where the war was being fought. I was puzzled and angry.

I went to the American embassy and demanded to know from a senior official if there was a conspiracy to befog with lies what I had seen and heard.

Said the official: "How can the reporters document this so-called deterioration? None of the resident press corps have been out of Saigon—except for a couple of day-long helicopter trips—since June [when the first Buddhist suicide took place]. Men like Major Kelly [of Quang Ngai] are busting to have reporters come up and see what they are doing. But the press isn't interested. And if we should try to get them interested, they would say that we are stage-managing things."

In fairness it should be said that from the point of view of a journalist trying to file daily about the Buddhist revolt, it was almost essential to stay close to Saigon, for its central telegraph office was the only place to get the story out. I was exempted from Saigon deadline pressures because my assignment was to write a series of articles. Consequently, I could spend more of my time in Krulak's country (theater of war) than in Mendenhall's country (theater of intrigue). There were only five or six permanent American correspondents in Saigon. Most of the bureaus were staffed by one reporter (an astonishing state of affairs considering the importance of the story). This, of course, accentuated their need to stay close to communications. For the big daily headlines in the United States concerned the flaming suicides and demonstrations, most of which either took place in Saigon or were quickly reported to Saigon.

So while the resident correspondents covered the war bravely (and won plaudits and Pulitzers) before and after the Buddhist crisis, they were seldom, judging by their datelines, at the scenes of battle in the period when stories appeared linking the Buddhist crisis to the war effort. Hence, in midsummer, 1963, these judgments passed in Saigon on the state of the war were in some part based on secondhand evidence, which in Vietnam is precarious in the extreme. The evidence was doubly suspect because it was all too often made available by ambitious young Vietnamese generals and colonels who wished to paint the war situation as darkly as possible, the better to justify their *coup d'état*, if and when it came.

As a lesson on how our government functions (or fails to function), let us consider for a moment the impact of these "deterioration" stories on Washington.

On August 14, 1963, for example, Assistant Secretary of State Roger Hilsman, in a broadcast over Voice of America, declared that the *Buddhist crisis was "beginning to affect the war effort* [italics mine]."

I took Hilsman's statement to Ambassador Nolting, who was then about to leave for the United States. He was in conference at the time with William Trueheart, his deputy, and John Mecklin, director of the United States Information Service.

The ambassador shook his head in bafflement. "I'm telling you in all honesty, Marguerite," he said, "that all our reports show that the Buddhist crisis is not having any impact at all—though of course it could if riots should become severe enough to necessitate diverting front line troops."

"We have made a special check," the ambassador continued, "of the rumor that Buddhists and Catholics are eating apart in army messes. Nothing to it. I don't know what Hilsman based his statement on. But he isn't basing it on anything that went out of this embassy, the military mission, or the C.I.A."

He looked around at Trueheart and Mecklin for confirmation, and they nodded in agreement.

But Mecklin suggested gently that perhaps Nolting should not press the matter in a public denial because Hilsman was, after all, Nolting's boss.

And thus Hilsman's curious version of events was allowed to stand.

I encountered a revealing sequel to the story when I myself returned to New York. I was still so perturbed over the contrast between Hilsman's broadcast and the embassy findings that my first act on landing in New York (it was a Saturday morning) was to telephone Hilsman. Despite the hour (eight A.M.) he was in his office.

"The embassy says the Buddhist crisis is having no effect on the war," I opened. "But your VOA broadcast said there is. What did you base it on? The *New York Times*?"

"Partly that," said Hilsman. "The *Times* and other press dispatches out of Saigon."

And thus is history recast. All those Vietnamese-speaking Americans circling the countryside for the purpose of testing Vietnamese opinion; all those American officers gauging the morale of the troops; all those C.I.A. agents tapping their sources (hopefully) everywhere; all those dispatches from Ambassador Nolting—an army of data-collectors in reasonable agreement had been downgraded in favor of press dispatches stating opposite conclusions. It was the first time that I began to comprehend, in depth and in some sorrow, what was meant by the *power* of the press.

The American embassy's contention that "the Viet Cong are losing" was a tricky judgment if based solely on statistics. For most statistics are meaningful only in a comparative sense. And often we had only a fragmentary notion at best of the Viet Cong losses and gains.

Under our system of verification, the Viet Cong had a certain advantage. For instance, with regard to loss of weapons, only those Viet Cong rifles, grenades, etc., actually captured and in our physical possession were counted as an enemy loss. Thus if the Vietnamese navy sank a Viet Cong sampan, there was usually no way of knowing about or getting credit for the Viet Cong rifles that went to the bottom with the ship.

On the other hand, we knew and announced how many weapons our side lost. Every American adviser—not just the Vietnamese commander—was responsible for verifying these losses. The assumption was always made (sometimes no doubt inaccurately) that the lost weapon actually fell into Viet Cong hands, instead of, say, to the bottom of a canal.

Weapons losses and gains became an important issue because so much nonsense has been written about how the Viet Cong equipped themselves militarily by capturing U.S.-supplied weapons from the Vietnamese army. The Communists nourished and spread this nonsense, recognizing its importance as propaganda. And many Westerners swallowed it without question. The unfortunate consequence was a portrayal of ineptitude that made the Vietnamese army look bad and the United States look silly. The Viet Cong, on the other hand, were made to look ten feet tall and unbeatable.

The portrayal was a blatant distortion from the beginning.

When the fighting started in 1959, American and French weapons in the hands of the guerrillas dated back to the *first war in Indochina that ended in 1954.* If you will, these arms had been captured from the *French*, not the Vietnamese army in the South. Up to that point the loss of weapons by the Vietnamese army was negligible.

The best summation of the entire situation was made by Secretary of Defense McNamara, who in April, 1965, said:

"Since 1960, the Viet Cong have captured approximately 39,000 weapons from troops of the South Vietnamese government.

"During that same period of time, the Viet Cong lost to those [Vietnamese] troops about 25,000 of their weapons. Thus the Viet Cong had *a net gain* of about 14,000 weapons during this period. [Captured weapons] supplied only ten to fifteen per cent of their [Viet Cong] overall requirements as represented by regular Communist troop strength of 46,000 [a figure later substantially revised upward] and 100,000 irregulars. The *remainder of the weapons— eighty-five to ninety per cent—have been supplied from outside.*"

The losses of weapons (in terms of Vietnamese soldiers under arms) amounted to less between January and November, 1963, than during the same period the previous year. It is certain that far fewer weapons were lost by the Diem regime in 1963 than in the two succeeding years, 1964 and 1965.

From a statistical standpoint, General Harkins could take great pride in developments between February, 1962, and the summer of 1963. The Vietnamese air force was flying one thousand sorties a month as compared with one hundred a year earlier. The Vietnamese navy, which had been nonexistent when the Americans arrived, now had a junk fleet plus a river fleet and patrol ships at sea. Three hundred and seventy-five civil-guard companies totalling one hundred thousand men had been formed. In addition, a village self-defense corps of about sixty thousand persons had been created. The Vietnamese army itself totaled about two hundred and thirty thousand men. Nearly eight million persons, out of a population of fourteen million, were in strategic hamlets.

Standing alone, the statistics were impressive. The effectiveness of the government buildup, however, had to be weighed against the fact that Ho Chi Minh had by no means been idle. He had escalated his infiltration of men and guns from the Communist north. Enough Red army soldiers had come south to replace losses and keep the Viet Cong hard core at a strength of at least thirty to forty thousand full-time soldiers.

In January, 1963, the most publicized military setback for our side occurred—the humiliation of the Vietnamese armed forces at Ap Bac. This battle in the Mekong delta, near Mytho, marked one of the first instances in which the Viet Cong stood its ground against government assault, rather than resorting to the old hit-and-run tactics. Sixty Vietnamese and three American lives were lost and five helicopters downed at Ap Bac. These losses were small by the standards of 1965, but some of the Vietnamese officers in the Ap Bac battle exhibited incredibly bad leadership, prompting Lieutenant Colonel John Vann, the brilliant and idealistic U.S. adviser at the time, to complain bitterly. One Vietnamese colonel, reportedly a Diem favorite, simply refused orders by his Vietnamese superior to move up his forces to close the trap on a crack Viet Cong unit. The Viet Cong thus were allowed to escape. In the framework of the times, the splashy headlines with their inevitable oversimplification were more or less justified in calling this a "defeat."

And yet in the North four months later, the Twenty-fifth Vietnamese Division at Quang Ngai not only stood its ground but also fought four days and nights running. When the battle was over two hundred and twenty-six Viet Cong dead were picked off the field with their weapons (including Chinese and Czech machine guns), and another idealistic and brilliant adviser, Major John Kelly, was full of praise for the Vietnamese division's performance. If Ap Bac was a "defeat," Quang Ngai was surely a "victory." But Quang Ngai got no headlines at all.

This accent on the negative was a recurring phenomenon, and it embittered the United States mission and upset young military advisers like Major Kelly, who felt that what happened at Ap Bac should not detract from the valor and accomplishments of "his men" —for that's the way he felt about them.

During a dinner at the Admiral Restaurant in Saigon I got into a discussion on this subject with Charles Mohr, then of *Time* magazine. To my surprise he subsequently quoted me in *Time* as having said: "Reporters here would like to see us lose the war to prove they're right."

My memory is different. I feel sure I never made so calloused and harsh a remark, because I don't believe it. I don't think any American *wants* us to lose the war in Vietnam or any other place.

I do think, however, that there was a demonstrable preoccupation of the resident press corps in Saigon with Vietnamese failures under Diem and that it can be argued that the space and attention given to the regime's shortcomings in the war (Ap Bac) were rarely balanced by equal attention to its successes (Quang Ngai). And there are many parallel examples.

During the dinner, Charlie (whom I had known for years) summed up his feelings on the regime, saying: "Anything—even a military junta—would be better than Diem." He expressed what I understood (from other conversations) to be the view of the close-knit group of resident American correspondents in Saigon. Other published reports of that time were accurate in stating that a vast difference of opinion existed between myself and the American resident journalists in Saigon on the wisdom of replacing Diem with a military junta in the midst of a war.

Much has been made by some critics of the fact that in February, 1963, the number of Viet Cong attacks rose to more than one thousand. Professor Fall has pointed to this spectacular number of Viet Cong incidents to support his contention that the United States was losing all along in Vietnam. It seems to me that Professor Fall is a bit overeager here in his attempt to prove American failures. Failures we have had, plenty of them, but a spectacular rise in Viet Cong incidents *in any given month* doesn't prove anything.

Surely any valid comparison must take averages, and in the spring and summer of 1963 Viet Cong-initiated attacks had dropped to about two to three hundred a week, whereas in 1962 they had averaged five to six hundred a week. So by mid-1963 Viet Cong aggressiveness had noticeably waned.

When I read stories to the effect that the "Vietnamese won't fight" I think almost automatically of the helicopters bearing dead and wounded that touch down in endless procession at air strips like Tan Son Nhut and Bien Hoa. The Vietnamese casualties in 1963 were running at a rate of fourteen thousand a year, which is higher, in terms of population, than the United States has ever suffered in any war. Such casualties bespeak a whale of a lot of fighting!

It was the contention of the American mission that the tide had started turning in our favor in the fall of 1962, when the Vietnamese army went on the offensive.

It is not without interest that for once the Communists agreed—up to a point. Wilfred "Peter" Burchett, the Australian reporter with Communist sympathies who has passed much time with the Viet Cong, quotes Communist guerrilla leaders as saying that "1962 is the year we concede to the Americans."

In 1963 Hanoi sent fewer Viet Cong officers and men south than in 1962, a development that encouraged those Americans who thought that Ho Chi Minh was getting ready to throw in the towel. Great importance was attached by these Americans to a broadcast by Hanoi radio in July, 1963, of a Ho Chi Minh statement hinting at a cease-fire and some kind of coexistence between North and South. The July statement was certainly the most conciliatory made by the Communist leaders before or since. It is fair to assume that Ho Chi Minh would not have hinted at conciliation had he felt the Diem regime was on the ropes.

It appears to me that the optimists were as wrong in 1963 in contending that the Viet Cong were *losing* the war as were the pessimists in claiming the Viet Cong were *winning*. Those terms didn't apply at that stage. For the terms "winning" and "losing" imply that one side or another could have forced a decision in its favor at a predictable date and that the *situation was irreversible*. But the situation in Vietnam was—and possibly still is—too fluid for that. For example, even when truce talks come, as they inevitably will, it may be that we will yield at the conference table what the enemy has not wrested and cannot wrest from us in war, so long as we are determined to use our power to prevent it.

Robert Thompson, of the British advisory mission, came closest to expressing the reality of the time when he said, "there is light at the end of the tunnel"—an expression that must allow for the fact that the tunnel might cave in before you get to the end.

Discarding these terms about "winning" and "losing," a convincing case can nonetheless be made that in 1962–1963, when the war in Vietnam was in phase two (mainly guerrilla and terrorist), the Vietnamese army made important gains in the countryside. In 1962 much of the coastal area of Vietnam, including Quang Ngai, had been Viet Cong hunting preserve. By 1963 the area was largely ours; Highway One (known to the Vietnamese as Route of the Mandarins, to the French as Street Without Joy) was open from the Seventeenth Parallel to deep in the delta, to cite an example or two.

This wariness about the concepts of "winning" or "losing" is not a matter of hindsight. In my first series on Vietnam in the New York *Herald Tribune* I took care not to use such yardsticks in giving my own assessment and wrote instead:

"Despite the strident anti-government campaign spread to provincial towns from humming mimeograph machines at the Xa Loi Pagoda in Saigon, despite the tragic suicides by fire, despite the defection of most citified intellectuals, President Diem's Vietnamese armies continued this summer *to gain* in those areas of the countryside where the war is fought the hardest."

This series was highly controversial. Even in journalism swimming upstream isn't easy, especially when the contrary currents are so massive and when there is a monster (as many still considered Diem) lurking about. All summer long the wire services, some news magazines, and the *Herald Tribune*'s main competition had poured out stories that seemed in contradiction to the central points I was making.

As late as August 25, 1963, UPI carried a dispatch dicussing "the government's move in *crushing the Buddhist religious movement* [italics mine]."

In July the Associated Press referred to "*religious conflict* between President Ngo Dinh Diem, a Roman Catholic and Buddhist leaders."

My Saigon summary, of course, contended the opposite on this and many other points.

The central themes of my newspaper articles were that the revolt was political, not religious; that Diem was fighting to save his government, not to persecute anybody; that the activities of some thousands of Buddhists and students in the city had no effect on the continuing war gains in the countryside; and that the perils of dumping Diem in midwar were greater than the perils of sticking with him.

My first cables from Saigon, I was later told, raised a few eyebrows and created some amazement in the *Herald Tribune* City Room. But when my documentation was presented, my editors backed me to the hilt. They were the triumvirate—Jim Bellows, Dick Wald, and Si Freidin—whose telegram had originally sent me to Saigon. And at the end of the journey, they printed every one of the thousands of words I wrote. Can one ask for anything more?

In the series I did quote the views of the American mission, including General Paul Harkins, to the effect that "the Viet Cong are going to lose." This was much criticized by the resident correspondents in Saigon, who felt that the U.S. mission was lying and undeserving of being quoted. I remain unrepentant. I believe that any responsible director of a vast enterprise, whether it be the American commander in Vietnam, or the dictator of Cuba, should be quoted on what he has to say. Let time and history be the judge. Who knows? History might be perverse enough to decide that the men fighting the war in Vietnam know as much about the battle as the typewriter strategists. I happen to believe our leaders there should be given a hearing.

As an integral part of the whole picture in 1963, it must be added that one of the biggest gains in Vietnam was economic rather than military. Instead of having to import rice, as was the case a year earlier, the Vietnamese peasants had been able to export three hundred thousand tons of rice by late fall, 1963.

The overriding point, in sum, is that in 1963, so long as there was a strong firm rule, *gains were* made in the Vietnamese countryside, the theater of war, the "country" of General Krulak, and the place where the battle for Southeast Asia will indeed be "won" or "lost" when the situation reaches the stage where such finalities have meaning.

It is important to realize that the tide of battle in Vietnam has not been one of unchanging reverses. Gains that were made once can be made again. If Quang Ngai was liberated from the Viet Cong once, it can be again. So can Highway One. And Pleiku province. And Binh Dinh. It is also important to realize that each time the Communist Viet Cong escalates the quantity of men and quality of weapons—as Ho Chi Minh has so spectacularly done—the cost of such gains gets steeper.

Could the gains made in Vietnam in 1963 have been consolidated and enlarged if there had been no coup against Diem? There are many informed Americans, including President Johnson and General Eisenhower, who deeply believed so then and believe so now.

Indeed Johnson, as we shall see, did his intense best to prevent this unprecedented American betrayal of an ally in midwar.

CHAPTER **8**

The Peasants and
the Commissars

It is certain that in the summer of 1963 an unprecedented number of Communist Viet Cong had decided that they were losing the war. For in that period they deserted in quantities to the Diem regime and sought asylum under the amnesty program President Ngo Dinh Diem proclaimed in April, 1963.

"There they are—real, genuine, bona-fide, eighteen-carat Communist Viet Cong," said the United States army captain as we approached a schoolhouse near Quang Ngai, where sixty of the returnees from the Viet Cong were sitting in prim rows. They were singing a patriotic Vietnamese song that required rhythmic clapping. They looked amazingly young, fresh-faced—and bored.

These Viet Cong were among eight hundred who had passed through the Quang Ngai camp since Diem's proclamation in April, 1963, of a policy of "forgiveness and rehabilitation" for those Communist soldiers who gave themselves up. Throughout the country the Chui Hoi (amnesty) program brought in more than ten thousand Viet Cong in 1963.

It seems to me that the story of the deserters from the Viet Cong remains one of the great untold epics of the war in Vietnam. I have never understood why so few Americans bothered talking to them, or for that matter, why so few officials made the effort to bring such authentic accounts of life with the Viet Cong home to the American public.

What has amazed me most about the Vietnamese amnesty program is that Viet Cong deserters continued to give themselves up even in the post-Diem period, when turmoil and riot ruled the country and many Americans were writing off the war as lost. In the turmoil and chaos of 1964 and early 1965 the rate of desertion diminished—of course. But as of this writing at least twenty-seven thousand Viet Cong Communists, both regulars and irregulars, have voluntarily come over to the government side. And that represents a politically significant drain on Communist manpower.

The fact that the Viet Cong continued to surrender even when Hanoi's ace seemed high—in 1964—says a great deal about the state of Communist morale. Desertion in adversity is understandable. Desertion when things are rosy certainly demonstrates that the Viet Cong, far from being ten feet high, cannot hold the loyalty of some of their troops even in good times.

As early as 1963 I was able to learn from the deserters specific details of how Chinese, Russian, and Czech arms were supplied to the "invasion" forces and of how ammunition factories in the North had been converted to adapt to these foreign-made weapons. The deserters told in detail how they came south and how the cadres of officers and noncommissioned officers filled out their ranks.

The Viet Cong are persuaded to come over to the nationalist side by a variety of techniques and lures. In Quang Ngai light planes equipped with loudspeakers dip low each morning over the foothills where the Viet Cong are known to make their headquarters and broadcast repeatedly the offer of forgiveness and rehabilitation. Also, thousands and thousands of pamphlets are dropped. These pamphlets amount to safe-conduct passes for any Viet Cong who retrieves one.

In the first interviews I had in Quang Ngai I found that hunger often motivated the deserter as much as ideology. Food is hard to come by in the Quang Ngai foothills. Also—and let this be pondered by those who say that the strategic-hamlet policy has failed—most of the Communists I interviewed blamed much of their trouble on the fortified-village program, because this made it harder to get into populated areas and extort rice from the peasant.

"Which one do you want to speak with first?" asked the Vietnamese camp director as sixty pairs of eyes looked up expectantly, their owners clearly desiring to be liberated from the camp's usual routine of indoctrination.

I asked a Viet Cong master sergeant, one of the most recent defectors, to join me and my interpreter (a Vietnamese-speaking American). We went over to a far corner of the schoolyard so that we could talk without interruption or without being overheard by the American or Vietnamese officials.

The master sergeant, Vu Duy Liem, 28, was clad in the cotton pajamas that many Vietnamese traditionally wear as outer garments. They find it amusing to think that Americans use them only to sleep in. The master sergeant was slim and wiry, and his mind was razor-sharp.

His home originally was a village in the Quang Ngai area. His family were peasants and ancestor-worshipers, as were most of the people of the village. He joined the Communist Viet Minh armies in 1953 to fight the French. In 1954 his battalion, then operating near Hué, was ordered to Hanoi in observance of the Geneva agreements that partitioned Vietnam at the Seventeenth Parallel. At the time, all organized Communist Viet Minh military units were ostensibly ordered north by Ho Chi Minh. Very few ordinary South Vietnamese civilians chose to flee north as refugees. In contrast, refugees who fled North Vietnam out of fear of Ho Chi Minh's Communist rule numbered nearly one million officially and may have totaled two million unofficially.

In July, 1962, Sergeant Liem was among four hundred and fifty men of the Eightieth Viet Minh battalion who completed an arduous journey south to the mountains near Pleiku with the assignment to join with other regular Viet Minh units that were infiltrating at the time in peak numbers to ("liberate") South Vietnam.

Defectors like Sergeant Liem have described how in Hanoi a special infiltration unit, the Seventieth Transportation Group, is responsible for moving men from North Vietnam into the south via infiltration trails in Laos. Another special unit, the Maritime Infiltration Group, ships weapons and supplies to the south by sea.

All U.S. estimates about Viet Cong infiltration are subject to revision as defectors and prisoners provide additional information. From 1959 to 1960 an estimated 2,700 hard-core Viet Cong guerrillas came south. In 1961 the number of infiltrations rose to nearly 4,000. In 1962 nearly 6,000 came south. In 1963 the infiltration slowed somewhat to 4,200 confirmed infiltrators. In 1964, the number of infiltrators was at least 10,000 and in 1965 possibly three times that many.

As Sergeant Liem described his own experience:

"We came through Laos over a mountain pass that was so steep that one misstep would cause you to tumble to death in the chasm below. Fortunately, we had excellent guides—the Communists prepare everything thoroughly in advance. We carried with us mainly Chinese and Czech weapons that are modified in North Vietnamese factories so that they can fire ammunition manufactured in Hanoi."

Of the dozens and dozens of defectors with whom I have spoken in three trips to Vietnam during 1963-64, not one had the slightest doubt as to who was running the "liberation" effort in South Vietnam, namely, Ho Chi Minh and General Giap. Nor did any of them talk of the so-called National Liberation Front as anything other than an extension (by another name) of the North Vietnamese Communist party.

In 1965 the Reds did in fact abandon the fiction that the National Liberation Front, the political arm of the Viet Cong, was a popular coalition of patriots and democrats. The People's Revolutionary party of South Vietnam, which is the Communist component of the N.L.F., publicly announced in a radio broadcast of August, 1965, that it was the "correct leadership" of the so-called liberation movement. At the same time, the Communist People's Revolutionary party of South Vietnam announced that it would apply "fully and creatively" the theories of Marxism-Leninism in the south. This announcement merely confirmed well-known realities.

Hanoi has been far less diffident than many Westerners in acknowledging its role and responsibilities for the conflict in South Vietnam.

Ho Chi Minh's designs on South Vietnam have been publicly stated many times. Indeed in 1960 the Third Communist Party Congress in Hanoi set forth two tasks for its members: "To carry out the socialist revolution in North Vietnam" and "*to liberate South Vietnam.*" Three months after this meeting, Hanoi announced creation of the "Front for the Liberation of the South."

General Giap, the wily Vietnamese strategist, probably put it the most sharply and succinctly when he wrote in an article for the Communist party journal *Hoc Tap* in early 1960 that "North Vietnam is the revolutionary base for the whole country."

But to return to Sergeant Liem, why did he desert?

"I learned very gradually that the Hanoi government was one that denied freedom," said the sergeant. "But in any case, I had been unsure of my loyalty to the Communists for some time before I came south. In the North, they told us that the Communist system would bring a better life to the people. They told us that the Russians and the Chinese were coming to our country to help raise the standard of living. But everybody could see with their own eyes that in the North the standard of living is going down and the people are suffering.

"And besides," said Sergeant Liem, coming with a giggle to what was probably the most important reason, "I was hungry. Life in the mountains [foothills near Quang Ngai] became very hard. My battalion lost one hundred men in one year. We were not only short on food . . . there was no medicine. . . . I had been thinking for some time of trying to get away, though I could not speak of it, for the Viet Cong would have killed me. . . . Still, I was afraid of how the government would treat me. . . . Then I heard the broadcast from the plane about the amnesty camps. . . . And I decided I would run away the first chance I got."

The sergeant was asked whether the people of North Vietnam preferred to get their "assistance" from the Russians or the Chinese.

"As a rule the Vietnamese don't like foreigners of any kind," said Sergeant Liem. "But if they have to have them, they prefer the Russians because they are more skillful and prosperous than the Chinese. Everybody knows that the Chinese have failed and the Russians have succeeded. Everybody in Hanoi follows very closely the situation in

China and knows all about the terrible suffering of the Chinese peasant."

It was from Sergeant Liem that I first got a clear idea of how the Viet Cong officers and men sent south from Hanoi sustained themselves and managed to fill out their ranks with local "recruits."

"The first few months in the mountains," said Sergeant Liem, "were spent in getting organized in the matter of food and water. We planted our own rice and cornfields. At first the Montagnards gave us a bottleful of rice a day without too much complaining. Later, we *had to force them* [italics mine]. In the fall [of 1962] we had our first success. We attacked a Vietnamese army convoy near Kontum, and we captured three cannons and lots of other ammunition. But when the strategic hamlets began going up, we had increasing difficulty in getting into the villages to capture or persuade young men to come to the hills and fill out our ranks. By winter the village defenses had been built up so that it was risky to go into them even at night to get food. Then our battalion had heavy losses in the April battle [of Quang Ngai]. Morale was very low."

I asked Sergeant Liem whether he believed the American-backed nationalist regime was winning the war.

"Of course," he said, adding with refreshing candor: "I saw American power and decided your side was bound to win. Otherwise I might not have surrendered. For if the Communists should win and get hold of me again, it is finished [here he drew his hand across his throat as if it were being slit]. The Communists never forgive those who leave them—or try to leave them. With American power behind them, how can the nationalists help but win?"

Sergeant Liem was proud of the fact that he was already helping the Vietnamese Twenty-fifth Division in its battle against his former Viet Cong comrades.

"I have already gone on two missions with the Twenty-fifth Division. I led them to a secret arms cache and we captured three weapons, four Viet Cong soldiers, and two and a half pounds of documents. We destroyed two supply dumps. And next week I will lead them to the cornfields and we will destroy them, and that will make the Viet Cong even hungrier."

I asked whether weapons captured from the Americans were an important part of the Viet Cong arsenal.

"For regular units like mine," said Sergeant Liem, "these captured arms have marginal importance. Since we must be prepared for heavy sustained firing, we must have very substantial stores of ammunition on hand. And while it is sometimes possible to capture American-made weapons, it is more difficult to guarantee sufficient stores of ammunition. So we usually let the regional guerrilla forces [those who are farmers by day and soldiers by night] use any American weapons we get. For they do not get into lengthy battles, and big stocks of ammunition are not necessary. Their work is hit and run. Our regular Viet Cong units use mainly Chinese, Russian, and Czech weapons. We have plentiful stores of ammunition for them."

Like many defectors, Sergeant Liem, after "rehabilitation," was allowed to visit his family briefly. Then he was assigned to a psychological-warfare branch of the Vietnamese army.

The only ex-Viet Cong kept in camps "for the duration" are those suspected of being Communist agents. Most are held for reindoctrination periods lasting between six months and a year

Of the many conversations I have had in my recent trips to Vietnam, the most revealing took place in an amnesty camp near Saigon in November, 1964. This was, of course, a year after Diem's overthrow. The conversation was with Captain Tram Quoc Ba, who was a rare political prize because he was a provincial commissar, meaning the boss of all Viet Cong forces, both military and political, in his province. He gave himself up in June, 1964.

Captain Ba was sent south from Hanoi in February, 1960, with two other officers and a company of Viet Cong militia.

In between his assignment in 1960 and his defection nearly four years later Captain Ba operated on orders from Hanoi without benefit of pay, home leave, or hopes of returning north until the war was over. Although the guerrilla cadres were supplied by Hanoi with sums of money before being sent south, they were expected to sustain themselves thereafter by "taxing" the local peasantry.

It is instructive to contrast Captain Ba's situation with that of our American military advisers. American advisers are assigned for a mere year. It takes a month to learn the hang of things and a month to say good-bye. So they are on top of their jobs for only ten months. Further, they do not speak the Vietnamese language and must depend on their contacts with a Vietnamese interpreter, who may or may not be dependable. They are openhanded, openminded, openhearted and for much of the time, in open confusion.

When American advisers were first assigned to Vietnamese regiments, battalions, and so forth, they were under orders not to get involved in politics. Whoever gave that order must have been on cloud ninety-nine. In Vietnam it is *impossible* to know what is going on militarily or any other way without knowing something about the politics, both local and national.

For example, on September 13, 1964, an American adviser with the Seventh Vietnamese Division, normally stationed in the delta, didn't discover that he was participating in an attempted *coup d'état* until he recognized the silhouette of some of Saigon's main buildings. At daybreak, when he realized with a shock that he was heading into the heart of the city instead of on a military operation in the delta, he excused himself from the convoy and rushed belatedly to the embassy to report the situation. Nonetheless, if the American adviser had been clued to the going intrigues—and known his Vietnamese counterpart better—he might have been saved the embarrassment of being an unwitting accessory to a *coup d'état* that his government opposed. For the would-be coup-makers naturally tried to turn the fact that an American accompanied them most of the way into a token of U.S. support for their revolt, which, fortunately, was unsuccessful.

To this day many of the normal-as-blueberry-pie Americans in Saigon have trouble adjusting to the fact that the phrase "Oriental intrigue" was not invented to please the exotic fiction writers but to fulfill a deep grammatical necessity—a description of an art that has probably reached its highest stage of development in intrigue-happy Vietnam.

How can a non-Vietnamese stranger who doesn't even speak the language hope to compete with a Viet Cong who lives, eats, and sleeps with the people and is in for the duration?

Perhaps Americans cannot be asked to "sacrifice" for long stints in

Vietnam. But the wildly unrealistic and inefficient results of assigning
American advisers for only twleve months could be at least mitigated
by sending mainly volunteers to Vietnam and for a period of no less
than two years.

Granted, this would not close the gap between us and the Viet
Cong. But it would somewhat modify the bewildering chaos of the
present situation.

The length of service in Vietnam of U.S. combat troops fighting as
units under American commanders is an entirely different matter.
Here other factors come into play, such as how much of a mauling
any given unit takes from the Viet Cong.

In any case, to go on with Captain Ba, his story was an object
example of Communist thoroughness in the smallest detail and their
skill in playing on the weakness of human nature.

For example, in the entire first year in his province Captain Ba and
his handful of men were specifically enjoined not to use violence of
any kind. Instead, they were merely to go from one key village of the
province to another, and, as Captain Ba put it, "to learn the qualities
of personality and character that could be turned to our purposes."

"This process is very simple," the captain related. "We go into a
village and find out who is hated, and why. We find out who is liked,
and why. We find out who is vain and susceptible to being made to
feel important. We find out who has stolen something or cheated on
his wife during a trip. When we are very sure of our assessment of the
people, their faults and their secrets, then we go to work to recruit.
With the vain man, we tell him that if he will work with us there is a
chance to be a leader of the side that will win. In the case of the
farmer who has cheated, we tell him that if he does not join our ranks
and take our orders we will expose him. And so on. And once some
village men come over to us, they can no longer get away. If they
tried, then we would kill them or their families. And one or two
deaths are usually enough to keep the rest terrorized into obedience.
Then once the villagers are actually involved in actions hostile to the
government—an ambush, or digging traps for the army to fall into—
then they are guilty, and so, in a sense, is the whole village. They are
on the Viet Cong side, because having attacked the government, there

is no going back. They have become, so to speak, our partners in crime."

"How do the people feel about the Viet Cong?" I asked the former political commissar.

"The villagers hate the Viet Cong," said Captain Ba. "But they know that we hold life and death in our hands. So they do what we say. We infiltrate gradually, and at first in small numbers, to avoid alarming the people. By the time our power base is built and we come out in the open, it is too late."

Both before and after talking with Captain Ba I was witness to the hatred of the Vietnamese peasant for the commissar that the Viet Cong deserter so candidly conceded.

A particularly vivid memory is the tragedy in a Montagnard village that I observed on my return to Pleiku in November, 1964. This province is in the spectacular highland area near the Laotian border. The Communist Viet Cong had raided the village the night before and there had been unconfirmed reports of a number of deaths.

As we entered the village we could hear the sound of wailing and chanting from the large wooden log house on stilts that dominated the center of the village. Even though the noon sun burned hot, fires were lit at either end of the hut. Inside, in the flickering gloom, on a mat surrounded by jars holding incense sticks, lay the body of a truly beautiful and serene-looking Montagnard woman.

For a weird moment it seemed as if the reports of death must be wrong, for the women surrounding the beautiful Montagnard were fanning her elaborately and periodically mopping her brow.

"Oh, no, she is dead all right," said the village chief, seeing the puzzlement of his Western visitors. "She was the wife of our former village chief. The Viet Cong killed him in a raid on our village this time last year. Last night the Viet Cong attacked again. About one hundred of them cut the barbed wire and came into the village after midnight. They told the former chief's wife to come with them into the mountains. She refused, so they took her out to the edge of the village and commanded all the villagers they could get their hands on to come and watch. Then they stood her up and shot her in the back of the neck. After that the Viet Cong picked out four of our best young men and told them they could expect the same if they did not go with them. And being young and wanting to live, the young men went."

I asked the Montagnard chieftain if the Viet Cong attack would cause any of his people to abandon their village and go back to their nomadic ways in the mountains.

"We have much fear," said the Montagnard chieftain, "but our roots are deep now. We have our rice to grow. We have our animals. We have a new well. The Viet Cong will come back but we know how to hide. Perhaps they will kill only a few. And there is much death anyway. And perhaps the government will grow stronger again and will be able to protect us. Is that not possible?"

The terror to which that village was subjected is typical of how the hard-core Viet Cong cadres everywhere in Vietnam most often get their "recruits" nowadays. And the "recurits" only infrequently make their escape back to their families and their villages because they know that they will get a bullet in the back of the neck, like the Montagnard woman, if they try to get away and are caught.

In the Montagnard village the hate and terror felt about the Viet Cong was an instructive contrast to the fairly widespread belief among Americans that the Communists have won the "hearts and minds" of the Vietnamese peasants.

Some Americans, for example, are forever crediting the Communist Viet Cong with having applied Mao Tse-tung's dictum of turning villages into "friendly oceans in which guerrillas can swim." This is so much bunkum. In the hundreds of Vietnamese and Montagnard villages attacked and then liberated by the Viet Cong that I have visited, the Communists have left behind not one drop of friendship, but oceans of terror.

It is an insult to the intelligence of the Vietnamese peasants to think that they cannot distinguish between the Viet Cong—who take their sons and their rice and their chances of peace—and the Vietnamese government and the long noses (as the Americans are called), who for all their fumbling have at least managed to get rice and seeds and insecticides and other vital commodities to many of the people. A peasant may not know where Saigon is, but he has judgments about his village chief and district chief, who represent about all of government he really understands. And whether a village chief or district chief is "good" or "bad" depends on whether he collects taxes justly, hands down judgments (in criminal cases) with fairness, and acquits himself in other quite pragmatic affairs without ideological bias of any kind. Historically, villages in Vietnam have had enormous autonomy in handling their own affairs. The district chief or the province chief is involved in the affairs of the village only in those matters affecting the security of the nation.

In 1963 peasants had received more direct help in the way of fertilizer, insecticides, etc., than at any previous time in modern history. And they said so. But it is asking the impossible of the Vietnamese peasant—irrespective of how many schoolhouses are built or wells dug—to expect him to take overt action against the Viet Cong when he knows he can be killed for it.

Peasants start informing on Viet Cong only when they feel they have a protected base, a really secure strategic hamlet, for instance, in which they are safe from Viet Cong retaliation. In Quang Ngai province, for example, it was only after the victory of April, 1963, that the peasants began to volunteer information about the Communists.

Therefore it is meaningless to say that the war in Vietnam is primarily political. The first priority is to make the peasant secure from assassination and murder so that he can think about politics. That doesn't mean that the political side—giving a sense of participation, civic action, and all—is not vastly important. But none of these things can be meaningful until there is security.

There is a famous story in Vietnam of the Catholic church in the delta that flew a Viet Cong flag. When an American adviser suggested to the Catholic priest that he order one of his parishioners to take down the flag, the priest declined.

"If you want to take down the flag, that is your business," said the priest, "but if one of my parishioners takes it down, he will be punished by the Viet Cong. And it won't do any good anyway, since the Viet Cong will put it right back up—after making an example of whoever took it down."

What the attitude of the peasants may be in the huge areas of the delta in South Vietnam actually run by the Communists is more difficult to say. No doubt the Viet Cong make headway, initially, in those areas where they actually make a gift to the peasant of land held by absentee owners. But this is, of course, just a Communist trick. For the next stage is to collectivize the land and turn much of it into state farms, in the pattern of developments in North Vietnam. We know that Ho Chi Minh's oppression of the peasantry in North Vietnam became so intense that there was an uprising in 1956 which was bloodily put down. We know that many deserters from the Viet Cong came over to the nationalist side because they saw that the South Vietnamese peasant, for all his trials and tribulations, was better off than the peasant in the North.

The tragic situation of the peasantry in Communist Vietnam was candidly admitted in the newspaper *Nhan Van,* which is Hanoi's counterpart of Moscow's *Pravda.*

Describing the ruthless application of the Chinese Communist style of land-reform program, *Nhan Van* wrote: "People were arrested, jailed, and their property confiscated. Innocent children of parents wrongly classified as 'landlords' were starved to death."

According to the Hanoi newspaper a "mistakes-correction" campaign brought about the release of twelve thousand *falsely accused peasants.* Further, claimed *Nhan Van,* fifteen thousand who had been killed were given *decent graves and public funerals.* There was no mention of the tens of thousands of victims considered unworthy of posthumous rehabilitation.

Such cruelties must have left searing memories in the minds of North Vietnamese youngsters whose families were involved in this grisly repression.

French diplomats estimated that at the time of the anti-Ho rebellion of 1956 perhaps ninety percent of the population was against the Communists. How, then, did the canard ever materialize that if nationwide Vietnamese elections had been held that year (free and supervised elections, that is, not Communist-style elections), Ho Chi Minh would have triumphed? To the contrary, so hostile was the population in this year of open revolt that the Communists would have been trounced, which is precisely why Ho Chi Minh refused such elections.

As late as 1964 the Canadian member of the International Control Commission in Hanoi described how it was impossible to walk down the street of the capital city without having passersby approach furtively and whisper, "À bas les Communistes."

How, then, have Western intellectuals managed to work themselves into such an inferiority complex about the Viet Cong in the South? Does it stand to reason that the terror that alienated the Communist-ruled population in the North is going to make friends of the Vietnamese in the South? What is it about Western psychology that results in applying such a relentless magnifying glass to the warts of allies with so little attention to the warts of our enemies?

Terror of the kind perpetrated by the Viet Cong is difficult for the American people to comprehend, probably because, like most horrible abstractions, it must be experienced to take on reality. We understand terror in the form of crime: killing to steal, for example. But we don't understand terror as politics: killing to force people to obey your will.

Nor do Americans understand that terror often accounts for the marvelous grit and cunning with which the Viet Cong hard core can fight. The public is frequently the victim of the great American fallacy that men who fight bravely must always be motivated by noble and high purposes.

The Viet Cong is a class of army that few Americans understand—an army that often fights superbly because its soldiers are more afraid of their officers than they are of their opponents.

This was perfectly plain in talking with Viet Cong deserters. In every single case, the drama (to them) was how they conspired and dared at great risk to escape their Communist comrades. They all stressed that instant death would have been their lot had their escape plans become known.

When I had pressed Sergeant Liem as to why the Viet Cong fought so well, he replied with an air of astonishment: "It is very simple. When my officer tells me to storm a Nationalist position, there is no alternative but to do it. That way, I at least have a chance of surviving. If I should hesitate, death would be certain. I would be shot instantly."

Vietnam is not the only place where fear has been the main goad to the enemy's performance. In Korea, there were many instances where seemingly fanatical Chinese soldiers fought well in spite of the fact that they hated Peking. This was demonstrated when more than 14,500 of a total of 19,500 Chinese prisoners of war flatly refused to be repatriated from prisoner-of-war camps in Korea and chose instead to go to Nationalist China. The previous battlefield accomplishments of these Chinese as warriors were not an accurate reflection of their feelings toward Peking, which they hated.

Even in our own country there is a lot of overcomplicated malarkey about the necessity to teach our soldiers what they are fighting for. Any eighteen-year-old American with his wits about him can usually figure out without benefit of elaborate lectures that he is fighting because the United States could find no other way to cope with the Communist or Fascist aggression of the time.

During the amphibious landing at Inchon's Red Beach in Korea, some Marine Corps men and I took shelter in a dip in the sea wall to escape the relentless cross fire from machine guns that our landing ship tanks were trying to take out with their heavier guns.

Intending it ironically (because there had been many rude jokes about indoctrination sessions), I said with mock solemnity to a Marine with his nose pressed to the dirt a spot a few inches away from mine (also pressed to the dirt), "Do you know what you are fighting for?" The Marine said irritably: "I'm fighting because he (pointing to a lieutenant a few yards away) told me to get my ass over this seawall and help clear this section of the beach."

Concerning Vietnam, the general lack of American comprehension on the effects of terror was reflected by a U.S. Senator who asked me indignantly at the time of the Viet Cong attack on the American compound at Pleiku in February, 1965: "Why didn't the peasants warn us? After all, the Viet Cong set up their mortars in a village only two kilometers from the American compound. After all we have done for these people, why wasn't there a single Paul Revere to come and find us and pass on the warning?"

As it happened, I knew precisely why the Montagnard peasants had not warned the United States. For, with their diabolical psychological cleverness and thoroughness, the Viet Cong set up their mortars in February in precisely the same Montagnard village in which, the preceding November, they had killed the beautiful Montagnard woman and kidnapped four young boys. I had wondered at the time why they had picked a village so impudently close to the Pleiku compound.

With hindsight, it was obvious that the Viet Cong had selected that village as part of a longer-range plan. They chose to terrorize precisely this village in precisely this spot in November so that the next time they appeared, every single Montagnard would be so frightened that he would do their bidding or be in hiding. Everyone would want to avoid suffering the same fate as the martyred Montagnard woman and the kidnapped young men. In any case, the Montagnards had no way of knowing in advance that this time they were not the real target and that the Viet Cong were about to use their village as the site from which to attack the Pleiku compound.

As the Montagnard chieftain told an American adviser after the incident, "I was in a deep and secret hiding place that nobody else knew of. I heard the uproar but couldn't be sure what it was. And I did not dare to come out of hiding to find out."

I have heard many Americans scoff at the idea that the Viet Cong use force to "recruit" Vietnamese and Montagnard young men. There are certainly instances in which, as Captain Ba explained, Vietnamese peasants have been "persuaded" to join the Viet Cong by playing on their vanity, their frailty, and their vices. But that was true mainly in the earlier phases of the war in Vietnam, when there was more time, when the war moved at a more leisurely pace, and when villages were not fortified, so that it was simpler for the Viet Cong to get in and get out.

I once spent a whole day talking to Vietnamese parents of kidnapped youngsters in a village in the delta which had been seized and held by the Viet Cong for nearly eighteen hours.

According to eyewitnesses the Viet Cong had at one point in this eighteen hours rounded up all the villagers and then ceremonially disemboweled the district chief in front of their eyes.

Then the Viet Cong commissar had given a speech on the "evils" of the strategic-hamlet system and warned the village that if it tried to rebuild its defenses, "you will be punished."

There had been plans, the commissar said, to exterminate a number of "other lackeys of the Diem government," but because of human compassion, the Viet Cong would let these people go—this time. However, it would be necessary for fifteen young men to show the village's "goodwill" by joining the Viet Cong "to fight against the imperialists and their lackeys."

In this instance, when no young Vietnamese stepped forward to "volunteer," the Viet Cong commissar said that he would give the village a few hours to help decide on which "young men will have the honor of joining us."

At my request, the villagers led me to the home of one of the bereaved families. I was met at the door by an elderly man of perhaps fifty years of age, his eyes red from weeping. Two of his sons had "gone" with the Viet Cong.

"Is there any possibility," I asked the old Vietnamese, "that your sons might actually have wanted to go with the Viet Cong, that they volunteered?"

"Volunteered!" exclaimed the old man, breaking into tears all over again. "The Viet Cong came at dusk and put guns at their heads and tied their hands behind their backs," he said. "I begged them to let them go. My wife is dead. I have no one else. The rice has to be harvested. I am too old to do it by myself. What is to become of me? When is this terrible war going to end?"

Like peasants everywhere, of course, those in Vietnam also yearn to be let alone. They are the ones who suffer the most from being caught in the middle.

This is particularly true in areas where neither the government nor the Viet Cong has total authority.

In a strategic hamlet located on the road from Mytho to Vinh Long I talked one day to some peasants who had been relocated there from their original home near the much-fought-over village of Ap Bac.

I asked the elder of the relocated village to talk with me about the pros and cons of the transfer. He was a charming and wise old man who was the pride of the village because he could both read and write and speak a little French.

We sat on his tiny front porch and were stared at by muddy and naked children. A stone's throw away a water buffalo lumbered by, driven by a tiny boy astride its broad back.

"For an old man like me," began the Vietnamese elder, "it is difficult to be so far [six kilometers] from my ricefields. It takes me an hour to get there by bicycle and by walking. And the Viet Cong are still in Ap Bac. They do not harm old men generally. But one has to be very careful and very polite with them. Also, when the government relocated us here they did not give us enough money to make up for the losses we suffered. There is nothing for the chickens and pigs to eat, as we are just starting the growing season and nothing has been planted here. But it is safer here. Over in Ap Bac bombs were falling on us all the time. We knew that the government was going after the Viet Cong. But the bombs killed some of us too."

I asked the old Vietnamese whether, if he had it to do over again, he would have preferred to stay at Ap Bac. Quite a few villagers had gathered by now and seemed as interested as I in what the old Vietnamese would say.

"No," said the old man finally. "Even though it is difficult to be so far from our rice paddies, we are probably safer here on the main road. I do not think the Viet Cong would dare to come here to kidnap our youngsters, for example. Also, when we were in Ap Bac we had to pay two sets of taxes. We had to give the Viet Cong a bag of rice and two hundred and seventy piastres a year. And we had to give the nationalists about the same. Now we pay only one set of taxes. The Viet Cong do not try to collect from us here."

The picture of the Viet Cong that the old Vietnamese painted was one of a combination of calculated correctness and calculated terror.

"If you do as the Viet Cong say," said the old man, "they are very correct with you. They never steal. They only 'tax.' If they take a chicken, they pay you. But if you do not cooperate, if you do not keep their secrets, they shoot you in the stomach." This pretense at "correctness" was virtually abandoned by the Viet Cong in 1965 when they began sacking and looting villages of everything from chickens to mattresses.

Pointing to a middle-aged woman in the crowd, the old Vietnamese said, "Her husband was almost killed by the Viet Cong because they suspected him of talking to government forces. The Viet Cong were taking him out to the field to shoot him when a government attack came. And in the confusion he ran away."

It was often true, unfortunately, that the regular Vietnamese army did not behave as "correctly" as the Viet Cong. There were times when they took the peasants' chickens at the point of a gun.

Also, in the early stage of the war, when it was still mainly guerrilla and terrorist in character, the sometimes indiscriminate use of artillery against villages was inexcusable. Certainly, advance targeting —fixing artillery on prechosen positions—was ridiculous, because the guerrillas were so mobile that they could evaporate quickly from one spot and turn up in another.

But by the time Ho Chi Minh escalated the war into phase three, which included conventional-warfare units, the use of artillery became inevitable wherever the Communist Viet Cong showed up in battalion or regimental force. If a Viet Cong regiment holes up in a village with heavy weapons, such as mortars, there is no alternative to going after the village with both artillery and airpower, giving the peasants prior warning when possible. It would be nice if wars could be fought without anybody being hurt. But they can't.

"We know that war is war," said the old Vietnamese. "We know that the government has good intentions. We know that the white men are here to help us. Our village has received fertilizer and food from the white men. We know that the Viet Cong always take away and give nothing. But we must be polite to the Viet Cong until the government and the white men can give us certain protection against them. We have some protection here, but I am not sure that it is complete protection. And at my ricefields at Ap Bac there is no protection at all."

The old man did not know how fateful were his words.

Four months later, when I went back to see him, I was met at the edge of the village by the old man's son-in-law, who asked me to go away at once. He appeared to be trembling with fear.

"Why?" I asked, puzzled, since the old man had seemed to enjoy his previous conversation.

"Because," said the son-in-law, "the Viet Cong kidnapped the old man when he was working his ricefields [at Ap Bac]. They held him prisoner for two days on charges of having given information to white people. You see, the Viet Cong found out that you had come to this hamlet. So the old man begs you not to endanger him again by going to his house. For the Viet Cong said that if he talked to you again they would kill him. He says that the Viet Cong are very cocky now and are sure that with Diem dead victory is inevitable. The old man says he would like very much to talk with you but hopes you will excuse him and understand why it is impossible for him to receive you."

This was late November, 1963, and I understood very well.

The kidnapping of the old man was a technique that the likes of Captain Ba also understood very well. In discussing "scare kidnappings" in his coldly clinical way, Captain Ba claimed that they brought maximum result with minimum effort. For the person kidnapped could be counted on after his or her release to do Communist bidding unquestioningly. The kidnapping would scare the victim into unconditional moral surrender, which was judged (rightly) to be the price for staying alive.

Captain Ba was particularly interesting to me because he had served sixteen years with Ho Chi Minh's Communist Viet Minh army. It was therefore a momentous decision for him to break with the Communist regime.

Why, after so many years, did Ba decide to desert the Viet Cong?

"Because," he said, "the more I saw of villages and people of South Vietnam, the more I realized how much better off they were than the people in the North. I began to question the idea that these rigid Marxist-Leninist ideas were applicable to Vietnam. I saw that the people secretly hated the Viet Minh [called Viet Cong in the

South] for the terrorism and fear, even though the government did not know how to exploit this hatred. So I decided to come over to the Vietnamese nationalists and offer my services. I know enough of Viet Cong approach so that I believe I can find ways to counter it." And that is precisely the assignment he has been given.

Since what happened in Captain Ba's province more or less parallels what went on in many others, I asked him to go into some detail.

Captain Ba's first year in South Vietnam was, he said, spent settling into the province, casing the villages, recruiting farmers and youngsters, and staging minor harassments. By 1961 orders had come down (Captain Ba had a radio that connected with a regional headquarters, which in turn connected with Hanoi) to start selective assassinations of district chiefs, teachers, etc. All these terror attacks were designed to give the impression that the Diem regime was losing control of the situation, as well as to make it hard for the national regime to recruit officials. In 1961 more hard-core reinforcements began to arrive—Hanoi-trained officers and men of the regular Viet Minh army. By 1962 there were two Viet Cong battalions under Captain Ba's command, in addition to the guerrilla irregulars previously recruited. The Viet Cong battalions had the capability of staging ambushes and of taking on regular Vietnam army units. During 1962 the number of hard-core Red army soldiers in his province again increased substantially. But in 1963 infiltration tapered off somewhat.

"It was after Diem's overthrow that we saw a really important increase in the number of Hanoi's infiltrators assigned to my province as well as passing through it to other destinations," said Captain Ba. "Four days after Diem's death I had received orders to intensify operations on all fronts. I was told to try and get food and medical supplies stocked up and hidden in preparation for important inflow of reinforcements. We were told to expect a disintegration of government authority in the countryside and take maximum advantage of it. During the early part of 1964 more than one thousand Viet Minh cadres passed through my province en route to other destinations. The weapons they brought were far heavier and better than before. Many units came south in company strength ready to fight without further reorganization. And for the first time antiaircraft companies of about thirty men each came south to fight with each battalion."

Another deserter from the Viet Cong at the Saigon camp, Sergeant Le Van Quyen, told of the excitement at Xuan Mai, in North Vietnam, when word came of Diem's overthrow. Xuan Mai is the camp where Ho's Red army officers and men receive the special training to equip them for their operations in the South.

"I was working in the wireless room of Xuan Mai," explained Sergeant Quyen, "when the telegrams came in about Diem's overthrow. There was great excitement. Two days later a big meeting was held. One of Ho's top generals appeared to tell us that the ['liberation'] movement would have to be greatly intensified in order to take advantage of the confusion following Diem's death. Instead of finishing out their normal training, every soldier in the camp was to head south as soon as preparations could be made. They even decided to send me. And I was just a radio specialist. I had been at Xuan Mai for several years. I had no desire to leave. But when they say go, you go."

Information from Captain Ba and others to the effect that organized Red army units were coming south was fascinating in November, 1964, in light of the fact that the U.S. government was still denying or scoffing at these facts. Yet, since Captain Ba had surrendered in June, his information had been available for nearly six months.

Indeed, General Nguyen Khanh, who was then Prime Minister, stated correctly, in midsummer, 1964, that the Communists were beginning to field a whole new army in South Vietnam which included regular North Vietnamese army units, coming south not just as cadres but as combat-ready units. In other words, the North Vietnamese officers and noncommissioned officers no longer paused to fill out their ranks by "recruits" (kidnapping and terrorizing), but were ready to go into military action the moment they entered South Vietnam.

But almost immediately after General Khanh's declaration an Associated Press dispatch from Saigon on July 14 stated: "A ranking United States military spokesman denied Tuesday that there were indications regular North Vietnamese army units were moving into South Vietnam."

This had the predictable effect of infuriating our Vietnamese allies because it made them out to be liars when in fact they were very much telling the truth.

But, according to Captain Ba, "such denials also have a very bad effect in Hanoi. For if Hanoi thinks that Washington is trying to brush things under the rug, then it is encouraged to believe that the United States is unwilling to do anything about this intensified infiltration. And if it can count on American inaction, the Communists are emboldened to try and get away with even more than would be the case if they thought some sort of reprisal would result."

Whether or not Americans are simply incapable of grasping the elementals of psychological and political warfare, it is certain that repeated attempts of American officials during 1964 to cover up the rapidly escalating rate of Red army infiltration was very shortsighted.

To have admitted this infiltration, of course, would have brought forth the corollary question: What do you intend to do about it? And since, at the time, the United States intended to do nothing at all about it, the safest course perhaps seemed to be to deny that the problem existed. But in so doing we acted as our own worst enemies for two reasons: We deprived ourselves of an important and valid propaganda argument against Hanoi; and we looked ridiculous when the day of reckoning finally came and we were forced to put out a white paper (February 28, 1965) affirming all the facts that we had pooh-poohed most of the previous year.

No wonder many people thought that the State Department white paper was an invention! After all, it contradicted the line we had been spouting for all too many months.

But this is not the only thing that baffles and exasperates me about the American "gap" in understanding psychological warfare.

I have often wondered why, for example, an intelligent Viet Cong deserter like Captain Ba is not brought to the United States for a few months to tell his story. A man like this could quickly learn sufficient English. Let a Viet Cong like Captain Ba go to the university campuses and tell the doubters why he at great risk fled the Communists to seek haven with Vietnamese nationalists. Let men like Captain Ba tell those who want us to welsh on our commitment to Vietnam just what life is like under Uncle Ho's harsh rule. Let Americans question him at will. A man who has been a Communist political commissar is resourceful enough to handle both the students and their professors.

Captain Ba's story, told in person and under free questioning, would be a thousand times more effective than long, boring white papers.

But every time I have suggested that the American people be allowed to meet these former Viet Cong, person to person, I find my suggestion shrugged off as "interesting but impractical."

CHAPTER **9**

Ngo Dinh Diem: The Case
of the Misunderstood Mandarin

When Ho Chi Minh sent for Ngo Dinh Diem in 1946, he clearly expected to see a broken man, spiritless and compliant. Four months earlier Diem had been seized by the Communists, acting on Ho's command, and taken to their mountain stronghold at Tuyen Quang. During captivity he was half starved and suffered from high fevers.

When Diem entered Ho's office, the Communist leader said to his haggard prisoner: "I am ready to offer you a high post in my government. I want you to come and live in the governor's palace."

If Ho expected Diem to fall upon him in gratitude, he was in for a huge surprise. Diem's reply was deliberate and blunt.

"You and I want totally different futures for Vietnam," he said. "Can you guarantee you will not try and impose a dictatorship of the proletariat here? . . . I have seen your agents at work [while province chief in Phan Rang and Phan Thiet]. . . . They act like criminals. . . . How can I trust you? . . . Your agents have the blood of many honest nationalists on their hands. . . . You killed my brother [Ngo Dinh Khoi, governor of Quang Ngai province]."

Ho protested: "I know nothing about your brother. . . . The country is all confused. . . . You are upset. . . . Stay with me. . . . We must all work together against the French."

Stubbornly Diem retorted: "I don't believe you understand the kind of man I am. Look me in the face. Am I a man who fears?"

"No," said Ho, "you are not such a man."

"Good," said Diem, "then I will go now."

And Ho Chi Minh let his fellow mandarin go.*

Ho had urgent reasons for trying to get Diem to collaborate with him. He admired his administrative gifts, which were in desperately short supply in the Viet Minh administration that had seized power in 1945 and managed to hang on until 1946, when open warfare against the French was launched. The prestige of Ngo Dinh Diem was legendary, and it would have been a triumph for Ho to have had him in his government, especially since it was Communist-controlled behind its popular-front facade. Diem was known in political circles as totally incorruptible, broadly educated (scholars in Vietnam are revered as perhaps in no other country), courageous, and able.

Philippe Devillers, an outstanding French historian of contemporary Vietnam, says Diem "was known for his perfect integrity, competence, and intelligence." Paul Mus in his book on Vietnam describes him as "the most respected and the most influential nationalist leader."

Ho Chi Minh's offer was but one in a long series that Ngo Dinh Diem had turned down—and would continue to reject. The Japanese during the occupation of Indochina in World War II tried unsuccessfully to tempt him into collaborating with them in a national government. The French, both before and after World War II, attempted countless times to assign him high posts. (The French attitude was variable; on several occasions they issued orders for his arrest.) Emperor Bao Dai, in his turn, repeatedly called Diem to his side. Aside from a decade spent as province chief in Phan Rang and Phan Thiet, he accepted a high government post only once. That was in 1933, when he became Minister of the Interior on the condition that the French accept the "reforms" he proposed. These included the elec-

* Various versions of this anecdote have appeared in American publications, including *Time* magazine. My account is based on an interview with Diem and on information supplied by a French diplomat who discussed the incident with Ho Chi Minh.

tion of a national legislature that would govern the country. He stepped out when the French reneged on their promises. In every case he adamantly refused to serve unless he was satisfied that his conditions would be met and that independence for Vietnam would be reality, not fiction. This did not come to pass until 1954, when Diem finally took power.

Diem had inherited his aversion to French rule from his father, Ngo Dinh Kha (by Vietnam custom Ngo is the family name, Dinh the middle name, and Kha the given name), chief mandarin at the court of Emperor Than Thai (1889–1907). The patriarch of the Ngo clan deeply disapproved of French colonialism because of its cruel exploitation of the Vietnamese peasants (through, among other things, a monopoly on salt). Ngo Dinh Kha resented the progressively deep intrusion of the French into administrative matters and was gravely offended when the French arbitrarily deposed his sovereign, Emperor Than Thai, and replaced him with a more obedient puppet.

Diem's father was not only the highest-ranking mandarin at the court (something like a grand vizier), but a brilliant scholar and educator, and for a man of his position, something of an eccentric. Ngo Dinh Kha felt that his sons should learn about hard labor as well as poetry.

"A man must understand the life of a farmer," Ngo Dinh Kha used to say. And this apparently explains why Diem and his five brothers were sometimes sent into the muddy rice paddies to help the farmers in their toilsome planting.

Ngo Dinh Diem was born on January 3, 1901, in Quang Binh province, north of the Seventeenth Parallel, which is also the birthplace of Ho Chi Minh.

Perhaps three hundred years before Diem's birth the Ngo family had been converted to Catholicism. They were extremely devout, and Diem was no exception. In his teens Diem considered going into the priesthood. But as he explained it to me, he had sensed, even as a youngster, that the clash between Vietnamese nationalism and French colonialism would come to a climax in his lifetime. "And I wanted to be able to play a practical part in it," said Diem. "And besides, as my interests widened I saw that the life of the Church would not be enough."

Unlike many of his compatriots, Diem had no real Western overlay because he received his entire formal education inside Vietnam, though in high school he scored so well in examinations at the French Lycée at Hué that he was offered a scholarship in Paris. He turned it down.

Diem's mother once remarked, "Those of my children who did go to France came back a mixture of many things and many inner contradictions. But Diem is pure Vietnamese."

In 1921 Diem graduated at the top of his class from the Hanoi school for law and administration. He was a brilliant orator and debater and already deeply attached to the idea of political independence for his country. He went into the provincial administration reluctantly, for it meant working for the French. Diem was pushed into it by family and friends, who argued that it was necessary for Vietnamese of talent and intellect to gain some practical experience in government administration.

In Phan Rang (his first important assignment) Diem as province chief came to know something of the minority problem of Vietnam, for there are many Montagnards in this area, as well as Chams. Diem had a special affinity for the Chams, since the Ngo family had acquired a lot of Cham blood through intermarriage. The Chams are of Polynesian-Indonesian origin, that is, non-Mongol, which explains why Diem and especially his brother Nhu looked less Oriental than most Vietnamese.

Diem's experience as a province chief gave him a lasting interest in the Vietnamese countryside and in the practical problems of agriculture, water, dams, and schools. As President, these interests took him out of Saigon at least several days each week.

A curious legend of isolation and aloofness grew up about Diem in the latter stages of his Presidency, and many Americans mistakenly believed he refused to identify with his people.

Because of this prevailing myth, I include here a letter of July, 1965, from former Ambassador Nolting giving an intimate view of Diem's journeys among the Vietnamese villagers.

Diem was an indefatigable traveler. He was out of Saigon in the provinces two–three days out of every week. He ran us ragged trying to keep up with him. In addition to Army headquarters and outposts, he visited the remotest villages and districts, Camau, Montagnard villages and training camps, off-shore islands, 17th parallel, etc. As you know, Diem had been a Province Chief under the French (a darned good one) and he was intensely interested in local rural problems—healthy conditions, schools, water supply, roads, canals, seeds, fertilizer, crop diversification, land ownership, land rents, housing, etc. He was full of ideas and on-the-spot suggestions for improvements. He was especially interested in, and proud of, the agricultural improvement stations which his government had established, teaching many things, from fruit and nut-tree raising to fishponds, manioc-grinding, and even mushroom-raising in rice-straw stacks.

I accompanied Diem on many, many trips (and took many others to try to get reactions on my own). I am sure that he was genuinely and sincerely seeking out the truth about rural conditions and rural government, inviting the airing of problems and complaints and settling many matters on the spot. He was not a good orator before big crowds, but extremely effective with groups of peasants and villagers, informal, inquiring, genuinely interested and sympathetic, and usually coming up with practical remedies. He was anything but aloof as depicted. He frequently complained about the ceremonies laid on for him by provincial officials, preferring to talk to the people in small groups, to eat simply with a few of the village elders, to discuss real problems. *The fact that he didn't shake hands and slap backs, but bowed instead, was of course the result of his country's customs* [italics mine], not a reflection of an aloof or disinterested attitude (as some members of the press professed to think).

On trips with Diem, our usual schedule was to leave Saigon at 5 A.M., fly to the airstrip nearest our destination, take a car, jeep or helicopter (depending on roads), sometimes reaching a hamlet or village by foot or row-boat. For a short, stout man, Diem was a fast walker and no hill or underbrush stopped him. He used to say that his father taught him to run uphill and walk down. After visiting four or five hamlets, outposts, or villages during the day, we would generally return to Saigon around 8 or 9 P.M. Sometimes, on longer trips, we would spend the night. Meals were sometimes elaborate, sometimes simple. Diem preferred the simple ones. I remember many occasions which reminded me of camping trips when I was a boy in Virginia—watermelon, roasted corn on the cob, even skinned catfish caught in the river.

On such trips, we must have visited, between 1961 and 1963, all, or nearly all, of the then 41 provinces of South Viet Nam—many times in some of them. These trips were always refreshing and rewarding, and I am sure that there was a real rapport and mutual respect between President Diem and the large majority of the rural people. Unfortunately, this was not true of the 'intellectuals' of Saigon. Maybe that's why Diem was always eager to visit the countryside.

I have never been quite sure what the 'mandarin type' is, but if Diem is one, I'm for it. He was a good, honest, courageous, and respected leader—according to my close observation over 2½ years. Although I had many difficult and time-consuming negotiations with him, I always respected him and admired his tenacity of purpose and, strangely, his gentleness and compassion. (He used to spend his 1½ day Christmas holiday, the only days-off he took, in the remotest military outpost he could find, with the troops.)

In his conversation with me, Ngo Dinh Diem seemed far more the Confucian scholar than the devout Catholic, an impression that probably grew out of our discussion of a wide range of topics—world politics and developments, Asian attitudes, varying philosophies of government, earthly opinions. Religion—the Buddhist crisis and the Catholics—was referred to in this broad framework.

"Why does the Western press keep calling this government Diem's Roman Catholic government?" Diem asked irately at one point. "Kennedy is a Catholic but nobody calls his government the Roman Catholic Kennedy regime."

The night before my interview with Diem at the palace I stayed up late doing my homework on this controversial man who was at once the hope and the despair of so many Americans. Even though Diem's rule was never entirely free of controversy, his early years, I discovered, were generally regarded as a triumph over long odds. Even his most articulate critics, such as William Henderson, Far East specialist on the Council of Foreign Relations, agreed that "in retrospect the survival of Ngo Dinh Diem's anti-Communist government and the effective consolidation of its power throughout most of Free Vietnam constitute a political miracle of the first magnitude. . . ."*

"After Geneva," Mr. Henderson continues, "Free Vietnam seemed

* *In Vietnam: The First Five Years, An International Symposium,* by Richard W. Lindholm.

close to chaos. For all practical purposes, Diem's authority was con-
fined to Saigon and a few other urban centers. . . . Despite Geneva,
the Viet-Minh left behind a powerful underground organization in
Free Vietnam. Even after their ostensible withdrawal, Communist
cadres continued to dominate many rural districts. The Communists
had also extensively infiltrated the army, police, and civil administration. As rapidly as circumstances permitted, Diem set about the difficult task of uprooting and destroying them. An impressive array of
political and psychological warfare techniques was employed in this
effort, as well as all-out pacification campaigns against the main
pockets of Communist strength. . . . By mid 1956, most observers
had concluded that the Communists, whatever their original potential, could no longer endanger the Diem regime *without outside
support* [italics mine]. This was all the more true since Diem had
systematically reorganized and greatly strengthened the army and police services. While still not strong enough to hold out indefinitely
against an attack from the Communist north the forces at Diem's
disposal seemed adequate for the maintenance of domestic security."

But what had Diem done for the peasant, these remarkably durable
Vietnamese who formed eighty-five percent of the population?

Certainly by any fair judgment the Diem regime had made substantial progress in helping them—until Communist violence put a stop to
it. The land-reform program wasn't perfect. Much remained on the
agenda of the countryside. But a commendable, impressive beginning
had been made.

In December, 1959, Wolf Ladejinsky, the American expert who
supervised the land-reform program in Japan and Taiwan, as well as
in South Vietnam, wrote in *Reporter* magazine: "The slogan 'land to
the landless' used so effectively by the Communists in their drive for
power has been a source of bitter disappointment and tragedy to
many farmers of North Vietnam. Not so in South Vietnam. Beginning
two years ago, a sizable portion of the large landlords' holdings has
been distributed among landless tenants. . . . By now, approximately
35 per cent of the tenants have become landed proprietors. An earlier
measure which limited land rents to 25 per cent of the crops, or about

half the rentals formerly received by the landlords, has made land-lordism less attractive than it once was."

Additionally, during the early years, inflation in South Vietnam had been checked, highways and roads were built, railways and bridges were renovated, thousands of villages acquired new schools or additional classrooms, malaria was being eradicated, and at least a million acres of abandoned land had been brought under cultivation.

In the *Christian Science Monitor* for October 12, 1959, Arnold Beichman, then associated with the International Confederation of Free Trade Unions, declared that the labor movement in South Vietnam was "perceptibly moving in the direction of freedom from government domination."

A year earlier Robert Gullain, Far Eastern correspondent for *Le Monde*, wrote, "In my opinion, South Vietnam is, on the whole, an asset to the Free World."

Therefore, on the word of many qualified and objective witnesses the Diem regime had made a creditable start toward a genuine social revolution in the southern half of the truncated land, until the pace and progress were interrupted by the renewed outbreak of Hanoi-directed terror.

No evidence can be adduced showing that before the Hué incident of May 8, 1963, there was a religious issue in Vietnam. If there had been, assuredly the critics of Diem's leadership would have trumpeted it to the world. Complaints of alleged religious repression made by Thich Tri Quang and his accomplices in a campaign of letters to the United Nations and prominent foreigners had begun, but they represented no more than the early activity of determined propagandists.

Most hostile criticism toward Diem centered not on what he did but on his methods and techniques of governing.

Mr. Henderson, for example, declared that "from the beginning there was a dark side of the picture."

"Most manifestations of political opposition," wrote Henderson, "were vigorously suppressed. Civil liberties remained an unfulfilled ideal. Elections were far from free and many of the devices used to stimulate popular support for the regime bore the familiar stamp of modern totalitarian practice. No doubt these moves could be justified, at least to some extent, in terms of the overwhelming problems confronting Diem during his first two years in office and also the inexperience of Free Vietnam's people with the forms and substance of democracy. But . . . Diem had still to prove that his professed devotion to the democratic cause represented anything more than a facade to disguise the increasingly plain reality of stern dictatorship."

In other words, Diem was not conforming to Western standards of democracy. And this was really the heart of the case against him. Implicit in this criticism was the assumption that Occidental-style democracy was in fact the answer to Oriental Vietnam's problems. It was an assumption with which Ngo Dinh Diem disagreed on both practical and philosophical grounds.

When I entered the Presidential Palace on August 7, 1963, I did not realize that I would be one of the last American journalists to interview Diem before his murder.

He was a man devoid of surface charm. Cool courtesy there was. Studied self-possession there was. But when he said (in French) "How are you?" it was clear that he was not really interested in knowing the answer. He was going through the requisite rites. He was in a hurry to get on with matters at hand: the war, the Buddhists, the tumultuous conflict between American advice and his own best judgment of how to deal with the crisis.

He was much changed from the somewhat diffident and considerably sparer man I had briefly called on back in 1954.

On this hot August afternoon there was an unhealthy plumpness and pinkness about him in his white-sharkskin suit. It was hard to imagine him as the revolutionary who had exhorted his people upon assuming power in 1954: "If I advance, follow me! If I retreat, kill me! If I die, avenge me!"

I quickly found myself admiring his odd impassiveness, his marked self-control in what was a time of almost intolerable tension. In the small palace reception room Diem sat opposite me in a deep chair under a whirring fan. Only occasionally did he betray any nervousness, by fiddling with a tiny translucent cup of green tea.

I spent an incredible five hours talking with Diem. They were disquieting hours, but not because of Diem's famed habit as a monologuist, although as the large chunks of quotation in this chapter will show, he did tend to make speeches at you. But President Diem and I had far more of a dialogue than I had expected, possibly because I have developed (I am told) a certain expertise in the art of interruption. What disturbed me was that until this conversation I had not realized just how desperate a corner Ngo Dinh Diem was in.

I started with the obvious inquiry into Vietnamese-American relations.

"It would help," said Diem, "if the people of the United States would try and understand the complexities of this country and the nature of the Communist war we are fighting. You, Miss Higgins, have been in the countryside. You have seen the Montagnards, with their spears and their superstitions. The Chams. The Cao Dai. The Hoa Hao. The primitive villages where the ancestors rule—as they do most places in Vietnam. Tell me, Miss Higgins, what can parliamentary democracy mean to a Montagnard when his language does not even have a term to express it. . . ."

Here Diem leaned forward in his chair, his voice growing tense. "The French did not leave us a pretty legacy," he said. "In the days before colonialism, people could read and write even in the villages. Now we have to rebuild, and the Viet Cong are doing their worst to prevent it. . . . But we must build slowly, beginning with the villages. There is a tradition of democracy and autonomy in the village. . . . It is part of the Confucian tradition . . . and Confucian customs and duties have survived illiteracy, for they are bound up in worship of the ancestor. . . . And we want to tap these deep roots of our Confucian traditions in rebuilding our society. I know that some Americans try to tarnish me by calling me a mandarin. . . . But I am proud of being a mandarin. . . . It may not be similar to anything that you Americans have experienced—this mandarin-Confucian system. But it has its merits and its own inner democracy. We are not going to go back to a sterile copy of the mandarin past. But we are going to adapt the best of our heritage to the modern situation. You Americans have a finished, polished society built on entirely different ideas of the priorities and values because your needs are totally different from ours. After the chaos of our recent history and the subversion by the

Communists, Vietnam's priority is stability, central control, respect for authority, and law and order. Do you realize that when I took power, the central government had lost all control of the countryside? . . . What do Americans know of mandarins? Have you heard of the five virtues [Jen, Li, I, Chi'i, Hsing—generosity, politeness, steadfastness, reason, and trust]? The Americans are breaking Vietnamese psychology and they don't even know what they are doing. Your press and radio mock the idea of discipline and respect for authority and glorify so-called civil liberties and the right to criticize and the need for political opposition, but this country is in a life-and-death struggle. Even Western democracies suspend civil liberties during war emergencies."

At this point Diem sent an aide for a document, which I later deduced to be a memorandum of a recent conversation with an American official.

"Your ambassador," Diem resumed, "comes and tells me that it enhances my 'liberal image' to permit demonstrations in the street by the Buddhists and the political opposition. . . . I cannot seem to convince the embassy that this is Vietnam—not the United States of America. We have had good reason to ban street demonstrations in the middle of a war, and the reason is that the Viet Cong are everywhere. . . . What would happen if the Viet Cong should infiltrate a demonstration here in Saigon, toss a bomb, kill dozens of persons, including some American press? What would 'liberal opinion' say of me then? Would they believe my government when it said that the Viet Cong were responsible for the killings because only the Communists could profit from such an event? Consider what happened at Hué. Those plastic bombs were thrown by the Viet Cong. . . . But whom did the Americans blame? They blamed me—the President of Vietnam—and the Vietnamese army. Would they be any more charitable next time? This is not child's play; I am not inventing Viet Cong terror. Yet when I try to protect the people of this country—including the Americans—by *good police work,* keeping control of the streets, I am accused of persecuting the Buddhists!"

At one point Diem startled me by suddenly changing the subject to ask me point-blank: "What am I to think of the American government, Miss Higgins? Am I merely a puppet on Washington's string? Or—as I had hoped—are we partners in a common cause?"

"Why, exactly, do you ask?" I countered.

"Why?" said Diem, half smiling. "I ask because I am trying to be a loyal ally. Yet almost daily I hear of broadcasts over Voice of America or of inspired articles in the American press discussing whether Washington is going to retain my services or throw me out. We are a small power and America is a great power. But what would Mr. Kennedy think if our press were filled with inspired stories virtually urging the people of America to overthrow him? We admire America in many ways. But we cannot always take American advice, for many reasons. It is, much of it, often contradictory. Procedures applicable to one culture cannot be transplanted wholly to another culture. We appreciate American aid. But we would like to believe that it is not given as a favor or to serve as a lever for controlling this government. Surely there is only one justification for Americans to be in Vietnam—and that justification is that America's national interest requires you to help prevent Communism from conquering this country. If this were your attitude, then your aid would be offered as part of a wartime partnership to defeat the Viet Cong. But now I hear hints that this aid may be withdrawn if I do not do exactly what the Americans demand. Isn't there a certain arrogance in these demands? America has a magnificent economy and many good points. But does your strength at home automatically mean that the United States is entitled to dictate everything here in Vietnam, which is undergoing a type of war that your country has never experienced? If you order Vietnam around like a puppet on a string, how will you be different—except in degree—from the French? I am not unaware that some Americans are flirting with elements in my country that perennially plot against me. These elements cannot succeed without the Americans, and they know it."

"But do you really think the United States is plotting against you, President Diem?" I asked with some astonishment.

He hesitated. Then choosing his words deliberately and speaking slowly, as if making points in a debate, he replied: "I do not think Ambassador Nolting is plotting against me. I do not think Richardson [of the C.I.A.] is plotting against me. I *know* there are American officials who are preparing the way in the event the decision is taken to try and get rid of me. I cannot foresee the future. I cannot believe that America would turn against an ally under attack, engaged in a struggle for its very existence. But some people are crazy—and the world is crazy. Still, Miss Higgins, I hope that your government will take a realistic look at these young generals plotting to take my place. How much maturity or political understanding do they have—of their own country, let alone the world? I am afraid there are no George Washingtons among our military."

Until the militant Buddhists turned the Hué tragedy into a major crisis, the principal opposition to Diem had always been the intellectuals and assorted generals and colonels.

These groups—a tiny minority of the population—usually bickered among themselves, unable to agree on coherent alternatives or much of anything else. The act of "plotting" seemed almost an end in itself, an exercise in self-fulfillment, perhaps therapeutic. It was the time-honored discourse of the coffeehouse, disputatious, mischievous, unsettling, often without purpose. To ask these idle conspirators what their program augured for the future was to discover they would do very little different from the Diem regime except that they would be "more democratic" or "more efficient." The generals and the colonels harbored no grander visions of change and progress than the civilians, but they were far more dangerous because they had the engines of power at their disposal if they chose to betray Diem.

"It is impossible," Diem said, "for Americans to understand the virulence of ideological passions in this country—passions that are a product of both the primitive and the backward state of Vietnam, and the negative attitudes resulting from the hundred years of French rule in which the people were united on only one point: hostility to the French. In America, even the Republicans and Democrats are united on many things—on the general philosophy of government, on some parts of foreign policy, for example. Here there is not even agreement on what kind of government we should have. There are some members of the Vietnamese bourgeoisie who do not understand the profound attachment of the rest of the people to the idea of national independence. For these bourgeois intellectuals were part of the privileged class under the French and they have since refused to participate actively in the reconstruction and consolidation of this national independence. We have heard that some of these Vietnamese bourgeois have proposed the extension of a kind of American protectorate over Vietnam. Perhaps they hope thus to find favor for their intrigues. It would be a great mistake for the Americans to support them. Such intrigues go against the deep longing of the Vietnamese people to be truly free of foreign rule."

Diem has been accused of showing his contempt for the coffeehouse intellectuals too openly, a charge of some substance. Perhaps he could have placated them to some degree by being less publicly disdainful. His brother Ngo Dinh Nhu, who had the title of political counselor, no doubt alienated many Vietnamese unnecessarily by his rudeness. Nhu was not the type to endear himself to persons over whom he wielded power. And he had great power, because, among other things, he controlled the police and was the director of the strategic-hamlet program. It is fair to say that the intelligentsia felt far more venomous toward Counselor Nhu and Madame Nhu than they did toward President Diem. But in their plots and condemnations, the Vietnamese intellectuals probably could not have been swayed and silenced by an acquiescent Diem any more than they have been by such pliable and permissive successors as the gentle Dr. Phan Huy Quat (Premier from February, 1965–June, 1965).

Ton That Thien, Vietnamese writer and intellectual, has stated the problem very much as I have observed it when he wrote: "Independence for Vietnam marked the beginning of many difficulties, quite unlike those encountered during the near century of French rule. When the French ruled Vietnam, the problem for the Vietnamese was relatively simple: How to get rid of the French. . . . French rule resulted in the elimination of the Vietnamese from the effective running of the country. Thus, the people's sense of organization, leadership, responsibility were lost, or at least blunted. . . . In fact, during those years, the Vietnamese acquired a new mentality: that of the revolutionary nationalist—*bitter, uncompromising, destructive* [italics mine]. The Vietnamese learned how to destroy—materially, mentally, socially. Having no responsibility for the running of their country, they had no opportunity to learn how to preserve, to develop, to build—in a word, to think and act constructively."

Throughout our conversation President Diem acted the role of an aggrieved, misunderstood mandarin. He did not deny ruling his country with an authoritarian hand. But he argued that without this strong rule the country, with its strong strain of anarchy and factionalism, would fragment under the emergencies that perpetually assailed it.

President Diem had gone to the trouble of constructing a facade of democracy to placate the United States, whose aid was indispensable to him. The Vietnamese constitution promulgated in October, 1956, follows the United States model in some ways. The presidential system was adopted because it was obvious that Vietnam needed a strong executive. But elections were never free in the Western sense. How could they be when most villagers (eighty-five percent of the population) and many city dwellers could not even read the names on their ballots, much less understand such concepts as constitutionalism, consent of the governed, secret ballots, checks and balances, and other features of democratic government?

"We go through the form of the elections," President Diem said, "and gradually, with practice, this will help our people understand the substance."

Most of our interview was, inevitably, devoted to the accusations leveled against the government by the Buddhists.

"The West has had its religious wars," Diem said. "But that has never been true of Vietnam. Vietnamese have never gone to war against each other for religious reasons. We are a very tolerant people. Look at our relations with China. We fought and defeated the Chinese and finally repulsed their invasion. But even though we got rid of the invaders, we kept their religions (Confucianism and Mahayana Buddhism). Our Confucian Emperors fought the Catholics—not because of their religion but because they feared that Catholic priests were the claw of the crab of imperialism. . . . And although we got rid of the French, we kept Catholicism.

"I don't understand the Americans. Your ambassador has asked me to conciliate the Buddhists and not even speak out in defense against these absurd charges being made against me. I have kept my side of the bargain. But if I must keep silent, why don't the Americans tell the truth—that this so-called Buddhist affair has nothing to do with religion but is a fight to topple my government?

"Or is it conceivable that Washington really thinks I have gone crazy? Certainly only a crazy man would at this late date and at this crucial point in the war suddenly start a fight with an important segment of the population. But I assure you, Miss Higgins, I am not crazy. I have done everything within my power to placate these Buddhists. I have made an agreement with them concerning the flying of flags and property ownership. I have offered to have every single grievance investigated by an international commission, including the foreign press and the Buddhists themselves. Why won't they accept these offers? It is because they want, not a solution, but an excuse to continue agitation against this government. There are Communist Viet Cong in those pagodas, Miss Higgins, and we know it. You have attended some of those demonstrations. You have heard wildly subversive speeches that not even the United States government could tolerate, and certainly not in the middle of a war. And yet the United States says that the liberal thing for this regime is to sit silently and accept all this. But what happens if we sit silent and do nothing? There will be more suicides and more headlines around the world portraying me as some kind of devil. The more passive we are, the more the demonstrators will be emboldened. How can I, in the middle of a war, allow these disorders in the streets to go on? We have an obligation to put first things first: the war. And our soldiers who are fighting and dying."

With Diem, an interview was always at two levels. There were written questions submitted and answered in writing. They were on-the-record. The person-to-person conversation was not to be used until the current crisis was over, and what was said would no longer influence the course of events.

When I left the palace after five hours, I was mentally exhausted but not bored.

The conversation was fascinating, not just for the glimpse into the mind of an Oriental leader at bay, but because I sensed that the arguments he was making were matters of life and death for his regime. If he could not with similar persuasiveness make his case with Washington, a *rapprochement* with the United States would be impossible. And, of course, as it developed, he never managed to make the case that would have saved his regime and preserved some semblance of stability in Vietnam.

Whatever his faults, President Diem remained a brilliant scholar and intellect all his days. My notes show that in our conversation he buttressed one single argument (on the merits and/or demerits of total acceptance of Western ways) with quotations from Thomas Jefferson, Plato, Confucius, Buddha, and Tao.

"The West must give us a little time," he said. "Even though you Westerners do not recognize it in its Oriental form, the spirit of democracy has always been a key part of the best of Asian thought. It is related to all our Asian religions. Indian philosophy conceives of the transcendence of the human soul. Buddha preached the equality of all men. There is the freedom entwined in the spontaneous emergence of the Taoist being [*sic*]; and there are the cosmic as well as highly individual virtues of Confucian Jen [Jen meaning the great, or complete, man]. This spiritual basis of democracy is to be found everywhere in Vietnam, and especially in our villages, and we are building democracy there. The villages largely run themselves. Gradually, when the war ends, we can move to greater democracy on a national level, drawing inspiration from the permanent values of Western culture. But it is impossible—a delusion—to think that a solution for Asia consists in blindly copying Western methods.

"What the American public does not understand is that Vietnam is backward both economically and at the front lines of a terrible war that we are fighting against Communist guerrillas, who are the best in the world. No other country finding itself in this plight could act any other way than the government of Vietnam is acting. Show me a single Afro-Asian country that has at this moment adopted the kind of democratic regime that is advocated by the liberal Occidentals. You will note that in Moscow, which is the headquarters of the oldest Communist dictatorship in the world, the Twentieth Party Congress nonetheless had the gall to come out in favor of 'liberal democratic' regimes for the African continent. The aim of the Communists is clear. If these states were to adopt this kind of regime, they would become that much easier for the Communists to swallow up. We have our police and security forces because in this subversive situation the struggle against the Communists demands that we know, village to village, who are susceptible to pressures by the Viet Cong. What you call authoritarian measures are the only way this government and this war can be run. And anyone who comes after me will have to resort to the same methods—or lose to the Communists. And if the American people really understand our plight and our problems, I feel certain that they would no longer respond to the attempts to poison public opinion with regard to Vietnam."

More than once Diem inquired: "Do the American people really understand what this Communist war we are fighting is about?"

"This is a war both total and various," he said at one point. "A war that often refuses battle and works at the moral attrition of the adversary; a war that embraces all the domains of politics, economics, diplomacy, and the military and which is waged at a world level because its sword strikes in more than one part of the world. If one looks on a map of the world, one can see to what point in these last years this Communist war has altered the face of the earth since World War II. And if we here in Vietnam can defend this front successfully against the Communists, then we are helping the entire Free World. And this we are going to do. Do not forget that in this war he who is still fighting in the last five minutes is the one who will win!"

As I look back through my notes, I am struck by the references to "those who may come after me." For instance, Diem said: "A key to the good relations between a great power like the United States and a newly independent power like Vietnam, whether it be governed by myself or those who come after me, is first of all the diligent respect for the substance as well as the form of the sovereignty of the newly independent power. The newer national independence is, the more are people passionately attached to it, especially if it has been won in great travail."

As to the regime's philosophical doctrines, I concluded from our conversation that the Vietnamese expression "Nhan Vi" (literal tranlation: human dignity) should not be translated into English as "personalism," because this gives a wrong impression. Humanism is closer to the idea that the Diem regime was after.

Obviously on the defensive about his religion, Diem was at pains to deny that his philosophy of Nhan Vi had anything to do with Catholic religious doctrine. This had been written repeatedly; and it plainly annoyed him because it figured conspicuously, as he saw it, in the attempt to indict him on the charge that he sought to impose his own Christian religious mores on a non-Christian majority. As expounded to me, the doctrine of Nhan Vi has a lot more to do with the teachings of Confucius than anything else.

"The concept of Nhan Vi is really very simple," Diem tried to explain. "The Communists say that individuals exist for the good of the state. In contrast, we hold that the state exists for the good of the individual, whose welfare and liberty must be protected. But freedom is not a gift from Santa Claus. Our peasants must learn to cooperate in protecting this freedom by helping each other and their communities. Each village should provide forces for its own defense, building of necessary public works (like the moats dug around the strategic hamlets) to help stave off the Viet Cong. The voice of the peasants is expressed in the free secret elections in the strategic hamlets—elections held to choose village councils. In precolonial Vietnam there was in the villages a combination of communally owned property and private property. The communally owned ricefields made it certain that even landless peasants would not starve—and the hungry man does not have much human dignity. Economically, a big problem in the field of industrialization is to find the balance between nationally owned enterprises and private enterprises that best suit our needs, customs, traditions, and hopes. In Vietnam we have what you in the West call a mixed economy. But due to shortage of foreign capital, the state will probably have to play a large role in industrialization.

"In a situation where anarchy perpetually threatens, we need first of all a sense of security and order that will permit us to build a new Vietnam with a character and personality entirely its own. Our emphasis on Nhan Vi is our way of saying that all this can and must be done within the restraints imposed by a humanist approach."

I asked at one point about Ho Chi Minh's July, 1963, broadcast hinting at the possibility of *rapprochement* between North and South Vietnam and ultimate reunification.

"A lot of people talk about reunification," Diem said, "but very few bother to say how this reunification could be reconciled with continued liberty. Very few nations exert pressures for moderation on the Communists, which is the aggressor in my country. The pressures are reserved for us, who are the victims of aggression.

"We have been at war for twenty-three years, and yet we are determined not to bow before armed aggression, because we want to save our independence and our opportunity for liberty. Any plan for reunification that did not guarantee these values would be a betrayal of the sacrifices that our people have made since 1954 and continue to make."

After I left the Gia Long Palace, my communications with Diem were by no means at an end. In subsequent days I found myself the recipient of an avalanche of material intended to buttress his arguments: photographs of Americans allegedly pushing small uniformed Vietnamese policemen around, statistics on deserters from the Viet Cong, documents showing the results of the official investigation of the Hué incident, plus assorted books and pamphlets on all aspects of Vietnam life.

One communication was a mimeographed excerpt from an article by Ellen Hammer, author of *The Struggle for Indo China*, with a handwritten notation (in French) in pencil from Diem saying: "Miss Hammer at least tries to *understand* what we are doing. She takes account of the Oriental context in which we must operate."

The key points advanced in Miss Hammer's article were these: "Vietnam has little in common with Western society, so the language of Western politics cannot be transposed to Vietnamese life without *the greatest caution, and then only at the risk of confusion and misunderstanding* [italics mine]."

Miss Hammer continued:

Vietnamese society was characterized by both a highly developed autocracy and a remarkable degree of democracy. Although all power reposed in the Emperor, every aspect of his life, as with the least of his subjects was regulated by the moral precepts of Confucius. The Confucianist teaching which was grounded solidly on humanism and characterized by moderation, minutely regulated the behavior of the individual; it provided that the role of the citizen in government was only one facet of a carefully organized network of social relations and obligations. Even during the period of French rule, Vietnamese society remained surprisingly unaltered. Although the displacement of political power to French hands inevitably disrupted certain aspects of Vietnamese life, the social traditions of Vietnam managed to survive through the family which became the guardian of national traditions.

Confucianism was a way of life which impregnated the entire culture of Vietnam. It left an indelible imprint upon the Vietnamese, *regardless of their religion*, upon Catholics and Buddhists, as well as animists; and in its emphasis on the responsibilities of an individual to society (as in the Nhan Vi doctrine) it acted as a valuable counterpoise to Buddhism which was essentially other worldly and indifferent to social or political relations.

In this Confucianist world, political behaviour was logically deduced from a set of ethical equations which any servant of the state had to assimilate before he could qualify for office. There was thus no place for the concept of the right of the minority to become majority which is at the root of Western political democracy, nor of majority rule. There was no hereditary aristocracy to stand between the emperor and the people. With the Vietnamese state recruiting its governing elite, or mandarins, entirely through educational channels by a system of triennial examinations open to the entire population, its officials were selected to a striking extent on ability. This intricate society was permeated by a profound sense of popular sovereignty for all that it was expressed in ways unknown to the West. It affected even the emperor who governed according to a so-called 'mandate of heaven. . . .' Omnipresent rules of Confucianist doctrine imposed both a practical and theoretical check on the abuse of power . . . the Confucianist system took for granted a society in which each individual knew his place and duties. . . . Whatever rights an individual might have were derived largely from his functions and from the role he was called to play in the social system. . . .

In 1954 when Diem returned to power the duty of obedience to established authority had been undermined (in the cities).

But since that time Diem has set about building a regime, step by step, on foundations that go deep in what in the past was legitimate and decent for an Asian country, namely Confucianist ethics. In the present Vietnamese state . . . recourse to the basic Confucianist equations has been accomplished by special emphasis on the rights of the individual. . . . In this development of a political credo which draws its deepest roots from the traditions of which Asia can so legitimately be proud, the service rendered by Diem to free Asia may well extend beyond the frontiers of his Republic of Vietnam.

Another item of interest that I found one day in my box at the Caravelle Hotel were these lines of Buddha taken from verses of the Sutta-Nipata, a collection of the teachings of the Enlightened One.

> The Wise Man who fares strenuously apart,
> Who is unshaken in the midst of praise or blame
> Even as a lion that trembles not at noises
> Or as the wind that is not caught in a net
> A leader of others, and not by others led,
> Him verily the discerning proclaim to be a sage.

These lines had been neatly typewritten on stationery from the Presidential Palace. A handwritten note in French, apparently from a presidential secretary, said: "President Diem thought you would be interested in the fact that an *Oriental* like Buddha had ideas about the nature of a wise leader that are not unlike his own."

I judged the note to be Diem's way of saying that what seemed "aloof and stubborn" to an Occidental might seem wise and praiseworthy to many an Oriental, including Buddha.

Diem would certainly have agreed with a penetrating diagnosis of problems of East and West that I came across in the United States several months after his death:

"The special danger of the present time would seem to be an increasing material contact between national and racial groups that remain spiritually alien. The chief obstacle to a better understanding between East and West in particular is *a certain type of Occidental who is wont to assume almost unconsciously that the East has everything to learn from the West and little or nothing to give in return* [italics mine]. . . . There is an assumption of superiority based on the achievements of physical sciences and the type of progress it has promoted, a tendency to regard as a general inferiority, the inferiority of the Oriental in material efficiency. . . ." This passage appears in an essay "The Buddha and the Occident," written by the late Irving Babbitt, Harvard professor, humanist, and philosopher.

Were Diem's troubles with the West due, then, in part to "the certain type of Occidental who is wont to assume almost unconsciously that the East has everything to learn from the West and little or nothing to give in return"? Did such assumptions underlie our demands for the trappings of Western-style democracy? Did such assumptions underlie our contemptuous use of the word "mandarin" as a term of reproach as applied to Diem? Did such an assumption underlie our refusal to appreciate the Confucian values that Diem was trying to restore to Vietnam? Was there any merit in Diem's complaint—reiterated in myriad ways in our conversation—that the breakdown in good relations between Vietnam and the United States stemmed from impossible demands upon a backward Oriental country at war, demands that it meet Western standards that the vast majority of the tribes, clans, and villagers neither understood nor would readily accept?

The historical verdict on Diem cannot be forecast with any assurance. Whether he was a prophet, devil, saint, hero, or villain requires the long perspective of time and events to judge. But one can hardly gainsay the view that he was at least a much misunderstood mandarin.

CHAPTER **10**

Plots and Plotters—
Vietnamese-American Style

The raids of August 21, 1963, on the Xa Loi and other pagodas were a turning point in American policy toward Diem. They crystallized the feelings of a powerful faction inside the Kennedy administration that Diem had to be deposed and led to the fateful cable of instruction only three days later that was to be a green light along a path of tragedy and chaos. The bell had begun to toll for the Ngo brothers— and for those who rang it.

The pagoda raids produced stories from the Saigon scene that had all the inventiveness of an Oriental Ian Fleming. Soldiers in battle dress and wearing gas masks had "stormed" into the pagoda shortly after midnight. A bedlam of gongs, bells, and blood-curdling screams shattered the spiritual serenity. One eyewitness professed to see two monks thrown twenty feet from a balcony. Extravagant rumors about the number of dead and wounded spread like a wild malignancy. As it turned out, in proportion to the damage done, the din was distorted beyond belief.

When the United Nations mission to Vietnam investigated the rumors and charges three months later, it could find no evidence that anyone had been killed! And the UN investigators talked at length to

monks who had been present during the entire affair at the Xa Loi Pagoda and elsewhere.

The gap between rumor and fact, always chronically vast in Vietnam, is indicated by this paragraph in the UN report: "The mission took note of the names of Buddhist monk leaders and students who had allegedly been arrested, kidnapped or killed. Later it was able to interview Thich Tri Tu, Thich Quang Lien, Thich Tam Giac, and Thich Tien Minh, who in some communications were said to have been killed. The mission also interviewed one student who, according to some communications, had disappeared."

Still, even if the Diem regime had been able to prove that not a single Buddhist had been badly hurt in the proceedings, it probably wouldn't have curbed the dire reaction in the United States.

The U.S. reaction was based in part, of course, on the feeling that holy places of worship had been violated. I did not share this view because my own experiences at the Xa Loi Pagoda had led me to look upon it more as a political command post than a holy place. As I said earlier, it was the headquarters from which the militant Thich Tri Quang and others had defiantly masterminded and run their political war against the Diem regime. Even today a vivid memory of the Xa Loi is the persistent humming sound that came day and night from the mimeograph machines that made the entire building reverberate. During my visits there had been the constant hubbub and bustle of a GHQ—telephones ringing, orders being barked, messengers scurrying to and fro, manifestoes being issued, press conferences being held.

The Buddhist militants knew that the government would have to act sooner or later. The key militants among the monks were informed by journalists, among others, that certain units of the armed forces had been alerted for the raid. As previously mentioned, Thich Tri Quang told Australian journalist Denis Warner early in August that he hoped that in the process "they would kill one or two of us."

In Washington the State Department regarded the actions against a dozen pagodas as a betrayal of Diem's promise to try to conciliate the Buddhists. The worst was believed and the raids were considered as

barbaric in deed as Madame Nhu had been in words when she invoked the infamous word "barbecue" to describe the self-immolations. Washington was almost frenetically determined to disassociate
this country from the pagoda episode and Diem's so-called "repression" of street demonstrations.

The psychological gap between Occidental Washington and Oriental Saigon surely had never been wider. The New Frontiersmen of the
Kennedy administration had come to admire the civil disobedience
movement in the United States. Many appeared to equate the Buddhist movement with the American Negro drive for his long-sought
rights. They remained skeptical of reports that the Buddhist movement had nothing to do with human rights and was instead a deliberately orchestrated campaign to use the false issue of religious
persecution for the precise political purpose of toppling the government. They could not understand that what the extremist Buddhists
wanted was not reform but revolution. The almost instinctive reaction
in many layers of our government—and in some sections of the U.S.
embassy in Saigon—was that if Negro demonstrations in our country
were a good and progressive development, then Buddhist demonstrations in Vietnam must also be a good and progressive development.
"How can I convince the American people that Vietnam is not the
United States?" Diem had asked me plaintively during our interview.
Unfortunately, from his point of view, it wasn't always easy. Even
many State Department officials remained unmoved by arguments
that demonstrations in the middle of a war in a beleaguered capital
like Saigon could hardly be compared with a peaceable march on
Washington.

To arguments that Communists were bound to take advantage of
such turmoil (as they do sometimes even in the U.S.A.), the idealist
sternly replied that "seeing Communists under every bed" was merely
an excuse to justify authoritarian ways. And because the civil-
disobedience movement in our own country was so deeply admired,
many New Frontiersmen felt that America's liberal image required
that our principal client in Asia act accordingly. For a while these
voices prevailed. Illegal demonstrations, hunger strikes, and a general
defiance of authority by an articulate, camera-conscious minority

were tolerated by Diem—on Washington's demand. Thus in the summer of 1963 mobocracy came to the streets of Vietnam for the first time since Diem had taken power almost a decade earlier.

It would have astonished these Americans, no doubt, to be told that within months after Diem's death the Buddhists and students would be back on the streets fighting their own Buddhist-led government and each other, and—what heights of ingratitude—even denouncing Uncle Sam. History was to record that impossible, if well-intentioned, American demands for meaningless trappings of democracy were to bring chaos, political instability, and confusion. And we are not out of the woods yet.

The raids by the Vietnamese army on the pagodas took place five days after the departure of Ambassador Nolting from Saigon and a week before Henry Cabot Lodge was expected to arrive for his first tour of duty in Vietnam.

Why this timing? In a message to Washington, President Diem claimed that the raids were ordered at this time because: It had become clear that the Thich Tri Quang wing of Buddhists was intransigent and had no intention of coming to any agreement with the government, irrespective of how many concessions were made. (For five long weeks the Buddhist extremists had refused to accept a government offer for joint, internationally supervised investigation of any Buddhist grievances if any were found to exist. This refusal was significant since it was the Buddhist extremists who initiated the demand for just such an investigation.) Since the raids would create an anti-Diem propaganda explosion, it would be less embarrassing to the United States if they took place when no ambassador was present in Vietnam. For the same reason, great care was taken not to inform the United States of the pagoda plans. The reasoning was that Washington could hardly be blamed for something about which it knew nothing.

President Diem also stated that the moves against the pagoda had been made at the express request of senior Vietnamese generals who felt that martial law was necessary to prevent a continuation of the turmoil which was being exploited by the Viet Cong and which was intolerable in time of war.

It was certainly true that Buddhist extremists had persistently boasted in August that they would bring their agitation and suicides to a peak to coincide with the arrival of Ambassador Lodge.

After the raids, when General Ton That Dinh, then military governor of Saigon, brought the small arsenal of weapons found in the pagodas—spears, daggers, plastic molds (for making bombs)—to a press conference, the foreign press laughed at him. Moreover, no attention was paid to the documents showing the involvement of a few monks with the Vietnamese liberation front, the Hanoi-created political arm of the Communist military campaign.

In this case I fear the Viet Cong will have the last laugh. Even Thich Duc Nhiep,* who was spokesman at the Xa Loi in the summer of 1963 and who at this writing is studying at Columbia University, confirms now that certain militants like Thich Tri Quang have on occasion used Viet Cong supporters to further their ends. Thich Duc Nhiep gave this view in a conversation at Columbia University with Dang Duc Khoi, former deputy minister of information of the Vietnamese government. Mr. Khoi interviewed Thich Duc Nhiep at my request in April, 1965, in New York.

Further, the Communists themselves openly boast of having helped the street demonstrations of the summer of 1963. Wrote Wilfred G. Burchett, the Australian journalist with Communist sympathies, concerning these events:

"The size of the demonstrations was a great shock to the U.S. command in Saigon. *The Viet Cong was right amongst them* [italics mine], in Saigon itself, in many tens of thousands, slugging it out with Diem's shock troops."

This is an absurd exaggeration. The so-called demonstrations usually *averaged* around three or four thousand persons or less. But Mr. Burchett is no doubt correct in saying that "the Viet Cong was right amongst them."

Under a Saigon dateline in the spring of 1965 Cyrus L. Sulzberger wrote in the *New York Times:* "Political tactics of South Vietnamese

---

* In 1964 Thich Duc Nhiep broke publicly with Thich Tri Quang, when it became clear that this Machiavellian monk would pursue chaos and undermine governments—any government—whatever the effect on the war effort.

Buddhists, combined with a *generally negative attitude toward all Saigon governments* [italics mine], afford the Viet Cong admirable chances of exploitation. There have been numero*us reports of known Communist agents* [italics mine] provoking violence during Buddhist demonstrations and there is some suspicion that the clerical hierarchy has been infiltrated. . . . Organized Buddhism here . . . is inherently hostile to Washington and sympathetic to announced Viet Cong aspirations. And, essentially, this significant trend is directed from Hanoi, not Peking."

These observations applied in 1963 as well as 1965. Without a doubt Diem was correct in charging that a minority of extremist Buddhists used the pagodas for subversion and that the Viet Cong had penetrated the Buddhist movement to some degree.

Even in 1963 many monks and nuns genuinely disapproved the militant politicking of the Buddhist extremists, although many were physically afraid of Thich Tri Quang's wrath. For this militant monk was a hero to the toughs in the Buddhist youth groups, and not a few monks who have spoken out against Thich Tri Quang have been violently beaten up within a day or so of their "indiscretion."

Following the raids on the pagodas, the two most prestigious of the nonpolitical monks—Thich Thien Hoa and Thich Tinh Khiet—publicly called on their followers to get out of politics and back to religion.

The pagodas were reopened within days after the raid. The Diem regime followed a policy of releasing into the custody of the senior monks anybody for whose loyalty they would vouch. Of the thousand monks and nuns picked up on August 21 all but a few dozen extremist leaders had been released within thirty days.

Despite all this the United States rushed into instant and almost total condemnation of Diem. Shortly after his arrival (August 22) Ambassador Henry Cabot Lodge seemed to personally and publicly place the U.S. embassy on the side of the Buddhists. Lodge seems to have called on the Buddhists even before presenting his credentials to Ngo Dinh Diem.

Later some administration insiders claimed that Lodge just happened to "drop in" at the Aid Mission compound and discovered the

Buddhists there. Since the USOM compound is miles away from the embassy and U.S. ambassadors rarely, if ever, have been known to "drop in" there, such a visit was highly unusual.

Further, when a U.S.I.A. official called Mr. Lodge's office about what to tell reporters, the reply was: "Tell them the Ambassador went to call on the Buddhists." While at the USOM compound, the Ambassador passed a good deal of time posing for photographers in the company of Buddhists. Accidental or not, Lodge's much-photographed session with the Buddhist monks was universally viewed in Saigon and the rest of the world as showing where America's sympathies lay.

At the time, some policy makers in Washington explained that this was necessary not just to safeguard America's image with Buddhist Asians but also to detach a Catholic American President from the "taint" of what a fellow Catholic had done. The Buddhists in question were two monks who had taken refuge at the United States aid-mission compound which is right next door to the Xa Loi Pagoda.

In Washington, partly to justify Lodge's call on the Buddhists, one official asked me plaintively: "Don't you realize that Diem is tarnishing our image everywhere in the world?"

"But," I countered, "if the United States were to state the facts—that this is a political, not a religious matter—wouldn't that in itself help to put the matter in perspective and help everybody's image?"

"The rights and wrongs don't matter," said the official; "it's what people believe."

Or as Roger Hilsman, Assistant Secretary of State for Far Eastern affairs put it (in a talk with Hearst's Frank Coniff): "After the closing of the pagodas on August 21, the facts became irrelevant." So, evidently, did a sense of perspective. What, for example, about the fact that President Diem was far more lenient to his political opposition than President Sukarno of Indonesia or Premier Sarit Thanarat of Thailand, both recipients of American aid? Whereas some three hundred political prisoners, at most, were found in Diem's jails, the prisons of Thailand, Indonesia, and Burma were filled—and still are—with tens of thousands of political victims.

"But," explained a pro-coup State Department officer, "the world spotlight is not on those countries, and it is on Vietnam. What we have to do is divorce ourselves from the pagoda business and from Diem."

I did not realize how far the disassociation was to go until Friday, August 23, when an old friend at the Department of State told me that "Diem will be overthrown in a matter of days."

This proved a bit premature. But not for any lack of effort on the part of certain factions of the U.S. government. Indeed, the second miracle of Vietnam involving Diem was that he was able to survive the pressures unleashed against him for as long as he did. (The first miracle was that his regime survived the doom-sayers who in 1954 gave South Vietnam six months to live.)

Whether President Kennedy fully realized that these pressures must necessarily seal Diem's doom will now remain forever unanswered. The President's attitude appears to have fluctuated greatly. It is clear that he was hampered by lack of any personal experience of Asia and plagued by wildly conflicting advice.

As Edward R. Murrow said to me not long before his death: "President Kennedy was very badly served on the issue of Vietnam. Feelings ran so high between the Diem-must-go school and the Diem-must-stay school that the processes of reason could not function."

". . . I was at one National Security Council meeting," Murrow continued, "when a supposedly responsible State Department expert got up and gave a long spiel about Diem's unpopularity. The basis for this attack on Diem were reports alleging that army officers were changing into civilian clothes to take food and other packages to their relatives among students detained after staging demonstrations. This fact was supposed to show of itself that the army was becoming disaffected with Diem. But how could we know what the attitude was of the officer visiting the camp? Maybe he was telling his younger brother to straighten up and fly right and show some discipline in time of war. In any case, although I rarely speak much at Security Council meetings, I finally challenged our Asian expert as to the source of the allegations. It turned out that the source was one *Paris-Match* photographer whose allegations were unchecked and unevaluated. Now, I ask you, is that the kind of evidence on which to base decisions?"

At the Department of State the leaders of the Diem-must-go school were Averell Harriman, Undersecretary of State for political affairs, and Roger Hilsman, Assistant Secretary for Far Eastern affairs.

Their advice was opposed by Vice-President Lyndon Johnson, Secretary of Defense Robert McNamara, General Maxwell Taylor, then chairman of the Joint Chiefs, and John McCone, director of the Central Intelligence Agency, among others. As between the often bitterly contending forces inside the government, Secretary of State Dean Rusk seems to have stayed somewhere in the middle.

When the secret files are opened, history will show that Vice-President Johnson made very strenuous, though secret, efforts to try to stem the tide—not out of any particular love for Diem, but out of fear of what his overthrow might do to the war effort and political stability. Indeed the man who was soon to be plunged into this maelstrom by an assassin's bullet appealed personally on several occasions to key State Department officials not to try to play God in Vietnam for the reason that Americans, being Occidentals, were too inexperienced in the ways of the Orient and too unsure of their facts to be omniscient about what was best for Vietnam. According to those who heard the Vice-President state his views, he further expressed fears that the Americans risked opening a Pandora's box in Vietnam. There were times to act, and also times not to act, the Vice-President argued. There was a war on. Who could be sure that government by a committee of generals could succeed better than a man whose personal incorruptibility was legendary and who, after all, had already overcome what many had described as insuperable odds? And unless we could be *sure* that the successors to Diem would be better, the prudent course was to stick with the known—even though troublesome—quantity. Who was there with the will and force of character to do as well as he?

As events have demonstrated, it was a good question and still is.

As the drama in Saigon moved inexorably to its tragic climax, I became increasingly baffled by the role of Attorney General Robert Kennedy. After all, it was he who recommended that I ask General

Krulak for a briefing, and General Krulak, of course, reflected the Taylor-McNamara view of the situation. I would have thought the Attorney General would be against taking the risk of overthrowing an ally in the middle of a war, accepting the strictures of Al Smith: "Don't change barrels going over Niagara Falls." In talking with him since then, I have concluded that Robert Kennedy, now a senator from New York, hoped and believed that the problems between the Kennedy administration and Diem could be solved short of the violent overthrow of the Vietnamese president. Robert Kennedy is at his best when he has mastered the minutiae of a crisis. He was simply never deeply enough involved in and informed about the small, vital details of the crisis in Vietnam to be able to play a decisive part in halting the inexorable march toward coups and chaos. Kennedy was not able to keep track of the Vietnam minutiae because in the summer and fall of 1963 he was preoccupied with a crisis more directly affecting his own Justice Department, the civil-rights battle.

A policy of overt political warfare against Diem was begun at the State Department the day after the pagoda raids. In a formal statement the Department accused Diem of breaking faith with his announced policy of conciliation and charged him with the repression of Buddhism. No effort was made to balance this indictment with the fact that the Buddhist extremists had for five weeks rejected every conciliatory move. Nor was any acknowledgment made of the fact that the pagoda incidents were isolated acts designed to track down subversive leaders in monk's clothing. For the first time, the State Department's phraseology gave credence to the theory that some sort of action against Buddhism itself was being undertaken. Since out of a total of 4,766 pagodas only twelve were affected by the raids, the charge seemed patently out of line with the facts.

These harsh accusations by the Department of State had an important effect inside Vietnam. They helped to incite precisely the kind of political agitation Diem was trying to damp down. For under a policy of so-called "impartiality," the Voice of America daily beamed into Saigon U.S. newspaper accounts of these State Department denunciations. Thus "impartial" rebroadcasts of news items were in reality very partial inasmuch as most American newspapers were extremely hostile to Diem and so was much of the Kennedy administration.

In Saigon, university students, high-school students, and even ordinary citizens could hardly be blamed for thinking that the anti-Diem broadcasts coming in over the Voice of America were a signal for even more antigovernment agitation. Many Vietnamese parents told me that their sons and daughters would listen to the Voice of America broadcasts before deciding whether to join in demonstrations. The day's anti-government slogan was often based on what the Voice of America was saying.

This produced another of those perfect vicious circles of the Diem era. For each new demonstration by students in Saigon brought fresh assertions from the Diem-must-go school in Washington that student unrest proved what they labeled his "massive unpopularity"; but by its anti-Diem broadcasts and statements, Washington nurtured this unpopularity. It's a little like spreading a rumor that a supposed friend is a liar and a cheat and then disowning the friend because the rumors exist!

The trickiest U.S. maneuver against the Diem regime was launched by Washington in statements on the weekend of August 25. These statements formally and pointedly absolved the South Vietnamese military leaders of command responsibility in the raids on the Buddhist pagodas and fixed the blame on Ngo Dinh Nhu and the special forces.

Said the State Department spokesman: "Current information makes it clear that these attacks on the pagodas . . . were carried out by the police, supported by small groups of special-forces troops *not under the command of the Vietnamese armed forces* [italics mine]."

But this effort to shift blame was deceitful, and the State Department knew it. In their files were dispatches from the U.S. embassy in Saigon—for once unanimous in appraisal of events—detailing how the pagoda raids evolved and assigning command responsibility to precisely those Vietnamese generals that the Department claimed were innocent of the whole matter.

Why did the Department of State choose the bizarre course of falsely rewriting this phase of history?

The obvious answer is that the faction in the State Department working toward a *coup d'état* knew that the Vietnamese generals were the only respectable group that could unseat Diem and therefore had to be cleansed of all impurities and suspicion. The game was "clean up their image," as one official put it, so that when the generals took over they could be pictured as a virtuous lot, innocent of the pagoda raids that caused such panic in some quarters of the Kennedy administration.

President Diem immediately countered this ploy of the Department of State by asking his generals to sign a document attesting to the truth—that the closing of the pagodas and the declaration of martial law had been proposed by them. And they did.

General Tran Van Khiem, who was at the time Chief of Staff of the Vietnamese army, has provided me with an inside account of how the pagoda decision was reached:*

"On August 20, all the key generals were called to the Presidential Palace for a discussion of the situation caused by the demonstrations in the cities. Ngo Dinh Nhu, the President's brother, put the question of what to do up for discussion. The first to take the floor was General Tran Van Don (acting commander of the Vietnamese armed forces and a Buddhist). The general said that continued disorders could not be tolerated. These disorders deeply undermined the people's faith in the power of the government to keep the situation under control. The ring leaders of the disorders had to be rounded up. . . . The pagodas could not be privileged sanctuaries for subversion. The Viet Cong were exploiting the situation. It was not possible to give one group the privilege of breaking laws (demonstrations were illegal). Soldiers in battle had the right to expect a certain discipline on the home front. . . ."

After General Don had spoken, Khiem related, there was a long discussion among the generals of just how the subversive Buddhist militants were to be taken into custody and the pagodas changed back into religious rather than political centers.

When the discussion was finished, the generals decided *unanimously* to send a written petition containing all their individual sig-

* In conversations at the time with American officials in Saigon, Major General Don, acting Army Commander, and several other generals gave reports similar in all essential details to the account of General Khiem.

natures to President Diem asking permission to proceed with the plan. The petition was taken that same evening to Diem by Ngo Dinh Nhu and approved by the Vietnamese President and enforced within hours.

In addition to army troops, special forces and police were called in to augment the operation. Acting army chief Tran Van Don was the overall commander. Tactical operations were directed by General Ton That Dinh, a Buddhist whose mother is now a Buddhist nun.

Many military men in Vietnam had long felt great concern over the permissiveness of the Diem regime with regard to anti-government demonstrations in the midst of a struggle for survival. As reported in previous chapters, the principal criticism of Diem that I heard from generals and colonels at the front lines was that he had allowed the disorders to go on too long.

There might have been a gentler, equally effective way to haul in the Buddhist extremists who were converting the pagodas into havens of subversion. But the hard fact is that the two Vietnamese generals in command of the operation (both Buddhists) were unable to think of any less forthright way of dealing with the pagoda-directed agitation.

The State Department's instant rewrite of history absolving the generals of any responsibility for the raids was only the first part of the drama.

The crucial act, with its overtones of Greek tragedy, opened with a cable. It was dispatched to Saigon late in the evening of August 24, 1963, a date made more significant because it was a Saturday. Washington usually empties on summer weekends or lapses for a few precious hours into a somnolent mood as officials desperately seek relaxation.

The telegram contained spectacular new instructions for the U.S. embassy in Saigon. It was drawn up at a meeting called by Under-secretary of State Averell Harriman and Roger Hilsman, Assistant Secretary of State for Far Eastern affairs and head of the Vietnam task force. The President's senior advisers were, for the most part, out of town. C.I.A. Director John McCone was in California. Defense Secretary Robert McNamara was on vacation. Secretary of State Dean Rusk was attending a baseball game in New York. President

Kennedy was at Hyannis Port. General Taylor says he knew nothing of the meeting until it was over and the telegram long on its way.

The circumstances suggest that the timing of the meeting was not accidental.

According to one responsible official at the Defense Department: "The Diem-must-go school deliberately scheduled the meeting for that empty weekend because they wanted to send instructions to Saigon that they knew would never have left this city if McNamara and Co. had been around."

State Department friends of Hilsman dispute this, contending that the Vietnam task force merely was in a hurry to get on with the business of repairing the U.S. image in the wake of the pagoda raids.

In any case, the cable proved historic. For the first time it gave the signal to "unleash" the Vietnamese military, flashed a green light for the *coup d'état* against Diem of which the generals had been talking for so many years.

As noted before, plotting to the Vietnamese is as much of a pastime as chess is to the Russians. Ambassador Nolting has remarked, "Not a day passed in Vietnam without some general or colonel or politician inquiring in effect if the United States would be so kind as to cooperate or passively accede in the overthrow of the Diem regime. What the generals were after, of course, was a flat assurance that if Diem were overthrown the military could continue to have U.S. support—that we would not punish them by withholding aid or recognition. In my period as ambassador my instructions were to put every possible obstacle in the way of a *coup d'état*. The embassy forcefully asserted that we could not turn against an allied government, that we were not going to rock the boat in the middle of a war, and that indeed one war at a time—the war with the Viet Cong—was quite enough. My instructions were to tell those plotters to get back to the business at hand, a war that demanded the best in everybody."

But the cable of August 24 was a radical revision of this previous philosophy of one war at a time. It envisaged the general's making war on their own government, and with the implicit blessing of the United States.

The substance of the cable was that the U.S. embassy was to make an effort to persuade Diem to fire his brother, Ngo Dinh Nhu, release the Buddhist rebels, end press censorship, and restore other democratic liberties suspended under martial law. And if, as the cable anticipated, Diem would not do these things, then the embassy was to contact the Vietnamese generals and tell them that the United States would no longer stand in the way of a revolt. The leash thus would no longer hamper the would-be revolters. "Rocking the boat" was no longer a U.S. taboo.

Another cable that went out about the same time made oblique reference to an earlier query of that August by the Vietnamese military about whether there was, in Washington's opinion, any truth to rumors that Nhu was trying to make a secret deal with Hanoi or the Communist liberation front. Washington was equivocal on the point of Nhu and Hanoi, but Lodge was told to stress that the United States was always interested in supporting anti-Communist governments.

According to the Department of State and the C.I.A., Counselor Nhu did on occasion have contacts with certain Communists, both in Hanoi and in the Viet Cong national liberation front, but there were for the purpose of encouraging defections. Details of these contacts were always conveyed by Counselor Nhu to Ambassador Nolting and John Richardson, who remained as C.I.A. director until October 6. In other words, while the United States government heard plenty of rumors, it never seriously accepted as a matter of policy and judgment the accusations that Nhu was attempting to make a secret deal with Hanoi to end the war behind America's back.

Concerning the U.S. demand that Ngo Dinh Nhu be exiled, I remember that Secretary of State Dean Rusk asked me during a talk in Washington in late August "whether it would be possible to separate Diem from his brother."

It was a question that startled me because I could not imagine even Ambassador Henry Cabot Lodge, who is not exactly awash with timidity, having the brass to tell a proud leader like Ngo Dinh Diem whom he should hire or fire in his supposedly sovereign government.

With some hesitancy I finally answered: "With all due respect, Mr. Secretary, I think it would be even harder to separate Ngo Dinh Nhu from President Diem than it would be to separate Bobby Kennedy from President Kennedy. Our President feels that he needs Bobby. President Diem, who is in a great period of crisis, also feels a need for his brother, especially since Nhu is handling the strategic-hamlet program."

"Oh, I don't deny that Nhu has a certain efficiency," said Rusk grimly, and we turned from that topic to the rumors that Nhu had taken over the reigns of government from his brother and planned to become dictator of South Vietnam.

This was absurd, because President Ngo Dinh Diem, whatever his faults in American eyes, was too strong and tough and stubborn a person to cede power to anyone else. Further, Ngo Dinh Nhu was too realistic about his own position to imagine that he could depose his brother.

"I am hated in this country," Nhu told me once in an interview. "I am hated and so is my wife. That is among the reasons why all the stories about our power-seeking are crazy. A man hated as much as I am would not last five minutes. . . . Every government has to have the tough guy, the man who does the dirty and unpleasant work. Even Eisenhower had to have a Sherman Adams,* in a country as advanced and unified as the United States of America. In Vietnam, where violence and virulence are everywhere, I am the person who takes on the unpleasant jobs. It is I who am vilified, so that others may be spared."

It can be argued that Nhu would have been vilified less if he had used his power more benignly and had been less overbearing in his ways. But Nhu's general description of his role in the government is more or less exact, and it was interesting to me, despite the self-pitying tone, that he should be candid about it.

There is controversy about the Kennedy administration's attitude toward news stories from Saigon concerning Nhu's alleged loss of rationality and its impact on the regime's viability. Nhu was certainly a desperate man, for in truth he was in a desperate situation. But in his interview with me he was completely rational, in control of his thoughts, even cool, albeit undeniably bitter. I have talked to literally

* Nhu took great pride in following closely the inner workings of the U.S. government.

dozens of persons who saw Ngo Dinh Nhu in the last few days of his life—friends and enemies—and his sanity was never doubted by any of them. Nhu has been accused of galloping megalomania because he claimed, among other things, to be the "motor of this strategic-hamlet program." It may have been an unseemly thing to say, but it happens to be correct. He was no master of Anglo-Saxon understatement, to be sure, but his boastfulness quite possibly sprang from a defensiveness not uncommon to a man aware of efforts to dispose of him. Nhu had no monopoly on egotism; in fact, he was a shrinking violet compared to the flamboyant young General Ton That Dinh, who after the anti-Diem coups took over many of the powers previously exercised by Nhu.

In any case the controversial August 24 cable was dispatched from Washington Saturday evening after being cryptically summarized to President Kennedy at the summer White House at Hyannis Port by Undersecretary of State George Ball, who interrupted the President in the midst of a shower. Mr. Ball was apprised of the cable when Undersecretary of State Averell Harriman and Assistant Secretary of State Roger Hilsman materialized around five P.M. at the edge of the golf course at the Chevy Chase Country Club, where he was playing. The three men took the cable to Undersecretary Ball's house and he talked to the President from there.

The acting Secretary of Defense, Roswell Gilpatric, who was at his farm on the outskirts of Washington, also had the cable described to him over the telephone after a bit of startling byplay by other actors in the unfolding drama.

To "clear" the cable with the Defense Department, Mike Forrestal, White House aide and a menber of the Vietnam task force, first placed a call to Vice-Admiral Herbert D. Riley, director of the Joint Staff (the executive committee for the Joint Chiefs of Staff). Admiral Riley did not pretend to be a specialist on Vietnam and sensed that the cable might contain international dynamite. So he tracked down General Krulak, the Pentagon's specialist on Vietnamese affairs, who was also at the Chevy Chase Country Club (the locker room). General Krulak, who until that moment had heard nothing about the telegram, also felt a sense of alarm and told Forrestal at the White

House that he would come down immediately to read it over. Once at the White House, and gravely concerned about the content of the message, Krulak insisted that Forrestal then call Undersecretary Gilpatric at his country place.

Mr. Gilpatric says he was frankly surprised that such an important set of instructions should be rushed out on a weekend. But he did not feel that he ought to veto the telegram since Forrestal told him flatly that it had "the approval of the President."

In McCone's absence, the cable was described, again cryptically, to Richard Helms, deputy director of the C.I.A., who also did not feel disposed to veto something "approved by the President."

All these details are of great importance because they are the basis of the arguments of those inside the government who assert that one of the most crucial documents of the Vietnamese war was sent out of Washington without being read, let alone thoughtfully considered, by the officials having deepest responsibility for the actual conduct of the war—Secretary McNamara and General Taylor, for example. The supporters of Hilsman are correct in the remotest technical way in saying that the telegram was "cleared" with Defense and the C.I.A. in the sense that officials of those activities were made aware of its content. But awareness and concurrence are two quite different things, and there is no shred of evidence that the telegram had any concurrence from Defense or C.I.A. officials. In any case, there can be little debate about whether such an incendiary cable should ever have left Washington in such a rush and with such perfunctory treatment by the government.

If my facts are correct, and I have done a lot of detailed checking, the manner in which this cable was sent raises a lot of questions. Is this really the way to run a war, let alone formulate national policy?

The telegram hit Saigon like an unexpected declaration of war. Because of the time difference, it came into the Saigon embassy the same night, Saturday, August 24. Ambassador Lodge had arrived only three days before and had scarcely had time to get his bearings. Indeed, when the telegram arrived Lodge had not even presented his credentials to Diem. Further, the Voice of America broadcast virtually inviting the generals to revolt was already being beamed into

Saigon hours before Lodge's scheduled first call on Diem, which had been arranged for eleven o'clock Monday morning, August 26.

It was, to say the least, an extraordinary way to do diplomatic business with anyone, let alone an erstwhile ally.

The first Voice of America broadcast was in Vietnamese and reached Saigon at seven-thirty P.M. Sunday. The second was in English and came into Saigon at eight A.M. Monday.

The Voice of America broadcast said: "High American officials blame police, headed by President Diem's brother, Ngo Dinh Nhu, for anti-Buddhist actions in the Vietnam republic. The officials say *Vietnam military leaders are not, repeat, not responsible for last week's attacks against pagodas and the mass arrest of monks and students* [italics mine].

"Washington officials say that Vietnam secret police carried out the raids and arrests and that some of them were disguised as army troops or members of the Youth Corps.

"They say the military leaders agreed to martial law in the hope that it would lead to a peaceful settlement. But, they say, *the military men were not advised of secret police plans to attack Buddhists* [italics mine].

"The officials indicate that the U.S. may sharply reduce its aid to Vietnam unless President Diem *gets rid of secret police officials responsible for the attacks* [italics mine]."

The broadcast created a Donnybrook of sorts in Washington. Angry questions were raised in Congress and by some reporters about the wisdom of issuing such an inflammatory invitation to revolt in a period when the new American ambassador had not even yet had a chance to call on the President of the Vietnamese Republic.

The State Department made a halfhearted attempt to blame the timing of the broadcast on the United States Information Agency, but its director, Edward R. Murrow, refused to be the fall guy. He instructed his public-information officer, Lowell Bennett, to tell reporters the truth. And this truth was that the Voice of America broadcast had been specifically cleared with Assistant Secretary of State Hilsman, who had in fact initiated it. Hilsman had called in Stewart

Hensley, the able diplomatic reporter for United Press International, on Sunday afternoon to brief him on policy developments. Hilsman then called the Voice of America and told officials there that Hensley's dispatch on Vietnam would be an accurate reflection of American policy. The Voice, of course, took the hint.

Says a State Department career officer: "On that weekend Hilsman was a man in a hurry—and perhaps out of the most idealistic reasons. He thought that if he could publicize the threat to cut aid the generals would be bound to act quickly against Diem. The revolt would be quick, clean, and neat. Diem and Nhu would be out. Failing that, the heat would be so intense that Diem would at least get rid of Nhu. And with him gone the United States could tell the world that it had eliminated the villain of the piece. Our image would be repaired, or so some imagined, and we would get on with the war."

It is true, of course, that stripped to its essentials, the broadcast could mean only one thing: "Get rid of Nhu or else." And since it was ninety-nine to one that Diem would never bow to such an edict, the emphasis was on the "or else."

Diem's shock at the Voice of America broadcast and the C.I.A. poll of the Vietnamese generals can be imagined only by turning the tables around. Suppose the United States were engaged in a war against the Communists in which we depended almost totally on aid from Vietnam. Suppose, in the middle of that war, that Vietnam issued a broadcast calling for the American Joint Chiefs of Staff to overthrow the American government.

In Saigon at a meeting on Sunday, August 25, at the embassy, Ambassador Lodge very sensibly decided that before "unleashing the Vietnamese generals" it might be prudent to inquire if the generals were really ready to be "unleashed."

Key Americans at the embassy were assigned to take soundings of the most openly revolt-minded generals. These included Lieutenant General Duong Van (Big) Minh, who had the title of chief military adviser to the President but who had actually little power, and Lieutenant General Tran Van Don, the acting commander in chief of the army and Brigadier General Le Van Kim. It took all of Monday and

Tuesday (August 26 and 27) to complete this "poll" of the Vietnamese generals. A total of seven generals were asked whether or not they were ready to revolt.

Meanwhile, back in Washington, an internal combustion flared Monday morning when the top officials at the Pentagon and C.I.A. realized the full import of the weekend cable. When General Taylor, for example, learned about the "fire-Nhu-or-else" ultimatum, he staged a scene that was, according to an aide, "blood-curdling to behold." Secretary of Defense McNamara shared the general's fury, as did C.I.A. Director McCone when he finally found out about it from an aide who flew to the West Coast with the controversial cable in his hands. Vice-President Johnson was equally appalled. All at one point or another argued at the White House for a repeal of what amounted to a decision to invite the political destruction of an ally if he did not submit to American dictates.

For a brief time it appeared that fate was siding with those arguing against the risk of setting the Vietnamese military at the throat of the Diem regime in midwar.

For, as it turned out, the American poll of seven Vietnamese generals taken in Saigon produced some very disconcerting reactions. The Vietnamese generals seemingly had talked a better revolutionary game than they were prepared to play. When told that the United States would withdraw its objections to a coup against Diem the generals didn't grab at the opportunity to revolt, as anticipated, but drew back. It was too dangerous, they told the Americans. Not only was it perfectly plain to Diem and Nhu what was going on, the generals said, but there were some military still loyal to the regime. Certainly the matter of staging a *coup d'état* in the immediate future was impossible. Maybe later, said the reluctant generals, but not now.

General Minh reportedly summed up the attitude of the generals to one U.S. official: "After all those years of being told not to rock the boat in the middle of a war, it was hard for us to really convince ourselves that this was precisely what the United States now wanted us to do."

The United States knew, of course, that there were various other plots and subplots being cooked up around Saigon. Remarked a cynical U.S. official: "An intelligent Vietnamese military man without a plot is as unthinkable as a prosperous Frenchman without a mistress." And he was exaggerating only slightly. But the point was that the successors to Diem had to have the outward air of respectability and dignity. Only senior generals could offer that.

The reluctance of the Vietnamese generals to be unleashed put a new face on the whole issue. The cable describing this reluctance reached Washington in time for consideration at a full dress meeting of the National Security Council held Wednesday, August 28.

That National Security Council meeting was a Babel of cross purposes and mutual suspicion.

Says a sensitive observer of the scene at the time: "For Harriman and Hilsman, the Lodge cable was a body blow. They lost face. They had gambled on a quick surgical *coup d'état*; they had hastily unleashed the generals only to be shown up as premature. On the other hand, for General Taylor and others opposed to a coup, the cable was a reprieve from disaster. They hoped to use it as a means of turning the policy around."

Everybody at that National Security Council meeting agreed that the Lodge cable indicated that there was no possibility of a quick *coup d'état*.

All the rest is confusion, because in the effort to compromise the violently opposing views the decisions were couched in such a way that they could be subject to widely differing interpretations.

For instance, the National Security Council meeting decided that Ambassador Lodge in Saigon should be told in effect that the policy of unleashing the generals was being reviewed. In the meantime, he was to shift emphasis to a policy predicated on the assumption that Diem was in power to stay. His priority was to unleash pressure (rather than generals) to compel the Diem regime to reform (i.e. fire Nhu and release his Buddhist and other political opponents). Yet at the same time Lodge was told that the United States would not stand in the way of an "indigenous revolt."

But what was an "indigenous revolt"? A revolt by generals could well be "indigenous" if Lodge judged that they commanded a large enough following.

According to McGeorge Bundy, White House assistant for national security affairs, President Kennedy went along with this policy of pressures against Diem because he was persuaded that the "Vietnamese ship of state could not weather the storm without changing course."

Whatever the intentions in Washington, the pressures applied by the United States did in point of fact turn the storm into a political hurricane that no Vietnamese could long have weathered. The depths of U.S. involvement, or put another way, the depth of Vietnam's dependence on the United States now, as then, is such that no Vietnamese leader could long survive an American government willing to wage intensive political and economic war against it. The pressures, which were of course both psychological and economic, led inexorably to Diem's undoing, and those who had any contrary idea simply understood little about Asia or Asians and the volatile situation in Vietnam.

President Kennedy contributed mightily to the political warfare against Diem in a statement of early September (made during a television interview) in which he called for "changes of policy and personnel." The key points of this statement were based on a briefing paper prepared for him by Assistant Secretary of State Hilsman.

President Kennedy claimed among other things that Ngo Dinh Diem had "gotten out of touch with the people."

"The repressions against the Buddhists, we felt, were very unwise," the President said. "Now all we can do is to make it very clear that we don't think this is the way to win."

The statement was a bombshell on both sides of the Pacific.

As the *New York Times's* James Reston observed: "Now if Diem changes his policies and his government, it will be said that he did so under public pressure from the U.S.; and if he doesn't change, the President will be charged with backing what he himself has called a losing policy."

The statement raised serious questions about the quality of some briefings received by President Kennedy in this period.

Did he realize that the only "Buddhists" being repressed comprised no more than several dozen political agitators who had openly boasted they were going for Diem's jugular? Why did he talk of a "repression of Buddhism," which certainly implied discrimination for religious reasons, when only politico priests openly boasting of toppling the Vietnamese government were kept under detention? Why did President Kennedy imply that the war might be lost as the result of what was happening to a few thousand persons in the cities when Secretary McNamara and others were insisting that in compartmentalized Vietnam the countryside did not know or care what was going on in the metropolis and that the war was holding its own in spite of the Buddhists? What "people" was Diem out of touch with—the Buddhist extremists? Students? Citified intellectuals? But Diem had never had their support. Neither would the support of these intrigue-prone groups be available to any of the eight future regimes that were to struggle unsuccessfully to stay in power in the next two years. For it is axiomatic that any regime in Vietnam, military or civilian, rules *in spite* of the cosmopolites of the bars and coffeehouses, who are congenital plotters, intriguers, and "aginners." They are, most especially, against government—any government.

It seems probable that these vital characteristics of Vietnamese urban and rural society had not been clearly brought home to the President at the time of the telecast. Had he realized the political and subversive nature of the Buddhist extremist minority, he surely would have stated the case differently and conceded that any government at war has a right after all to protect itself against subversion.

Kennedy's call for "changes of policy and personnel" was a landmark in modern American history in the treatment of a wartime ally. Seldom has there been such a blunt public intervention of one government in the internal affairs of another supposedly friendly power. Intervention to prevent the takeover of a hostile pro-Communist government (Guatemala) is an entirely different subject. In Vietnam we were dealing with an anti-Communist government joined in a common cause—the fight against the Viet Cong.

There are no exact comparisons, of course, but supposing General de Gaulle were to call for a "change of policy and personnel" in the American government as a price for cooperation in NATO? It would cause a furore, would it not?

The atmosphere in Vietnam was later described this way by one of Diem's top aides, presently in exile in Paris: "It seemed like the whole world had turned against us. Not only the American press, but now the official organ of the American government, the Voice of America, kept pouring in ugly accusations that made us out to be evil and in the wrong. It was a little as if the BBC had suddenly begun in World War II to denounce the United States and call for Roosevelt's overthrow. The miracle was that so many of Diem's cabinet stuck by him for so long. The massive disapproval of America was a deep psychological shock. You could not help but be affected even if you felt that the accusations were utterly wrong. I knew that Diem had had no alternative but to act against the Buddhist extremists because they were going after his political head. Yet I myself was tempted to try to resign and be applauded by the Americans like Vu Van Mau [the foreign minister] when he shaved his head and resigned. . . . It had been charged that the Diem regime became rattled. . . . Of course the regime became rattled. . . . Never the President himself but Nhu and other officials. . . . How could they help it? . . . It is difficult enough to fight against the Viet Cong. . . . But when the most powerful democratic country and your supposed ally leads the chorus of denunciations of your country, the situation becomes impossible. . . . I am amazed that Diem lasted as long as he did."

Ambassador Lodge also contributed to the atmosphere by his conspicuous air of aloofness to the Diem regime. The assignment to Vietnam was not one that most men would have welcomed, and Lodge must be complimented for his courage in taking it on—not just once but twice. In 1963 he had told President Kennedy that he wanted a tough and challenging assignment and his wish was more than granted. Nobody could have fully foreseen the turmoil, tension, and tragedy that were to plague his first mission to Saigon.

His task in Vietnam was infinitely more complex and demanding than his previous position as ambassador to the United Nations (in the Eisenhower administration). The reason was starkly simple. At the United Nations it was perfectly plain who were the good guys (the Free world) and the bad guys (the Communist world). In Vietnam the whole problem was to decide who the good guys and bad guys were in the Saigon jungle. The criterion should have been of course this question: Who among the Vietnamese best serve the cause of fighting the Communists and in the process the national interests of the United States? In those days Lodge acted as though Thich Tri Quang and his brand of Buddhists were the good guys, Diemists the bad guys.

Some of Lodge's Republican colleagues in Kennedy's cabinet were surprised at the fact of his apparently instant hostility to the Diem regime. For one thing, Lodge had had no experience in Asia since World War II. His basis for judgments thus was necessarily narrow.

One highly placed Republican in the administration, for example, commented at the time. "I had thought that Lodge would at least take a couple of weeks and look around a little before he made up his mind. But he took up the cudgels against Diem from the moment he arrived. From the first day, his telegrams were all on the side of radical surgery. There are some of us who were disquieted by Lodge's gung-ho approach in this matter. Lodge was an important obstacle to those of us who were trying to put a brake on the moves to topple Diem."

It is reportedly Robert Kennedy's view that Lodge's performance as ambassador during those crucial months prior to the *coup d'état* was terrible. It is said that his complaint is based on the ambassador's free-wheeling ways and the evidence that in his zeal he sometimes exceeded or ignored his instructions. Kennedy's opinion is shared at some high levels at the Department of State. According to one senior official, there were several occasions prior to the November 1 *coup d'état* when Lodge was instructed to keep in close communication with President Diem. But Lodge replied in effect, "My policy is not to go to Diem but to let Diem come to me."

The resultant breakdown in American-Vietnamese communications, some argue, allowed the coup situation to get out of hand before the policy of "reforming" Diem had had a fair trial.

It is a contention that will be controversial for decades.

President Johnson, who opposed the *coup d'état,* nonetheless does not agree with Senator Kennedy's judgment that Lodge's performance as ambassador "was terrible." It is President Johnson's view that

Lodge was merely executing Washington policy, for which no ambassador can be held responsible. What was "terrible" in President Johnson's eyes was the Kennedy administration policy that brought such terrible pressures to bear on Diem that they finally snapped the twig and provoked the *coup d'état*.

In 1963, Lodge's critics in the Kennedy administration were remarkably silent and for obvious reasons. He was a walking political land mine for the Democratic administration. He was given the assignment to Vietnam partly because of Kennedy's hope that his very presence there would deflect Republican criticism should the war become prolonged. By the same token, the Kennedy administration could not risk antagonizing Lodge and have him turn against U.S. policies. Therefore Lodge was not subject to the ordinary disciplines of a foreign-service officer. And the things he said and did had far more impact inside the United States government than those of any other ambassador could hope to have. His priority was always the highest.

After Kennedy's assassination on November 22 President Johnson also showed himself highly sensitive to the potent political force that Lodge represented. President Johnson ordered every single cable from the ambassador to be sent to him at the White House. Presidential priority was given to making sure that every reasonable request from Lodge was promptly fulfilled.

As a White House aide put it: "We were going to make dead sure that Lodge could never quit Vietnam and come home and turn on us with the accusation that the White House had failed to back him up."

To his immense credit, Lodge never once tried to play politics with Vietnam. He has never wavered in his adherence to the proposition that South Vietnam can and must be saved from the Communists.

This was noted with appreciation by President Johnson. After Lodge's return to the United States in July, 1964, to do battle against Goldwater, President Johnson named him a special counselor on Vietnam and then reappointed him as ambassador to Saigon to succeed Ambassador Maxwell Taylor in August, 1965. There remains a certain mystery about the Taylor resignation, for it is out of character. He was a soldier who had written a book about the dangers of sounding "an Uncertain Trumpet." Then he himself sounded an Uncertain Trumpet, for any change of ambassadors at a crucial time in the war in Vietnam is unsettling, as Taylor with his wide experience certainly realized. His resignation right in the midst of the Viet Cong monsoon offensive of 1965 startled such old friends as General Earle Wheeler, chairman of the Joint Chiefs of Staff, who only days before the announced resignation had been proclaiming his confidence that Taylor would see the worst of the crisis—the monsoon offensive—through.

Lodge's reassignment to Vietnam was controversial in the Democratic party. Senator Thomas Dodd, Democrat of Connecticut, a member of the Senate Foreign Relations Committee, sent the President a long memorandum warning that Lodge's earlier involvement with Thich Tri Quang would be certain to cause dismay among the anti-Communists in Vietnam—not just to the Catholics but to the Hoa Hao and Cao Dai, which are numerically important in the Delta. He cited the demoralizing effect inside the U.S. embassy of Lodge's 1963 feuds with General Paul Harkins and others. But the President felt that Lodge's Republicanism and his strong stand against the surrender psychology of some Americans were the overriding considerations.

On this first tour in Saigon Lodge scored one notable success that should not pass unmentioned. He did something that Ambassador Nolting had failed spectacularly to do. He got the resident American press in Saigon on his side. For once the ambassador and the resident press seemed to have had the same anti-Diem foreign policy. Also he made a special point of cultivating the correspondents and listening to their ideas.

There are some knowledgeable Americans who believe that Lodge had been given instructions for "radical surgery" against the Diem regime before leaving Washington.

The principal instrument of this policy proved to be the cutback in economic aid that was initiated in late August but which became public knowledge only in early October.

The aid cutback involved counterpart funds used to pay the salaries of the Vietnamese army. And although the United States argued correctly that the reductions would not immediately hamper the war effort, the action was a psychological time bomb.

At least six of the generals who masterminded the revolt, including General Duong Van (Big) Minh, the leader of the first junta, told me and others that the reduction in U.S. assistance was the decisive event that persuaded them to proceed with plans to overthrow the Diem regime.

"The aid cuts," said General Minh, "erased all our doubts."

According to Major General Tran Thien Khiem, the army chief of staff, "we looked on this U.S. decision on aid as a signal from Washington that the Vietnamese military had to choose between the Americans and Diem. . . . And with a war on, there could be only one choice. . . . After all, the very bullets for our guns depended, so to speak, on the United States. . . . And if the United States was so angry with Diem that it would cut off aid, it was even possible that the United States would pull out of the war. . . . And that would have been the end of everything. . . ."

General Tran Thien Khiem, who later was named Vietnam's ambassador to Washington, adds: "The revolt was staged to please the United States. We thought that was what the Kennedy administration wanted. We thought it was the only way to save the war effort. We thought that was what the Americans were telling us in taking action that affected aid to the military!"

Ironically, at this point, well-meaning efforts of Diem's good friends ended up hurting him. For example, General Paul Harkins, head of the U.S. military mission, was aware that a main argument of the Diem-must-go school in Washington was that unrest in the cities (affecting less than one percent of the population) was bound to impair the war effort in the countryside. To General Harkins' despair, it seemed impossible to convey to the sophisticates of Washington the utter disconnection—as well as alienation—of the city from the countryside and the fact that progress could be made in Quang Ngai province and elsewhere despite demonstrations in Saigon and Hué. In the fall of 1963 a token of how little the countryside was affected by events in the city was the fact that despite the rugged political warfare waged by the powerful United States against the Vietnam regime, the government troops held their own in the field. Government-initiated offensives slowed down in September and October because some officers in the field were looking over their shoulder toward Saigon trying to figure out which way personally to jump. But the distractions were insufficient to cause an overt breakdown in discipline. Diem, in other words, still had the situation under control. So the Viet Cong found few openings to exploit. The curve of Viet Cong attacks in September and October, 1963, rose only slightly.

To emphasize the progress the war was making, General Harkins insisted that Secretary McNamara, after a September inspection trip to Vietnam, include in the communiqué an announcement that many Americans involved in training could be sent home by 1965. General Harkins hoped that the result of this statement would be to demonstrate irrevocably that the counterinsurgency campaign was progressing. And if the prospects had brightened, then, Harkins hoped, President Kennedy would see the danger of upsetting the regime that was presiding over this progress.

Whatever the impact on President Kennedy—and it appears to have been negligible—the prospect of a U.S. withdrawal of any kind in 1965 had the effect inside Vietnam opposite to that intended by Harkins. It only deepened the sense of alarm among the Vietnamese military, and a near-panic reaction began to take hold.

"We took it as a sign that unless we got rid of Diem, the United States would wash its hands of the war no later than 1965," says General Khiem.

What is to be made of statements by Ambassador Lodge and others disavowing any American "involvement" in the November 1 *coup d'état*? On June 30, 1964, Ambassador Lodge said in a widely quoted newspaper interview: "The overthrow—of the Diem regime—was a purely Vietnamese affair. We never participated in the planning. We had nothing whatever to do with it. I—*there were opportunities to participate in planning and give advice, and we never did* [italics mine]. We were punctilious in drawing that line."

The generals obviously consulted him about their coup in advance and thus provided the opportunity to "give advice." According to the generals, the Vietnamese military had been given to understand in advance of the *coup d'état* that a military junta would be recognized by the United States and economic aid restored once the "reforms" demanded of Diem (like letting Buddhist rebels out of jail) were accomplished.

The best that can be said for claims of noninvolvement is that in a technical and physical sense they are correct. No American soldier shot at President Diem. No American general drew up the plans for the assault on the palace.

The "punctilious line" reflected a terrible gamble. Here was the United States intervening deeply enough to signal the destruction of a friendly government but unwilling to plunge in far enough to make sure that the succeeding government would be an improvement by demanding exact accounts and commitments in advance about what it would do. Here was a classic case of falling between two stools.

If Diem was running the war badly, then surely the wise course would have been to insist before signaling his destruction that the generals would instantly correct his mistakes. If the United States had exacted such conditions in advance, it is barely possible, for example, that the military junta would not have dawdled so disastrously on the strategic-hamlet program which the United States wanted to see vigorously implemented. If the United States had probed more responsibly into the plans and personalities of the generals, it might even have found out before (instead of after) the coup just how vacuous mentally and puny morally were the men into whose weak hands the destiny of Vietnam was being thrust.

The fall of 1963 was no time for pressing buzzers and opening doors without knowing who and what was going to come in. It was certainly too late to "keep our hands clean." Everybody in Vietnam—and most especially President Diem and Counselor Nhu—understood that the United States was waging economic and political war and summoning the generals to revolt.

It is certain that the revolt against Diem could never have taken place without specific and sustained signals of American support. Policy was crudely and cruelly reversed; the halters placed on would-be plotters were removed with a jarring finality. Subsequent controversy aside, several key Americans on the receiving end of the fateful August 24 cable have lately stated that they never once construed it to be anything short of a command decision that Diem must go.

C.I.A. Director McCone, in the presence of other high officials, put the question point-blank to Ambassador Lodge in Saigon in September, 1963, as the group sat outside on the ambassador's terrace. All present agree that Lodge replied without hesitation that the cable was interpreted by himself, and every single member of his team, as representing a command decision in Washington; it was deemed, purely and simply, as an order to unleash the generals—if they could—and get on with the business of promoting sweeping "changes of policy and personnel."

In its private signals to the Vietnamese generals and in its public declarations and acts of political and economic warfare, the United States effectively opened the floodgates to revolt.

Would there have been any way to turn back the flood?

Robert Kennedy says that his brother had second thoughts about the August 24 cable and hoped to the last that Lodge might find a modus vivendi with Diem. If so, President Kennedy was ill-advised to make his public demand for "changes in policy and personnel" and to institute aid cuts.

It is possible that President Kennedy might have diverted the momentum of revolt if sometime before November 1 he had made a strong declaration of confidence in Diem, emphasizing that it superseded his televised declaration of no confidence in September. Also, economic aid would have had to be fully restored. Neither of these things was President Kennedy willing to do.

Was American fury over the pagoda raids justified? Would it really have been wise for any government in Vietnam to have allowed the Buddhist extremists and the agitators who gathered under the umbrella of their revolt to remain indefinitely at large and unchecked?

Supposing the Buddhist extremists had made good their threats to stage "thirty, forty, or fifty" suicides by fire? What would this have done to the image of both Vietnam and the United States? Public demonstrations have a way of gathering momentum, and the Buddhist extremists were experts at crowd management.

The longer the government restrained itself, the more violent became the anti-Diem tirades at the pagodas. The demonstrations attracted not just Viet Cong but all sorts of well-meaning, excitement-seeking youngsters of Catholic and other faiths, as well as hoodlums and professional agitators. It was all very exciting—and potentially dangerous. In time of war the government that loses control of the streets of its capital city tempts anarchy, as later events were to show. The post-Diem regimes learned the grisly price of permissiveness in the streets as they dealt faintheartedly with the demonstrators and rioters.

Diem ruled with a strong authoritarian hand. But never under his regime did Buddhists and Catholics hack each other to death in the streets of Saigon while the police looked the other way in compliance with their instructions. At least nine youngsters died horrible deaths in the streets of Saigon in the summer of 1964 when the then premier, Nguyen Khanh, was in one of his *laissez faire* moods designed to show that he was a liberal and unlike Diem.

In no country can a leader allow himself to be cowed by the mob. His authority is eroded, and respect withers away. In the streets of Saigon the extremist Buddhists fattened on their successes in deposing governments, and they found their ability to stage demonstration after demonstration—and get away almost scot-free—very heady stuff indeed, long after Diem and Nhu were dead. It was so heady, in fact, that at least two successive governments of Vietnam (General Khanh's and Premier Tran Van Huong's) were toppled and countless fine patriotic persons exiled as a result of the extremists' riotous defiance of any government that did not truckle to their demands.

But quite apart from the rights and wrongs and ultimate wisdom of it all, was it possible to expect Diem—as the August 24 cable demanded—to let loose once again the Buddhist extremist forces dedicated to his subversion? Further, could Diem be asked to separate himself from a brother who was not only the head of the crucial strategic-hamlet program but was the effective head of secret police, and thus the buffer between the palace and the endemic intrigues that have always plagued Vietnam and always will until its primitive tribes and squabbling intellectuals attain some sense of nationhood? If

Diem defied the Americans, he risked his doom. But if he had fired Nhu, his day of reckoning would have been no less inevitable. Nhu was the strongman who shielded Diem from the plotters. That was one reason the plotting generals schemed to get the United States to get rid of Nhu for them. It seems to me that what some Americans were asking of Diem in the summer of 1963 was that he sit quietly, his hands tied behind his back, while his enemies continued unchecked their campaign against him. As he viewed the demands made of him and their inexorable consequences, Diem was being asked to do nothing less than preside over his own downfall.

CHAPTER 11

Coups and Consequences, Human

Three and a half hours after the revolt began, President Ngo Dinh Diem put through a telephone call to Ambassador Lodge. It was four-thirty P.M., Friday, November 1, 1963, and Diem, referring obliquely to the fury of gunfire ripping the Presidential Palace, asked the ambassador: "What is Washington's attitude to all this?"

". . . I cannot say," said Ambassador Lodge. "After all, it is four-thirty A.M. in the morning in Washington."

"But," replied Diem, a mixture of irony and coldness in his voice, "you must have some idea of what the policy is?"

"I know that I am concerned for your safety," said Lodge. "I'd like to get you safely out of the country. . . ."

Was there any starker way for Diem to learn that the United States had washed its hands of him as the leader of Vietnam?

Lodge posed one final question: "What will you do?"

Diem's response was typical of the man. "I shall do," he said, "what duty and good sense dictate. I shall attempt to restore order."

And with those words the Vietnamese President sealed his doom.

When Ambassador Lodge told me of this exchange—his last—with Diem in a conversation in his Saigon office several weeks after the coup, it was clear to me that he had sincerely hoped that Diem's murder could be avoided. It had also been President Kennedy's hope.

Perhaps it was too much to ask that such infinitely civilized Occidentals as Lodge and Kennedy, with their Boston-bred concepts of the gentlemanly response in good times and bad, could have understood the savage laws of the Vietnamese political jungle. Under the circumstances prevailing in Vietnam it would have been a great political risk for the generals to permit Diem or Nhu to live. The two brothers were men of stature and power, feared and respected men who would haunt their foes forever with the threat of a counter-coup.

In a conversation with an American months after the *coup d'état,* General Big Minh, one-time head of the military junta, who, in his turn, was exiled, stated frankly: "We had no alternative. They had to be killed."

"Diem could not be allowed to live," General Minh said, "because he was too much respected among simple, gullible people in the countryside, especially the Catholics and the refugees. We had to kill Nhu because he was so widely feared—and he had created organizations that were arms of his personal power." General Minh was referring to, among other things, the Can Lao Workers party and the Republican Youth, both controlled by Nhu.

Prime Minister Tran Van Huong (in office October, 1964–January, 1965) had another view. In a discussion with a British diplomat, Prime Minister Huong said: "The top generals who decided to murder President Diem and his brother were scared to death. The generals knew very well that having no talent, nor moral virtues, and no popular support whatsoever, they could not prevent a spectacular comeback of the President and Mr. Nhu if they were alive."

It is an interesting comment coming from a man who passed a number of months in prison because of political opposition to Diem.

The overthrow and murder of the brothers Ngo resulted from two successive betrayals. The first was the defection to the plotting generals of Major General Ton That Dinh, commander of the third corps, which embraces Saigon. General Big Minh played on the enormous ego of this flamboyant young general with great skill. First General Minh persuaded General Dinh that he should go to Diem and

Nhu and, in light of his "great service" to the family (he had been military governor of Saigon during the pagoda raids), demand the post of Minister of Defense. When he did so and was refused, as Minh foresaw he would be, General Dinh was by turns furious, humiliated, vengeful. He joined the plotters without further ado.

When the shooting at the Presidential Palace erupted at one o'clock, Diem had barely said farewell to Ambassador Lodge and Admiral Harry Felt, commander in chief, Pacific, who had paid a call in late morning. There is special point in recalling that meeting. For at the end of it Diem drew the ambassador aside and said, in effect, "Perhaps we have been too inflexible. Perhaps we have made a mistake. We want you to know we are ready to try and accommodate you."

But Lodge, who must have known that a coup was imminent, did not take Diem's words seriously enough to advise the generals to call off their revolution. A word from him—a strong, tough word—might have saved Diem even at that late hour.

There has always been a special poignancy to me in the fact that Ngo Dinh Diem sought refuge in the moment of greatest need not with one of his own countrymen but with a Chinese.

At eight P.M. Friday night President Diem and Nhu drove in a small Citroën to the home of Ma Tuyen, the Chinese-born trader and chief of a youth movement in the Cholon suburb of Saigon. Previously a call had been put through from the palace asking Ma Tuyen to stage a huge youth rally, a desperate last resort of the resourceful Nhu. He had hoped that such a rally in support of President Diem would buy time, divert the plotters, perhaps even discourage them. But the die had been cast—and the hour was very late.

It took great courage for Diem's Chinese friend to give refuge to the President and his brother during the night. He suffered for his loyalty. When the rule of law came to near collapse under Big Minh's rudderless junta, Ma Tuyen, although he had done nothing illegal, was jailed for some time.

An observer of the scene, a Chinese recalls: "In some ways Diem was much closer to the educated Chinese than to the educated Vietnamese, who, being so deeply influenced by the French, were more

Occidental in some of their reactions than Oriental. Some Vietnamese felt a sense of inferiority because they were Oriental. Men like President Diem and Ma Tuyen were proud of being Oriental. They represented all that was best of the Confucian tradition, including a sense of ceremonials and a total command of self. . . . Diem was a man who had long ago made his peace with death. . . . He did not expect to die. . . . He believed that the generals would make good on their offer of safe conduct for himself and Nhu out of the country. . . . He thought the Americans would at least grant him that much. . . . But Diem was prepared for death. . . . The tragedy is that he had to be killed with his hands behind his back."

After a night of fruitless telephone calls the Ngo brothers became resigned to their fate. They decided to go to eight o'clock mass at the Catholic church next door, to Ma Tuyen's home, and then call military headquarters to surrender.

At this point in time the rebelling generals were in a quandary. The palace had fallen. But where were Diem and Nhu?

The previous afternoon the rebel generals had telephoned the palace several times to try to persuade President Diem and Counselor Nhu to surrender. It was during these conversations with the embattled President that the Vietnamese military offered him—on surrender—safe conduct out of the country to a place of exile of his own choosing.

But the moment of surrender did not come until eight-thirty A.M. the next morning. At that time a telephone call came into general staff headquarters and the voice at the other end asked for Major General Tran Thien Khiem, the army chief of staff. It was Diem, sounding very cool, composed, and businesslike. The President said that he and his brother were ready to turn themselves over to the army and disclosed their whereabouts in the Saigon suburb of Cholon. The President asked specifically that Khiem himself come to escort them to headquarters.

"But General Minh would not let me go," explained Khiem later.

After Diem's call solved the mystery of his whereabouts, General Minh called a meeting of a rather conspiratorial nature, excluding Khiem and other high-ranking officers. Only a few close cronies of

Minh were invited to this confab. These reportedly included Army Commander Tran Van Don and Nguyen Ngoc Tho, the Vietnamese Vice-President. After the meeting General Minh ordered Major General Mai Huu Xuan to organize a convoy to go and fetch the Ngo brothers.

Apparently General Xuan suffered from a superstitious reluctance to handle the task and insisted that another officer join him. He was Colonel Duong Ngoc Lam, head of the Civil Guard, and it is from him that I learned the essentials of what happened to Diem and Nhu. Colonel Lam, like so many of the November 1 plotters, is in exile in France.

According to Colonel Lam: "The President and his brother were standing on the church steps when our convoy rolled up. There were some parishioners around but there was no commotion. Still, the presence of the convoy was bound to attract attention. So I wanted to get started quickly. President Diem, who had the impression he was going to be sent forthwith out of the country, asked if he could go by the palace and pick up some of his personal effects. General Xuan and I had to tell him that our orders were to take him at once to military headquarters."

According to Colonel Lam, as the convoy was turning around, several of the younger Vietnamese officers approached him and "asked me for permission to shoot Nhu."

"I told them," recounts Lam, "that nobody was going to shoot anybody. That we were going to take President Diem and Counselor Nhu back to headquarters as ordered."

Colonel Lam personally escorted the two brothers to an armored personnel carrier. He left them alone. As they climbed into the back of the vehicle *no Vietnamese officer* was with them and the only other Vietnamese in the vehicle was the driver.

Colonel Lam and General Xuan rode at the tail end of the convoy in a car that was four vehicles behind the armored personnel carrier. The convoy had to stop a few times, once at a train crossing.

When the convoy reached the junta headquarters, Colonel Lam started toward the armored personnel carrier. Others had gotten there before him. Both bodies were already stretched out on the ground.

Both were in civilian clothes. Diem had been shot in the back of the head, Nhu had been stabbed in the chest and shot numerous times in the back of the head and in the back. The hands of both victims were tied behind their backs. This was the second betrayal—the betrayal of the promise of safe conduct. To this day, Colonel Lam does not know precisely how or when the Ngo brothers were murdered. On the tense morning of November 2 it would have been dangerous to press the matter.

Later General Minh said that his aide, Captain Nguyen Van Nhung, had gotten into the personnel carrier and had been provoked into an argument by Nhu and shot the two leaders.

Nobody believed him. Junior officers in Vietnam do not take upon themselves such responsibilities. People killed in the heat of argument are rarely shot in the back. I have talked to eight members of the original military junta. They all state categorically that Captain Nhung was not the sort of officer who would ever have acted without his superior's specific order. And Captain Nhung's superior was General Minh.

The first story broadcast by the junta was that Diem and Nhu had been "accidental suicides." This transparent lie made the junta contemptible in the eyes of those who suspected the truth—and that was practically everybody in the higher echelons of the bureaucracy.

Many officers involved in the *coup d'état* were deeply resentful of the murders.

"It was days before I got over the shock," said Colonel Lam, "and many officers resented being made, in effect, criminals by association." So an important point of friction plagued the junta from the moment it was born.

Major General Nguyen Khanh, then a relatively obscure officer at second-corps headquarters at Pleiku, was so incensed that he vowed the crime would be exposed. When Khanh, in his turn, overthrew Minh's junta, on January 30, 1964, he was advised by the Americans to keep Minh on as a figurehead chief of state. But the enmity between the two men, in part stemming from the murder of the Ngo brothers, made it impossible for both to stay in the same government.

The murders preyed on the mind of the young assassin, Captain

Nhung. He committed suicide at the time of Khanh's *coup d'état,* evidently fearing that the new leaders were bent on vengeance against him. He reportedly left a suicide note expressing regret for the murders.

In Washington the murder of Diem and Nhu brought not a single public expression of regret on the part of the U.S. government. In Saigon the embassy's silence on this score was equally conspicuous.

To superstitious Vietnamese—and superstitious most of them are —it is not insignificant that virtually every single one of the key anti-Diem plotters has come to harm or fallen into political ignominy. General Minh is in exile in Bangkok, General Khiem is in exile in Washington, and Generals Don, Xuan, and Kim have been forced out of the army. The flamboyant General Dinh is under police surveillance in Vietnam.

The superstition-minded even found an eerie echo on the American side. President Kennedy's death before the month was out was wholly unrelated, of course, to Diem's downfall. But the distraught Madame Nhu, in bitterness and wrath, was moved shockingly to liken her feelings to those of the slain President's family. Kennedy was deeply and emotionally admired by the Vietnamese intellectuals. But in their parochial way, many instinctively related the two tragedies. Said a Catholic professor at Hué—an enemy of the Diem regime: "My first reaction was one of almost primitive terror. I felt as if God was taking revenge on us." It was also noted by the superstitious that within months after the *coup d'état* Assistant Secretary of State Roger Hilsman was out of government and Undersecretary of State Averell Harriman removed from a position of any responsibility for Vietnam. He was named "roving ambassador." Thus, less than a year after the end of the Diem regime two of the Americans most eager for its overthrow no longer had any real power over the course of events in Vietnam.

On November 2 in Saigon the bodies of the Ngo brothers were delivered to a niece and a nephew. They were Mr. and Mrs. Tran Trung Dung, and the unwanted responsibilities given them were enveloped in a certain irony. For Tran Trung Dung, a former Defense Minister under Diem, had had a falling out with President Diem many years before. It was so serious that Counselor Nhu had even refused Mr. Dung a passport for a business trip to Hong Kong. Madame Dung had additionally had a battle with Madame Nhu because she refused to assist with the Paramilitary Women project. So strong was the sense of family duty, however, that since there was no one else to do it, the couple carried out the difficult task of giving the two fallen leaders a decent burial.

Mr. and Mrs. Dung's description of the wounds received by Diem and Nhu confirm the story told by Colonel Lam that the two leaders had been shot in the back.

Tran Trung Dung and his wife, plus a priest, were the only ones present when the bodies of the Ngo brothers were secretly buried in a corner of the large parklike grounds that surround Vietnamese military headquarters.

There is considerable controversy over the reaction in Saigon to the *coup d'état.* The resident American press corps carried stories of an "explosion of joy" in the streets. It is certain, of course, that no Vietnamese would have been inclined to *complain* to an American about the *coup d'état,* which was universally assumed by the washed and unwashed of Saigon to have been plotted in Washington.

The European press was more cautious. Suzanne Labin, a French photographer-writer who was in Sagion at the time, writes in her book *Vietnam, an Eyewitness Account* the following:

"I spent a great deal of time wandering through the streets of Saigon, taking numerous photographs. Not more than a few thousand people came out to celebrate spontaneously the fall of the Ngos. . . . Any specialist can see that the pictures produced to illustrate the alleged popular explosion reveal in reality very shallow crowds—no true masses such as, for example, erupted in Brazil following the overthrow of Goulart."

Madame Labin is one of the few to have reported the existence, among the demonstrators, of organized bands.

"Fifteen minutes after the last shot, at seven A.M.," she writes, "I observed disciplined groups marching in order. . . . They attacked even some buildings *that had absolutely no connection with Diem, such as the building in which the Asian People's Anti-Communist*

League held its congress [italics mine]. Then, an hour later, some of the groups which perpetrated these raids started shouting Communist slogans: 'Down with the strategic hamlets! Stop the war!' These same bands arrested and killed a number of anti-Communists. This went so far that, on the fourth day after the coup, General Dinh issued an order instructing anyone threatened with arrest to telephone at once to a designated number published in all newspapers, or to shout and call on his neighbors for help."

In America the reverberations to the *coup d'état* centered around Madame Nhu. By November 1 she had reached Los Angeles, in the last of a series of public appearances designed to regain U.S. support for the Diem regime.

If anything, President Kennedy's attitude was probably hardened by Madame Nhu's crusade. This had taken the form of a round-the-world trip beginning in Europe in October, 1963. It got off to a joltingly bad start. For example, in Rome she described Americans in Vietnam as "little soldiers of fortune." She subsequently denied the quotation during a long interview with me. It is, of course, possible, as Madame Nhu claimed, that words were sometimes put in her mouth by journalists determined to document their preconceived notions of a "wicked Dragon Lady," which has been widely parodied in comic strips. But the reality is that the bad press that she had previously received while in Vietnam conditioned the American people to think the worst of her.

In Washington Madame Nhu received a totally cold shoulder from the Kennedy administration. This was calculated and deliberate. Not even a protocol officer met her train, and this was an extraordinary snub for the "first lady" of a wartime ally.

Several officials at the Department of State, including Walt Whitman Rostow, head of the Policy Planning Staff, felt that this snub was another important factor in screwing up the courage of the Vietnamese generals to overthrow the government.

As usual, with Madame Nhu the trouble was not so much what she said as the way she said it. For example, in New York on October 9, in one of her first public statements, she declared that "The United

States Information Agency . . . and the Voice of America are working feverishly" to overthrow the Diem regime.

This kind of imprecision undermined the credibility of what she had to say, although there was, in a sense, something to it. If she had said that the Voice of America was broadcasting incendiary commentaries deeply hostile to the Diem regime, she could have made a believable case. A simple reading of the famous August 25 broadcast virtually inviting the Vietnamese military to overthrow Diem would have been ample documentation, and there was much more available.

As between the Diem-must-go school, now in a sense victorious, and the Diem-should-stay school, now defeated, things could never be the same again. Events took strange turns. The pessimists became the optimists, and vice versa.

In Saigon the previously pessimistic embassy was elated, albeit regretful, about the murders. This elation was still dominant when I returned to Saigon in mid-November, 1963. Ambassador Lodge's crystal ball was so cloudy that even three weeks after Diem's death, and at a time when the Communist Viet Cong were commencing to make furious gains in the countryside, he told the press that "prospects for defeating Communism are better than they ever were."

By contrast, the once optimistic military mission in Saigon headed by General Harkins was full of private forebodings and anxiety.

The relations between Lodge and the U.S. military must have been, to say the least, interesting. Lodge, who expected the *coup d'état* had not mentioned this to Admiral Felt when they went to call on President Diem at the palace on the fateful morning of November 1 a few hours before the shooting started. Shortly after the *coup d'état*, stories from Saigon began to appear in the American press asserting additionally that the revolting generals had kept Harkins in the dark because they didn't trust him. Some stories said that Harkins had dissented from a cable sent out the morning of November 1 by the embassy and the C.I.A. forewarning Washington of the *coup d'état*. The idea began to get around that Lodge would not be sorry to see Harkins go. But the anti-Harkins stories so incensed President Kennedy that he extended the general's tour for several months.

In point of fact, General Harkins knew, he says, of the coup and had conveyed to its key leader, General Tran Van Don, some of his fears as to the effect on the war effort of a violent change of government in mid-war. This was, of course, to no avail. In the post-coup era, Harkins' dark misgivings and apprehensions were shared in Washington by the Pentagon, the Central Intelligence Agency, the Office of the Vice President, and some White House aides.

But at the Department of State the Diem-must-go group was heady with a sense of accomplishment. Their ebullience spilled out at various background briefings I attended. Mainly there seemed to be satisfaction that the deed was finally done, even though not quite as cleanly as everybody had hoped.

My first personal involvement in the repercussions of the Diem overthrow came late Saturday night, November 2, when, returning from a party, I found an urgent message to call Madame Nhu at the Beverly Wilshire Hotel in Los Angeles. Her pretty teen-age daughter, Le Thuy, who had traveled the world with her mother, answered the phone.

"Mother is upset," said Le Thuy, as if this was a source of surprise to her. "She wants to talk to you about the children."

In Saigon I had met Madame Nhu's four-year-old daughter in the Presidential Palace. I knew there were also two boys, Son Quyen, 11, and Son Trac, 15.

But when Madame Nhu came on the line, she spoke first of her husband and brother-in-law.

"Do you really believe they are dead?" she asked.

"I am afraid so," I answered unhappily.

"I could spit upon the world," Madame Nhu said bitterly.

Silence. What was there to say?

"Are they going to kill my children too?" she asked.

"It's the last thing President Kennedy would want," I said in some agitation as the horror of the three Nhu children being murdered was, alas, not impossible in the crazy, vengeful world of Vietnam, where rioting, looting, and senseless burnings were going on.

"Then why doesn't the United States government do something to help me get them out?" said Madame Nhu, who by now was quite plainly speaking through sobs, a broken warrior if ever there was one.

"I'll put the question to the State Department officer in charge of Vietnam," I promised.

"Hurry," said Madame Nhu. "Please hurry and ask about Can." Ngo Can is Diem's brother, who was in control of Central Vietnam.

It was two A.M. I roused Assistant Secretary Hilsman out of a sound sleep.

"Congratulations, Roger," I said. "How does it feel to have blood on your hands?"

"Oh, come on now, Maggie," said Roger. "Revolutions are rough. People get hurt."

"What about Madame Nhu's children?" I asked. "Are they going to get hurt?"

"If you will find out from Madame Nhu where her children are," said Hilsman, "we will have General Harkins send his personal plane to get them. If you will find out, further, where Madame Nhu wants the children sent, we will get them tickets and see that they are delivered to any address she names. The President is deeply shocked over the death of Diem and Nhu. He will do anything he can to safeguard Madame Nhu's children."

"What about Ngo Dinh Can?"

"He can have asylum if he wants it," said Roger.

In the case of the children, the United States kept the promise made by Hilsman to the letter. Within days Madame Nhu's three children were duly deposited in Rome.

With regard to Ngo Dinh Can, the real power in Central Vietnam, the story was different. In due course Diem's brother sought asylum at the American consulate at Hué. But the American consul sought to send him to Saigon, pleading that he did not have adequate means to protect him. At first Ngo Dinh Can refused.

Madame Tran Trung Dung, his niece, was present during the conversation between Can and the American consul. Madame Dung speaks excellent English: "The American consul persuaded my uncle to go aboard the American airplane by promising he would be taken

to a 'safe place' in Saigon. The only possible safe place was the
American embassy in Saigon, or exile. It was my understanding and
that of my uncle that if he agreed to leave the American consulate he
would be given asylum at the American embassy."

At Hué Counselor Can was driven from the consulate to the airport in an American jeep under escort of an American officer. He
was immediately put on an American plane that the U.S. embassy
had sent up from Saigon. But when Can's plane landed at Saigon, he
was met not by American officials but by Vietnamese police. They
had a hospital stretcher with them, as Can had been reported by the
U.S. consulate to be in poor health (diabetes and bad heart). Can
was instantly arrested by the Vietnamese and taken to jail.

He was later tried and executed. It is possible that Can was guilty
of some abuse of power, but nothing presented at the trial would have
brought a verdict of guilty anyplace else in the world—East or West.
Counselor Can was ordered before a firing squad on a verdict based
on the acceptance of unsubstantiated rumor and innuendo.

Despite their falling-out with the Diem regime, Mr. and Mrs. Dung
stuck by Counselor Can to the end. Both told me that they made it a
personal crusade to go to Hué and check out each accusation.

"There was no truth to them," said Madame Dung, "but who is
interested in truth?"

At the time, there was a rather muted U.S. attempt to rationalize
turning Ngo Dinh Can over to his executioners by saying that asylum
was impossible because he was "a fugitive from justice." Such rationalizations really put Vietnamese tongues in Vietnamese cheeks. After
all, Thich Tri Quang, the militant Buddhist extremist, had been very
much a fugitive from justice at the time that he was taken in by the
U.S. embassy. He was wanted by Diem's police on charges ranging
from subversion to incitement to suicide.

It was the prevailing view among Americans in Saigon that Can
was turned over to the junta's police out of consideration of the
American image. When Thich Tri Quang was given asylum by the
embassy he represented the Buddhists who were being painted by the
majority of the resident press in Saigon as the "good guys," with
Diem the "bad guy." After the coup, the military junta represented

the good guys and the Diemists were still the bad guys. And the United States didn't want to sully its image and/or strain its relations with the military junta by giving a haven to a "bad guy."

Ambassador Lodge did make an effort to save Counselor Can's life. This was done at the personal request of Pope Paul VI. Lodge called on the Pope in Rome en route back to Saigon from Washington after attending the funeral of President Kennedy. By the time Can's execution was drawing near, General Nguyen Khanh was head of the Saigon government. But General Nguyen Khanh was afraid that a stay of execution would bring him trouble with the militant extremists among the Buddhists, who were even then beginning their effort to topple him, an effort that will be described later. General Khanh refused to save Can's life unless Thich Tri Quang, whose trouble-making power he feared, would publicly accede to the act of commutation.

Lodge flew to Hué and passed most of one day trying to talk Thich Tri Quang into displaying some of the compassion that Buddhists claim as a main tenet of their religion. Thich Tri Quang refused flatly. Such bloodthirstiness, let it be noted, is very un-Buddhist.

The death of Can left two of the six Ngo brothers alive. Archbishop Ngo Dinh Thuc had been in Rome during the *coup d'état.* Another brother, Ngo Dinh Luyen, was ambassador to London.

Travesties of justice were plentiful in that turbulent, often anarchic span of time. One rank injustice was the arrest and imprisonment of Tran Van Khiem on no other grounds than the fact he happened to be a brother of Madame Nhu. In fairness, the junta might have taken into consideration the fact that Tran Van Khiem was, additionally, the son of Tran Van Chuong, who resigned as ambassador to Washington in August, 1963, and bitterly opposed the Diem regime as well as his daughter and son-in-law. Further, Tran Van Khiem had actively made trouble for the Diem regime. In the fall of 1963 Counselor Nhu had threatened to bring him before a military court-martial on charges of passing material unfavorable to the regime on to Western journalists. There is no doubt that Tran Van Khiem was guilty of the charge, having passed on much anti-Diem material to his good friend Denis Warner, the free-lance Australian journalist. If Nhu had staged his trial, Khiem would probably have been convicted. The trial was never held, probably because Nhu had more formidable opponents to deal with at the time or possibly because Madame Nhu interceded. But the fact remains that Khiem did work against the Diem regime. How does that square with his arrest by a supposedly anti-Diem junta? It doesn't, of course. And it is, alas, one of thousands of examples of the irrational atmosphere of the time. The ancient credo of revolutions prevailed: Vengeance now, justice later (maybe).

At a National Security Council meeting in the White House shortly after the coups, General Krulak, the top specialist in counterinsurgency, and John McCone, director of C.I.A., were asked to give their estimate of the military junta's chances of survival. They infuriated the pro-coup enthusiasts by predicting that the junta's chances were "fifty-fifty." As it turned out, they were overoptimistic.

What was their reasoning? Summarized at the time (November, 1963) by an authoritative source, the reasons given by the two men ran roughly like this: American insistence on the trappings of democracy is out of step with Vietnamese realities in time of war. Diem did what he did, not because he liked having a secret police or press censorship, but because of the geographic, racial, economic, and historic nature of the problem. A tight rein was the only way to control a country prone to anarchy, political fragmentation, and chronic intrigues, and so primitive in many areas that it was a struggle to make the central government's existence even vaguely felt. No future Vietnamese government could, for example, permit hostile demonstrations in the streets, Buddhist or otherwise, and survive. One day, certainly, Vietnam would be able to have enough of a consensus so that unity would not have to be enforced by an authoritarian ruler. Someday a Montagnard might come to regard a Vietnamese as a friend rather than as an automatic enemy. Someday a Vietnamese from Saigon would cease to be suspicious of a Vietnamese from Hué. But until such a time, the Americans ought to remove such phrases as "popular support" from their measurements of Vietnamese governments, because this term implies positive assent from a majority— more than fifty percent—and this is simply impossible for any Vietnamese government to achieve. In Vietnam the term "popular support" is meaningless. Whose support? Support of the Montagnards? But the Montagnards could never give their wholehearted support, at this stage of tribal development, to any Vietnamese citizen. The same is true of Cao Dai and Hoa Hao—in the countryside they reserved loyalty for members of their own religions. In urban centers there are more sophisticated Confucianists, Catholics, Buddhists, Cao Dai, and Hoa Hao who do understand what central government is all about. But the citified intellectuals, like the military, are in great part incapable of loyalty to anything except their own ambitions and vanities. In short, Diem's overthrow did not change the nature of the Vietnamese dilemma. The most any central Vietnamese government can expect is to obtain the respect—and obedience—of differing groups.

At this writing the question of whether any Vietnamese leader has the stature to command such respect and obedience remains in doubt.

This diagnosis of the problems of Vietnam, however galling to Washington's coup-makers, was prophetically correct. In our interview, Diem had told me: "If they overthrow me, whoever comes after will have to be far more of a dictator than I."

He was right. Martial law was invoked more often in the two years following Diem's death than in the entire nine years of his rule!

CHAPTER 12

Post-Coup Vietnam:
Jungle Without Law

The walls of the nearest thatched hut trembled slightly even though the artillery bursts to the north and west were at least three miles away. Near us was the torn and twisted village bridge that had been blown up when the Communist Viet Cong had been driven out the night before. The sharp, sporadic crackle of an automatic weapon could be heard not far away.

The white-haired Vietnamese peasant sitting cross-legged on a bare bench beneath the small altar bearing portraits of his ancestors went on with his conversation, unperturbed.

"Yes," he said. "A cousin in the next village told me something about changes in the big village [sic]."

"Do you think the changes will be for good or for bad?" I asked through my interpreter, a Vietnamese-speaking American.

"I don't know yet," the old Vietnamese replied. "We will have to wait and see."

A sniper's bullet suddenly crashed nearby into a concrete urn filled with a magnificent bush of orange bougainvillaea that obviously had the loving care of some flower fancier among the farmers. It barely chipped the concrete. But in a moment there was a louder, more ominous explosion—a grenade or a mine. Grimly holding onto my aplomb, I called out, "What's going on?" to the Vietnamese army sergeant who served as interpreter for the small military convoy that had brought us to the village.

"ARVN [the Vietnamese army] is clearing the rest of the village," he explained, "and stirring up a little trouble."

Venturing out for a better view, I noted that the Vietnamese soldiers seemed reasonably disciplined and polite toward the villagers as they made their house-to-house search. Even many hours later, when it came time to leave, there were no chickens and ducks tied to the soldiers' belts. The peasants here had been lucky. Vietnamese soldiers did not always resist the temptation to "help themselves."

Suddenly there was a whir of several helicopters. Sharp gusts of air told us they were landing nearby. The province chief was coming to inspect the village, which had been free (more or less) of Viet Cong control for only a matter of hours. With the province chief was my acquaintance of the previous summer, Major Olen O'Connor, his adviser.

We were only a few miles from Mytho, a key capital in the Mekong delta. I had gone there almost immediately after returning to Vietnam in November, 1963, several weeks after the anti-Diem *coup d'état*. The reason for the journey was a compelling one. In a land riven by rumor it is essential whenever humanly possible to write only of that which you have personally seen or heard at first hand. Valid comparisons can be made only by revisiting war fronts you have taken a hard look at previously. Some three months earlier, while Diem was still alive, I had covered the war in Mytho and elsewhere in Vietnam. Mytho was a good place to start comparing the post-coup situation with that which had obtained a few months back. I felt lucky that Major O'Connor's twelve-month tour was not yet up and that I would have the benefit of judgments I had come to respect.

As usual, Major O'Connor was cautious in his appraisal. "Down here in the delta," he said, "the V.C. have raised hell effectively since the *coup d'état*. But there are also some new things going for us—like a really fine new commander for the Seventh division. So the picture is very mixed."

My first request to Major O'Connor at that meeting was to revisit the saintly Buddhist monk in the little village near Tan Nhiep, whose pagoda stood in a timeless and indestructible posture next to a limpid stream gorged with water lilies. The major and I had driven there one hot summer day without escort and without trouble. I still remember the engagingly informal lecture the saintly Buddhist had given me about the differences between devout Buddhism and Buddhist politicians. I was anxious to know if the Buddhist monk had heard of the changes in Saigon, and if so, what he thought of it all. (Many villages in the deep rural countryside were unaware for many months of the changes in Saigon, unless, as happened to an increasing number in the next two years, they were overrun by Viet Cong forces. The Communists, as a standard tactic, gathered the villagers together at pistol point for an agitation or propaganda session. In these meetings the Communist eyeview of events was the subject of harangues couched in simplest possible terms. It was also standard procedure to terrorize peasants by making them witness the disembowling of village leaders. In one "liberated" village near Mytho that I visited, the Viet Cong had lined up not just the chief but also his wife, five-year-old daughter, three-year-old son, and one-year-old baby and disembowled them all, starting with the infant.)

In response to my request to go back to see my favorite Buddhist, Major O'Connor shook his head firmly. "Impossible," he said. "That whole area has been overrun by the Viet Cong."

"So quickly?" I asked in some disbelief.

"You've got to remember," the major said, "that the Seventh division, which has its headquarters here, is known as the coup division. Some of the key units of the Seventh division were sent to Saigon for the coup. You've also got to remember that the Viet Cong received orders [through radio-casts from Hanoi and regional Viet Cong headquarters] to make maximum assaults to take advantage of the expected confusion. So the Viet Cong hit us with maximum force at a time of maximum weakness when some of the Seventh division's units were playing coup politics up in Saigon."

In Mytho itself the Viet Cong's "maximum push" boldly included a mortar attack against the main bus station as well as the one-time seminary in which the military advisers made their headquarters.

Later, as the tempo of the war mounted, it became increasingly commonplace for the Viet Cong to attack district and provincial capitals
with organized military units, but in 1963 they limted themselves to
terroristic acts—grenades tossed into a bar, a delayed-action bomb
left in a crowded marketplace.

The Seventh division area, with headquarters at Mytho, was crucial
to the war because it embraced, among other things, Highway Four,
which is the delta lifeline over which shipments of rice, cattle, and
pigs travel to Saigon.

To illustrate the intensification of Viet Cong activity, Major O'Connor noted that in the last week of October, 1963, Viet Cong attacks
and harassing fires averaged four to five a night in the area of his
responsibility. But a week after Diem's overthrow, they were able to
stage seventy-six attacks in one night (fifteen times as many as in
October). And although they did not sustain this pace, they managed
to gobble up considerable real estate that was "clear" when Major
O'Connor and I had driven blithely down Highway Four to Vinh
Long, seventy miles away.

What was Colonel Pham Van Dong, the Seventh division's new
commander, doing to checkmate all this?

According to a senior American military adviser: "In Colonel
Dong's very first week he conducted three big operations, including
one that lasted five days. He's a real tiger. What really caused a
sensation in these parts is that he fought two battles at night. This is
unheard of. In the past we just could not get the Vietnamese to fight
at night. As you know, the ARVN, even when it had a daytime
victory, would abandon contact at dusk, and in the night the V.C.
would slip away. And what really encourages us around here is that
Colonel Dong has displayed the ability to make on-the-spot decisions
without having to go all the way back to corps or to Saigon. We hope
to Christ that this is a policy the military junta will apply everywhere.
Very often the ability to make on-the-spot decisions spells the difference between winning and losing."

This was cheering news, but in Vietnam's political quicksands the
ground can shift quickly and inexplicably. Within a few weeks of my
visit Colonel Dong, to the despair of the American advisers, was

yanked out of the Seventh division. He was exiled to Formosa, where for some time his great military talents were to atrophy in the inconsequential post of military attaché. Why? Was it because he had made on-the-spot decisions without consulting the junta? Was it because he was the protégé of General Ton That Dinh, Minister of the Interior, whose flamboyant ways were bringing him into disfavor with the rest of the junta? Was it because coup rumors were already starting? Were the generals of the junta, like Diem before them, beginning to discover the realities of Vietnam's intrigue-haunted society, making it a risky business to give too much autonomy to officers in command of key units? The Seventh, as an example, was called the coup division precisely because it had been—and would continue to be—the instrument of many efforts to overthrow governments. Nobody knew the real reason for Dong's banishment.

What was grimly clear, however, was that the process of purge and cannibalization had begun. Politically the generals and the colonels had begun to devour each other. Rudyard Kipling's jungle at least had laws; the political jungles of Vietnam were lawless.

The haunting part of all this is that it had been so accurately foretold.

In a dinner on the seventh floor of the Hotel Caravelle the previous August I had pressed Robert G. K. Thompson,* chief of the British advisory mission, and John Richardson, head of the C.I.A. (then identified only as the first secretary of the U.S. embassy), for an opinion about what would happen if there were a *coup d'état*.

"It would set back the war twelve months—maybe forever," said Thompson, and Richardson nodded agreement.

"But why?"

Because, they agreed, purges would be inevitable. At the very least, any new military junta would have to fire the forty-two province chiefs; to justify their coup they would have to discredit those who served Diem. They would want to appoint men personally beholden to them. The firing of province chiefs would in itself shake Vietnam's hard-won stability, the two officials said, because it had taken nine

* Now Sir Robert Thompson; he was given the Order of the British Empire in early 1965.

long, hard years to fill the bureaucratic vacuum left by the French and to develop reasonably competent rural officials. Both men feared that any future military dictatorship might also be tempted to junk good programs in their zeal to prove that all that went before was bad. The logic of any revolution is that it must be quickly justified.

"In revolutions of this kind," said Thompson, "the rule of law is usually the first victim."

"And," said Richardson, "military juntas are notoriously unstable."

I had written most of this (without attribution, in the summer of 1963), and it had caused anger and controversy in Washington and among pro-coup enthusiasts in Saigon.

Almost a year later I asked a senior C.I.A. official why Mr. Richardson's perceptive diagnosis of the situation had made so little impression on top policy-makers.

"Because," said the C.I.A. official laconically, "you can take policy-makers to intelligence, but you can't make them drink."

He could have added, accurately, that Richardson had also become a victim of the Saigon "jungle" (the Occidental part of the forest). This C.I.A. officer, as disciplined and honorable as he was prophetic, disagreed certainly with Lodge's apparent pro-coup enthusiasms. But he obeyed instantly and to the letter* when Lodge ordered him to take actions that many felt would contribute to the pro-coup atmosphere, such as breaking off all contact with the Diem regime.

Thus it came as a shock to the C.I.A., Richardson and his staff in Vietnam when a news story out of Saigon described him as having been "arrogantly defiant" of orders.

In light of these attacks, Richardson was recalled. President Kennedy decided that there was no sense in having hostility between the ambassador and the chief of the intelligence mission.

The plotting generals later said that Richardson's departure was useful to them because it erased a psychological block in the minds of some of the military. Richardson's objections to a *coup d'état* were well known around Saigon, and his mere presence in the embassy might have had a deterrent effect on the more nervous plotters.

* This was established by a subsequent Washington investigation.

After the Richardson incident, President Kennedy's attitude toward some facets of Ambassador Lodge's stewardship began in private to take on a jaundiced hue. President Kennedy let his displeasure at the slurs on Richardson become known when he went to great trouble at a press conference to praise him and his work by name. Never before in history has a C.I.A. man in the field been so publicly honored.

In post-coup Saigon the Thompson-Richardson prophecies began to take on a fearful reality even sooner than I would have imagined. Even though Diem was only a few weeks dead, the teahouse intellectuals and the *apéritif* set already were carping and sneering at the new leaders of Vietnam, who had not yet had time to find their way through the corridors of the Gia Long Palace. This was not too surprising, because the teahouse set thrives on crankiness and fault-finding.

Saigon's spoiled urbanites had not even been appeased by the junta's gesture in legalizing the Western dance called the twist. Nor were they impressed by the fact that young Interior Minister, General Dinh, had been persuaded by some Western photographers to go to a night club and do the twist himself to show that he was "liberal and in touch with the people," as one U.S. caption proclaimed. (An interesting insight into Occidental values.)

"The Interior Minister," said one Vietnamese student with supreme disdain, "is allowing himself to be played for a fool."

Such disdain was in no way surprising. For as the Minh junta, and all future governments in Vietnam, were to discover, concessions made to the Buddhist extremists and to students brought no returns at all so far as the war effort was concerned.

For the Buddhists, intellectuals, and students who marched the streets in anti-Diem demonstrations (and subsequently in anti-Minh, anti-Khanh, anti-Huong, anti-American and proneutralist demonstrations) could not have cared less about the war. Vietnamese college students, who total about seventeen thousand, tell you quite frankly that one reason they prize admission to a university is that it enables them to avoid the draft. If the success or failure of the war were to depend on these groups, Vietnam would have been lost from the start. All of which again shows the lack of comprehension of those at the State Department who argued that Diem must go because the disaffection of some students and some Buddhists in the cities impeded the prosecution of the war. Since the activities of the students and extremist monks mattered not in the slightest to those fighting the Viet Cong in the rural areas, and since the students and monks were draft-exempt, the only way their trouble-making could affect the war effort was in the minds of some Occidentals at the State Department, who kept measuring events in Vietnam by what they imagined would be the reaction in the United States if the same sort of thing were going on.

Far from being appeased by the Diem *coup d'état*, within two weeks of that cataclysmic development, ten thousand students at Hué demonstrated noisily against the military junta because it had not dismissed several professors who had served Diem "too loyally" for their tastes.

Such charges were utterly hypocritical. Almost every educated person in Vietnam, whether in the military or the civil service, had of course served Diem. When one is fighting a bitter anti-Communist war, what could be a fair measure of being "too loyal" to the government leading the fight? Such terms were sheer nonsense. Another black mark against the intellectuals was the smut and sheer mendacity of the post-coup free press of Vietnam. It proved too much, finally, even for the junta. Three Saigon dailies were closed before 1963 was out.

In view of the U.S. embassy's buoyant feelings over the results of the *coup d'état,* I was dismayed on my return to Saigon to find that for once the teahouse rumors were not empty; the military-junta members were, in fact, already intriguing and maneuvering against each other.

I discovered this at first hand in an interview I had with General Ton That Dinh, the Interior Minister and the officer whose last-minute defection from the Diem regime had made the success of the coup possible. General Dinh said nothing to diminish his reputation as an egomaniac, though it was leavened with a certain charm.

What was startling, however, was General Dinh's attempts to hint to me, a total stranger, that his supposed partner in government, General Big Minh, was not only guilty of Diem's murder, but incompetent. General Dinh even intimated that it might be necessary for him, as Interior Minister, to give this junta leader his walking papers one of these days. In view of General Dinh's attitude, it was perfectly plain to me that the triumvirate (General Dinh, General Minh, General Le Van Kim) would not last long. If he was so outlandishly disloyal to the triumvirate in a conversation with a stranger, what was General Dinh saying to close friends? The thought staggered me, and the Thompson-Richardson conversation was recalled with a shudder for the fate of Vietnam. As for General Minh, he impressed me as an amiable prevaricator, as illustrated by his sad story during our interview about having been "crushed" by the death of Diem (killed by his personal circle). More serious, though, was an apparent intellectual poverty. When I tried to draw him out on the strategic-hamlet program, General Minh observed, "Perhaps they were a good idea, but we don't know whether to go on with them, because they are associated with Diem."

"Well, the war against the Viet Cong is associated with Diem and you are going on with that, aren't you?" I said rather tartly. He evaded a direct reply.

The U.S. embassy had small success, too, trying to get General Minh to make up his mind. The Americans were unanimous in the view that the strategic-hamlet program was absolutely vital. The fact that it was overextended—too many had been built too fast—was a fault that could be corrected. Indeed, in September Diem and Nhu had already agreed to slow down the program and had given orders to that effect. This important and conciliatory gesture by the Vietnamese leaders was never announced to the press by Lodge. It is widely believed in Washington that he deliberately played it down because public knowledge of Diem's attempt to accommodate the Americans on the strategic-hamlet score might have given the anti-coup forces ammunition for saying that Diem was not so hopeless after all.

After the coup and despite heavy pressure from the U.S. military mission, months elapsed before the junta, after ridiculously long labors, finally brought forth the decision to change the name of the program to "new-life hamlet" (to remove the taint of the Nhu appellation) and get on with it.

The junta's inability to make up its mind, coupled with the Viet Cong's continuing gains in the countryside, so unsettled nine northern province chiefs that in December, 1963, they jointly wired General Minh, pleading, "Please send us orders."

But if Big Minh's committee of generals was unable to come forth with the kind of positive decisions required to push on with the war and hold the country together, it was unfortunately capable of negative and destructive decisions. Not only were massive purges of key (and scarce) officials instigated, but, in addition, a reign of terror was unloosed against officials who had done nothing beyond loyally serving the anti-Communist government of Ngo Dinh Diem when it was the legally constituted authority. This was, by any definition, ex post facto justice, applied arbitrarily and senselessly, in the way of all revolutions.

In Quang Ngai province, for instance, Province Chief Nguyen Van Tat, who was unanimously acclaimed by the Americans as one of the best officials in the country, was not only fired but dragged from his house, beaten (probably by Communist sympathizers calling themselves Buddhists), and for a time held in jail. Nguyen Van Tat had made life tough for the Viet Cong in Quang Ngai. It was logical that they should seek the opportunity of a breakdown in law and order to wreak vengeance on him. But was it really necessary for the military junta to play the Communist game by ridding itself of one of its best anti-Communist fighters?

Nguyen Van Tat was the province chief who had so skillfully and compassionately defused the potential crisis that might have been triggered by the Buddhist hunger strike in Quang Ngai, which had been proclaimed on orders from the Xa Loi Pagoda. One of his great admirers was Major John Kelly, who bitterly remarked: "Nguyen Van Tat's 'crimes' were to be a Catholic and a member of the Can Lao party [an elite society organized by Ngo Dinh Nhu]." But despite Major Kelly's sarcasm, it was not a crime, of course, to be either a Can Lao or a Catholic. Nor was religion a criterion for the Can Lao. The criteria included distinguished service in the fight against the Communists and loyalty to the Diem regime. In 1963 it was the fashion to condemn the regime for using such groups as the Can Lao, the Republican Youth, etc., to assure loyalty and discipline. Nowadays U.S. officials only wish that some Vietnamese government would find some organizational way to assure loyalty of some kind.

In the junta period one of the big dangers of the simultaneous and widespread firings, purges, jailings, and (all too often) arbitrary executions was that newly appointed officials, being strangers to their province, district, or village, could not know for sure how to distinguish the "good guys" from the "bad guys." Who were the Viet Cong sympathizers? Who had a son who went north with the Viet Minh regulars after the partition of 1954? Who might be most vulnerable to Communist pressures? Such knowledge, essential when fighting a subversive war, is not easily come by even for Vietnamese, especially if they are strangers to the area, or even if they are local boys but strangers to the problems.

In its careening course to eradicate all vestiges of the Diem era, the military junta plunged much of the countryside into the confusion from which it purportedly was trying to save it. It was no wonder that the Viet Cong took advantage of the situation to seize the military initiative for the first time in many months. It is no wonder that, in the two months after the *coup d'état*, the military junta lost more real estate, lives, and weapons to the Viet Cong than at any previous time in the war.

After President Kennedy's assassination, a U.S. expert on the Far East tried to convey to top officials in Washington some idea of the near chaos in Vietnam with a briefing paper that took this tack: "President Johnson, of course, put maximum emphasis on a sense of continuity. But supposing, instead, that President Johnson had started out by firing every governor of a state, every mayor of a city, every important police chief, and ordered a few of these executed for having repressed some rioters who had been carrying banners demanding the overthrow of the U.S. government. Supposing the new President additionally had fired the Joint Chiefs of Staff and the entire cabinet, several of whom were also executed by firing squads. Supposing he had fired J. Edgar Hoover, purged the F.B.I. and C.I.A. Supposing he even forced a purge of key labor leaders and religious figures [in Vietnam, for example, the pro-Diem Cao Dai pope was replaced, on junta orders, with a new pope supposedly loyal to the generals]. Supposing all this traumatic purging took place in the middle of a war in which the enemy was in sight of the Washington Monument. Consider what the results would be of such violent change in even so politically stable a country as the United States."

The Communists took great relish in all the confusion and were blunt to say so. Wilfred Burchett, correspondent with Communist sympathies, asked Nguyen Huu Tho, president of the so-called National Liberation Front, to evaluate in an interview the coup against Diem and the murder of the Ngo brothers.

Here are the essential quotes from Burchett's interview.

"They were gifts from heaven for us," said President Tho. "Our enemy had been seriously weakened from all points of view, military, political, and administrative. The special shock troops which were an essential support for the Diem regime have been eliminated. The military command has been turned upside down and weakened by purges.

"For the same reason, the police apparatus set up over the years with great care by Diem is utterly shattered, especially at the base. The principal chiefs of security and the secret police on which mainly depended the protection of the regime and the repression of the revolutionary Communist Viet Cong movement, have been eliminated, purged.

"Troops, officers, and officials of the army and administration are completely lost; they have no more confidence in their chiefs and have no idea to whom they should be loyal. From the political viewpoint the weakening of our adversary is still clearer. . . . Political organizations like the labor and humanist party, the national revolutionary movement, the young republicans, and the movement for women's solidarity and others which constituted appreciable support for the regime have been dissolved and eliminated."

In another appraisal that is fascinating and instructive of the Communist point of view, Burchett quotes another National Liberation Front leader—Tran Nam Trung—as saying, "The Americans chose the dangerous course of changing horses in midstream. But in fact they will search in vain for a more efficient horse than Diem. With all his faults and criminal stupidities, Diem did succeed in setting up and maintaining an army, an administration, and some sort of political machine, with all the reins of power in his hands. . . ."

It is certain that under the military junta many Vietnamese were jailed for far less than was necessary to send a person to prison under Diem. Said a European observer: "Under Diem a Vietnamese had to do something specific against the regime to get into trouble. Under the military junta a Vietnamese can be jailed without charge, simply under the suspicion that he was loyal to the Diem regime at the time when it was supported by the United States and recognized by the entire world."

Writing from Vietnam, Sanche de Gramont, a Pulitzer Prize-winning reporter in the New York *Herald Tribune*, estimated that in Saigon alone just after the first coup the arbitrary arrests numbered five hundred or more. In those days there was at times a Keystone Cop quality to the junta's justice. One dignified Vietnamese bourgeois lady in a chauffer-driven car came to Saigon's main prison to deliver a package to her recently arrested husband and was herself promptly clapped in jail along with her driver! Since the woman was a political neuter and her driver very pro-Buddhist, the incident caused some merriment among the cynics. The Vietnamese lady and her driver, however, were not amused.

In that period Mr. de Gramont and this writer were the only Americans to report in any detail the junta's reversion to some of the police-state tactics the Saigon press corps so bitterly criticized in Diem.

The U.S. embassy, practicing a disturbing double standard, remained strangely silent—a silence that also contrasted starkly with its angry denunciations of the Diem era. Perhaps, in the beginning, this was justifiable. Big Minh and his junta were "our boys." If we criticized them, we criticized ourselves, for hadn't we made it possible for them to take over?

Or, as one U.S. embassy official put it, this was not the time to start rocking the boat—again. But later, as the decline of law and order began to tear apart the very fabric of Vietnamese society—to the benefit of the Viet Cong and the peril of the war effort—America's incomprehensible silence was to prove one of the biggest blunders of all.

In any case, within three months of the junta's takeover, the Vietnamese boat was rocked again. The surgically swift and clean *coup d'état* staged by thirty-six-year-old General Nguyen Khanh on January 30, 1964, was to inaugurate a weird and turbulent year of off-again, on-again rule by this goateed military man whose relations with the United States were to be as fickle as an uncertain betrothal.

Except for Big Minh, the leaders of the previous military junta were all put under house arrest by General Khanh on charges of intriguing with the French and with neutralists. True? Possibly, but they were never brought to trial.

Vietnamese are specialists at getting rid of each other and at finding rationalizations for it, and the most spectacular example of an endemic plotter is Colonel Pham Ngoc Thao, an intelligent, charming Vietnamese who had once been an intelligence officer for Ho Chi Minh but who joined up with Diem's nationalists when he realized that North Vietnam was to be part of the Communist empire.

Colonel Thao was the key planner of the brilliantly executed coup that brought Khanh into power. He had also played a key role in the anti-Diem coup; it was he and his men who seized the Saigon radio station early in the afternoon of November 1, 1963, and began broadcasting pro-junta and anti-Diem statements. In September, 1964, Colonel Thao was planning a coup against General Khanh (for allegedly being soft on pro-Communist elements) but was foiled when another group of generals beat him to it. This "coupette" was clumsily executed and quickly put down, but General Khanh's suspicions of Colonel Thao were aroused finally, and he was exiled to Washington in September, 1964. By January, 1965, however, Colonel Thao was back in Saigon, having succumbed to his old addiction to plotting. A *coup d'état* he engineered on February 19 finally led to Khanh's own political destruction and exile abroad. Premier Phan Huy Quat was Khanh's successor, and against Quat the chronic conspirator resorted to more subtle methods, using Vietnamese President Phan Khac Suu as a vehicle for his trouble-making. President Suu was a blood relative of the colonel, though a somewhat distant one. Colonel Thao managed, like Iago, to whisper his suspicions and schemes to the old President, who in turn blocked Premier Quat's efforts to make key appointments. Eventually Quat, unable to overcome the obstructions, resigned, inviting the generals back into the political arena. Still another military junta emerged in the revolving-door politics of Saigon.*

It is the machinations of men like Colonel Thao that occasionally make Americans wonder despairingly if Vietnam is governable.

Vietnam is, of course, governable, if the United States will get over the idea that elections of themselves win wars, that "instant democracy" is an attainable goal, and above all, that Oriental leaders we support must wear halos and forswear such nasty things as public executions of the Viet Cong.

Peter Lisagor, of the Chicago *Daily News*, put it very well when he wrote: "Unfortunately, government leaders can't be bought across the counter like frozen food, pasteurized, cleansed of all scales and warts, sin-free.

"This is a fact that Uncle Sam seems to forget from crisis to crisis. He goes about righteously applying the puritan's yardstick to his choices. What he wants . . . is an Ataturk on the saintly side, plus halo, or a Simón Bolívar who understands balance of payments and turns his paycheck over to charity. . . . The United States has hamstrung and thwarted itself by a chronic tendency to attempt to dredge up out of a corrupt, empty, vengeful society a man of unassailable virtues. Not only must he be a man who has never yielded to temptation, but one who has never known it. The search is for a political eunuch suddenly and miraculously restored to his full powers. . . . It wasn't so long ago that U.S. policy makers thought South Vietnam's Ngo Dinh Diem might prove to be a sainted Bolívar, Sun Yat-sen, Ataturk, or name your own national hero. He was a symbol of

---

* Colonel Thao finally died a violent death. In March, 1965, he was tried and sentenced to death in absentia for his part in various *coup d'états*. But he evaded capture for many months. Finally in July, 1965, the government caught up with him at his refuge in a Catholic monastery outside Saigon, and he was allegedly fatally wounded in the ensuing struggle.

mandarin authority, religious scruples, and courage in the face of long odds.

"But all of a sudden, the symbol came unraveled and Diem had to go, with the result that Saigon has known no real stability since. Every new coup has brought a new Prime Minister who might just turn the corner in the wishful thinking of U.S. authorities, but none has turned it for long.

"Instant leaders, like instant democracy, cannot be packaged and preserved for use upon demand."

Hear, hear!

I never cease to be amazed at those Occidentals who believe that gimmicks and tricks of speech and personality can be decisive in the murky, nightmarish world of Vietnamese politics. In 1963 even the State Department was agog over the cable from Lodge in which he intimated that things were going to improve because he was giving Big Minh tips on elocution to help him project his personality better to the people.

Elocution lessons, yet, and in the middle of a war!

With Khanh, the United States finally got a chance to try out the conventional Occidental theory that support of the Oriental masses could be won if a Vietnamese leader would only go to the grass roots and shake enough hands. The corollary to this is the belief that if the masses really gave a leader such support, the Communists would be forced to pick up their hammocks and steal silently away.

This is a very unhistoric assumption. The opposition of the majority has never deterred a Communist minority. Czechoslovakia is a case in point. The Communists seized power there in 1947 and imposed their minority rule by police and terror in spite of the overwhelming opposition of the majority.

At Lodge's urging, General Khanh went on a number of barnstorming trips. If nothing else, they at least earned him some good press notices in the United States.

Said *Time* magazine in the issue of February 15, 1965: "From the way he buttonholed passersby on Saigon sidewalks, the pint-sized Vietnamese officer in green fatigues might have been Nelson Rockefeller campaigning in the New Hampshire primary . . . the folksy pleasant style surprised U.S. advisers, who have long urged grass-roots politicking on government leaders. At a village market in Ben Cat [twenty-seven miles north of Saigon] he questioned startled peasants about their health, housing, and work."

Boundless is the praise of Americans for Asians who act like Americans, especially in the realm of politics. But such praise is a denial of the Oriental mystique of leadership which demands a certain aloofness. It flies in the face of that reasonable aphorism that "familiarity breeds contempt." And it betrays an ignorance about the character of the struggle in Vietnam.

This was tragically demonstrated by an episode that followed General Khanh's visit to the village market at Ben Cat, which is in a highly insecure area deeply penetrated by the Viet Cong. It seems that General Khanh singled out one farmer for a somewhat lengthy chat. Two days later the farmer was found decapitated in his ricefield. The Viet Cong had pinned a note to his shirt announcing "This is what happens to peasants who collaborate with the dirty Khanh regime and the dirty American imperialists. Let the people be warned."

The decapitated farmer was not an isolated example of how grass-roots politicking in Vietnam can boomerang. Wherever the hearts and minds of the Vietnamese peasant may be, the realities of the dirty war make it highly impolitic, if staying alive is a consideration, to show enthusiastic support for the government—any non-Communist government—unless there are absolute guarantees that no Viet Cong or Viet Cong spy is about. And in 1964 and 1965 in Vietnam it became virtually impossible to be sure of this.

When Khanh staged his coup, he promised the stability-craving Americans not to order any more widespread shakeups of province chiefs and military personnel. It was an empty promise for the simple reason that to survive politically a Vietnamese leader must install in crucial posts officers personally loyal or in debt to him. It is a necessary act of survival in Vietnam's intrigue-drenched atmosphere.

As usual, the Viet Cong timed its maximum offensives for the period of maximum confusion following Khanh's seizure of power and the inevitable dislocations. During the relentless series of coups and coupettes that were to plague the country in 1964 and 1965, the graph of Viet Cong attacks showed a series of matching upward spurts.

In two separate journeys to Vietnam after the death of Diem I was most depressed by the Viet Cong reconquest of so much of the coastal plain north of Saigon, territory that had been largely free and clear during my first visit. In Phan Rang in the summer of 1963 I had been able to drive without military escort to the charming villages of the Cham tribesmen (of Polynesian descent), with their whitewashed mosques, and blue mosaic domes of stunning handiwork. Eighteen months later the province chief at Phan Rang told me that it would take a major military convoy to get back to these villages, and even than an ambush was likely.

In Quang Ngai province, in the summer of 1963, a sense of exhilaration and progress pervaded the villages, the direct result of the defeat of the Viet Cong in the April 15 battle and the feeling of security afforded by the strategic hamlets that (thanks to Province Chief That) had been carefully and intelligently constructed. Eighteen months later, the eleven strategic hamlets near Quang Ngai City (the province capital) that had, along with the Vietnamese Twenty-fifth division, fought the Viet Cong, were still free and clear, but it was impossible to get to them by road because the intervening territory was held by Viet Cong.

The volatility of the war in Vietnam is nowhere better illustrated than in the story of the short, happy life of Quang Ngai province.

In 1962, when massive United States military assistance was just beginning, the villages in the potentially lush coastal areas of Quang Ngai were easy prey to the Viet Cong, who could enter them at will to forage for food and kidnap young "recruits." Even Quang Ngai City had been subject to attacks by the Viet Cong based in the jungle-covered foothills.

In 1963 the densely inhabited coastal area in Quang Ngai province became largely immune to Viet Cong harassment. Although great improvement had also been made in liberating the Vietnamese coastal plains stretching hundreds of miles from Hué, near the Seventeenth Parallel in the North, to Phan Thiet, in the South, the improvement in Quang Ngai was so dramatic as to be called "a miracle" by no less a person than Roger Hilsman, the Assistant Secretary of State for Far Eastern affairs. Since Hilsman was, in this period, usually in hot pursuit of facts to justify Diem's overthrow, the compliment was sincere, even though the miracle of Quang Ngai was not sufficient to convince him that Diem might be worth keeping on.

The miracle endured so long as the Twenty-fifth division remained in that province in full strength and so long as the Communist guerrilla strength (two battalions in mid-1963 in Quang Ngai itself) remained static, both in numbers of personnel and quality of weapons. (Machine guns were the heaviest guerrilla weapon in that time and in that place.)

The miracle began to fade in the fall of 1963. Under American pressure Diem had reluctantly agreed to transfer some crack regiments of the Twenty-fifth division to the Mekong delta, where the Viet Cong was then giving maximum trouble.

There was one fundamental thing wrong with this transfer. Vietnamese soldiers, drawn largely from the peasantry, are understandably parochial and know little beyond their own village and province. The Twenty-fifth division had been recruited from peasants in Quang Ngai province. It was one thing for the men of Quang Ngai to defend their own villages, their own homes, the graves of their own ancestors. It was another to go to a strange country (as the delta seemed to them) and to fight for alien ground. As soon as the Twenty-fifth division hit the Delta, its desertion rate skyrocketed—as Diem had argued would happen.

Like Diem, Ho Chi Minh also attached great importance to deploying in each province military personnel who knew the terrain and who had family links with the villages. That is why in the beginning of his military assault on South Vietnam Ho Chi Minh took care whenever possible to choose officers and noncoms who had been born or had fought in the South. In the war against the French the wily Red leader had recruited many regular Viet Minh units from Quang Ngai province. Ho ordered the regular units to march to Hanoi at the time of the Geneva agreement partitioning the country. He selected the best fighters from the one-time natives of this province (but now in his Red army) to lead the first waves of Viet Minh (now Viet Cong) infiltrated into Quang Ngai. By mid-1964, however, Ho was to run out of such officers and noncoms. From then on most of the Red army officers and men captured were born and brought up in the North.

By the winter of 1964–1965 the miracle of Quang Ngai was no more. Already greatly weakened, the Vietnamese army units there were to be chewed up by an enormously strengthened Viet Cong enemy. Quang Ngai is in the first-corps area of the Vietnamese army, and in 1963 the number of hard-core Viet Cong—full-time soldiers under full-time discipline—in the first corps were estimated to be four battalions. In 1964 this jumped fourfold, to fourteen Viet Cong battalions, and in 1965 to at least twenty such battalions, probably more. The rise in Viet Cong strength was nearly five hundred percent in this corps area alone.

By returning always to war fronts previously visited I was able to measure for myself the differences between the Diem era and the post-Diem era. At Hué, Danang, Pleiku, Tay Ninh, Qui Nhon, Mytho, Can Tho, and Vinh Long, everything I saw and heard added up to alarming encroachments by an ever-stronger and more professional Viet Cong.

(By 1965 regular Viet Minh units were plucked in their entirety out of Ho's Red army and sent south. They began wearing regular Viet Minh uniforms complete with webbed belts and brass buckles engraved with a red star. Some of the units contained soldiers who had been with regular Viet Minh forces in Kontum province more than a decade ago when they cut up the famous French Force Mobile 100 that had just returned from Korea.)

What had gone wrong?

Had we failed to dig enough wells? Did we neglect to get sufficient medicine to the grass roots? Was the war suffering because of lack of civic action? Would more democracy (i.e. national elections) have helped to stave off the Viet Cong? Were we overemphasizing the military at the expense of the political, whatever that means, as Robert Kennedy claimed in early 1965? Had we failed in our campaign to "win the hearts and minds" of the Vietnamese people?

Such claims have been, and apparently will be interminably, advanced even by intelligent Americans as long as the Vietnam war is with us.

But neither a high IQ nor a Harvard (or any other) degree can take the place of direct experience of the grim Oriental realities of Vietnam. And the massive good intentions behind these accusations do not prevent them from being utterly naïve and nonsensical, as well as out of touch with these realities.

Of course the United States and its Vietnamese ally should and could do more by way of well-digging, school-building, peasant-courting. Of course there have been mistakes and omissions. But by and large, the United States has done very well in this matter of civic action, especially when contrasted with the Viet Cong's fiendish determination to wreck the schools and hospitals and wells and bridges and farm-to-market roads constructed with American help. It can be maintained with assurance that any omissions and mistakes made in the campaign to "win the hearts and minds" of the peasants had nothing decisive to do with the crisis that made American military intervention mandatory.

This intervention became necessary because the Communist forces were able to concentrate *superior military power* in crucial areas and the Vietnamese army, as we shall see, simply ran out of sufficient reserves.

Or as an American military adviser said after the grisly battle for the district capital of Dong Xoai: "It is all very well to win the heart and the mind of the peasant, but when there are three hundred on your side, and three thousand V.C. surrounding you on all sides, and when the V.C. has mortars, recoilless rifles, and heavy machine guns, the sympathies of the peasant are irrelevant to what happens. If the peasant is smart he'll go hide while he can."

Lenin once said that *"refugees are people who vote with their feet."* On this occasion he spoke a historical truth. It is a truth that Americans could well ponder, because it might be a corrective to the illusion that the Viet Cong have some magical formula to "win the hearts and minds" of the peasant that is unavailable to us.

The hatred of the peasant for the commissar is no better proved than by the fact that in 1964 and 1965 literally five hundred thousand

Vietnamese were again "voting with their feet" against the Communists and for the free Vietnamese and the Americans. In Binh Dinh province alone nearly one hundred thousand Vietnamese peasants have picked up their belongings and deserted their villages because of Viet Cong pressure. Most of them had to flee suddenly and on foot to escape Viet Cong rule that was widening as the result of increased Communist military power. Bowed down by the household belongings toted on their backs holding the hands of their children, the peasants journeyed down mountain trails, over dirt roads, and across rivers to reach places like Qui Nhon, a coastal town, that was relatively safe (at the time) from the Communists. The flood of refugees from Communist areas continues at this writing. After the battle of Dong Xoai every peasant family in that district begged to be evacuated to a government-held area. If the peasants were, in any case, to leave their homes, they could just as well have slipped over into Viet Cong-held areas. But they didn't. The latest wave of refugees constitutes a terrible new burden to both the Vietnamese officials and the United States. But the tide of refugees affirms (how many times is this going to have to be proved?) that, given a real choice of alternatives, the Vietnamese peasant for the most part seeks to evade Communist control.

Sometimes a peasant leaves an area because Viet Cong infestation brings on government artillery attacks. Many Americans automatically assume that such artillery attacks would turn the Vietnamese into friends of the Viet Cong. But usually the opposite is true. After interviewing two hundred persons who had fled Viet Cong control, the RAND Corporation, a highly respected American research outfit, discovered that villagers under artillery attack blame not us but the Viet Cong for their plight.

A 1965 RAND Corporation report to the U.S. government says: "We find that villagers increasingly tend to ask the Viet Cong unit to leave, refuse to sell them rice, refuse to allow them to sleep in their houses. In some cases, the villagers simply leave the area when the Viet Cong unit arrives. Criticism of irresponsible and provocative actions on the part of the guerrillas is fairly widespread, not only among the villagers but also among defectors from hard-core (Communist) units. Despite Viet Cong propaganda, there is no belief that the Vietnamese government or the Americans are deliberately bombing harmless villages. The villagers more often take the view that the attacks are part of the unavoidable existence of war. They believe the attacks result from the fact that the village is under Viet Cong control, so obviously—since it is enemy territory—it is an obvious target. Often the villager moves to the government area because that is where the artillery fire is coming from. If the villager moves into government territory, he knows he won't be shot at by the government."

During its extensive interviewing of refugees from the Viet Cong in the summer of 1965, RAND Corporation researchers found that Viet Cong brutality sometimes boomeranged, especially in cases where young villagers were hauled away to serve as soldiers or ammunition carriers. Defectors told of cases in which families tried to fight off recruiters (kidnappers) with knives.

Unfortunately, when it gets to be a duel between mortars and airplanes—that is, a semi-conventional war—the feelings of the population are not decisive. The Germans conquered France, Poland, and other countries of Europe in spite of the hatred of the people. China conquered Tibet despite the hatred of that devout Buddhist population.

Ho Chi Minh's Communist minority held on to North Vietnam despite the peasant revolt of 1956 which, according to French sources, was an eruption of anti-Ho sentiment held by *ninety percent of the people.*

In World War II, resistance movements, such as that in France, were virtually nonexistent until there was hope of liberation from outside. In France, there was no resistance to speak of until the United States entered the war against Hitler, thus affording hope of eventual liberation.

Whatever the feeling of the Vietnamese villagers, the Viet Cong made spectacular military gains in 1964 and 1965. These gains were aided and abetted, both psychologically and materially, by the confusion generated by the rapid succession of revolving-door governments in Saigon.

Whatever may be said of Diem, he at least *ruled* his people. Most of the generals and politicians that came after him were too busy playing their deadly political games in Saigon ever to get around to the essentials of administration and rule.

This political turmoil had been an obvious invitation to Hanoi to intensify its war effort, and Ho Chi Minh accepted the invitation, not just with pleasure but with speed and efficiency. So the situation has been that the Communist enemy increased his strength in spectacular fashion at a time when the political and administrative fabric of Vietnam was being increasingly torn apart by turmoil, purge, guillotine justice, arbitrary arrest, and the machinations of those extremists who put a parochial struggle for power above the national interest.

Indeed, because of political uncertainty, recruiting for the Vietnamese army simply ground to a total halt for many months in the spring of 1964, and this happened, tragically, when the Vietnamese army was about to be most savagely tested by the Viet Cong. The surprising fact in Vietnam is that the war effort continued as well as it did for so long.

For once the sheer primitiveness of much of the country proved an advantage. The very fact that Vietnam was so compartmentalized cushioned the impact of what was happening in Saigon. In a sense, there are forty-two different wars going on in Vietnam, because in each province it is fought in a different way. The militia (irregular forces) fighting to defend a village near Mytho, in the Mekong delta, is not affected by developments in Saigon because this village-based force usually neither knows nor understands the squalid politics of the big city. The village militia and the village chief are concerned with what to them are more vital requirements—that the ammunition, the rice seeds, and the insecticides get from Saigon to them. And despite all the frothings at the top, the second-level bureaucrats— with a big assist from the Americans—kept the essentials moving from the capital city to the countryside, and vice versa. In 1965, after Highway One was repeatedly cut, the United States had to resort to an airlift to keep certain provincial items supplied.

In the regular army most of the fighting fortunately is done by regiments and battalions whose commanders are majors and captains, men remote from the cesspools of intrigue and ambition. And while it has been commonplace in the two years since Diem's death for Americans to be unable to locate the commanders of an army corps or the chief of the air force, the lower-ranking officers were usually with their troops. American advisers who were present at every level, from headquarters to battalions, also supplied a kind of glue to hold the regular army together while the top brass was off playing politics.

These things helped us to forestall a total disaster in Vietnam but could not eliminate the hard reality of a macabre dance performed breathtakingly close to the edge of collapse.

Politically the situation got dangerously out of hand because for a long time both the Americans and the top Vietnamese leaders failed to realize that they were faced with two separate sets of enemies in Vietnam and two different wars. The first enemy was the Viet Cong, which was fighting a shooting war. The second enemy was the extremist wing of the political Buddhists, who on some occasions fought a political war of such subtlety and complexity that their foes could hardly feel the knife penetrate at all, while on other occasions they fought with such ferocity that the dead were left in the streets with hatchets in their heads.

General Khanh, of course, was wary of Thich Tri Quang, the extremist leader, not just because of his demagogic powers but also because he assumed that this monk was a special favorite of the United States. After all, he had been given asylum at the United States embassy. And what Thich Tri Quang wanted, he (in Vietnamese eyes) more or less got. Was it strange that so many Vietnamese generals thought that Thich Tri Quang must have friends in high places in the United States?

Also General Khanh made the mistake of thinking that he could buy Thich Tri Quang's goodwill by doing his branch of Buddhism special favors.

Thich Tri Quang's climb to power—such power that he has vetoed appointments of Prime Ministers, emptied jails of arrested Communist agents, toppled governments, to name a few special feats of strength—came as a jolting surprise to Washington when it was finally realized that this militant monk was in effect subverting precisely the goal we were trying to achieve: a strong and stable political regime.

Like the Viet Cong soldiers who hide under the muddy waters of the canals, breathing through reeds, Thich Tri Quang prefers to operate under the surface. This may be one reason why most American newspaper readers have rarely heard of him. His baffling and slippery modes of operation are nonetheless no excuse for the incredible naïveté of the Americans toward him and his activities that prevailed well into 1965.

That Thich Tri Quang fooled us once is not surprising. After all, he left the U.S. embassy with a big smile of gratitude and professions that with Diem gone he would devote himself to religion. But by January, 1964, he was playing politics among the various groups organized in the new Buddhist institute formed the same month to bring together some fourteen Buddhist sects.

He failed in his effort to be elected director of the institute. He was defeated by his sometime friend and sometime enemy, Thich Tam Chau, a refugee from the North. But Thich Tri Quang quietly extended his power base. He did so in Central Vietnam through the National Salvation Councils organized by his admirer and personal physician, Dr. Le Khac Quyen. In Saigon Thich Tri Quang wielded power through the Buddhist youth groups, to whom he was a hero.

In his first months in office General Khanh, a Buddhist, was confident that he had the goodwill of this powerful monk. After all, the general's entire cabinet consisted almost entirely of Buddhists or Confucianists. His government had made handsome gifts to the new Buddhist institute, including more than an acre of land in the heart of Saigon, worth many million piastres. A new law promulgated in January gave Buddhists special privileges in the matter of buying property, privileges not extended to Cao Dai, Hao Hoa, Confucianists, Catholics, or any other religion.

Thus strongman Khanh was totally unprepared when Thich Tri Quang issued what amounted to a declaration of war on him. This occurred when Thich Tri Quang wrote a long signed article in April, 1964, in the Saigon daily *Tieng Vang* (Echo) charging that General Khanh's Buddhist-dominated government was persecuting Buddhists more than Diem ever had!

Was this for real?

The charge was wholly mendacious, of course, but Thich Tri Quang made it with the melodramatic flourishes of the true demagogue.

He ended the article with this rhetorical paragraph: "Alas! What policy are Buddhists living under now? What times are Buddhists living in now? Have the Buddhists poured out blood and tears for nine whole years and fought for four months that resounded around the world just *to have to live a more shameful, a more unjust life now* [italics mine]? Why does persecution and repression of Buddhists and their faith still go on? . . ."

At first the Americans could not bring themselves to take Thich Tri Quang seriously. At the State Department in Washington an information officer for Far Eastern affairs, when queried about Thich Tri Quang's accusations, could not comment because he had never heard of the monk! After investigation, the officer said the State Department felt sure Thich Tri Quang was misinformed and that everything would be straightened out when the accusations were investigated by the Khanh regime and disproved, or so it was hoped.

It was many months before the Americans were to realize that the accusations were deliberate—not accidental—lies.

CHAPTER 13

Reprise at the Pagodas

> As in the Ocean's midmost depth no
>   wave is born
> But all is still, so let the monk be
>   still, be
> Motionless, and nowhere should he swell.
> —Buddha

An obscure item in a Saigon newspaper in October, 1964, reported a statement by a highly respected Buddhist monk accusing the Communist Viet Cong of fraudulently operating under Buddhist colors and falsely using Buddhist insignia.

When I reached Saigon a few weeks later I hurried to the new Buddhist Institute to investigate for myself the monk's statement. If the press account were correct this would be the first time that a Buddhist monk in good standing had openly admitted infiltration and exploitation of his religion by Communists. The circumstantial evidence on this score was substantial but not dramatic or sharply enough in focus to convince broad segments of the American public. At home I had been frequently asked how it was possible for *Communists* to infiltrate a *religious order*, as if somehow the two were mutually exclusive in practical fact as well as in philosophical theory.

The value of the Buddhist monk's statement was that it explained in vivid detail just how effective the Communists can be as infiltrators. The statement, dated October 15, 1964, was written by Thich Huyen Quang, a secretary of the Unified Buddhist Church. It was all the more illuminating because it described specific events in the monk's own province of Phu Yen.

Thich Huyen Quang wrote:

On August 20 and 26 Communist Viet Cong forced people of four villages in Phu Yen to carry Buddhist flags and block with their own bodies the passage of M-113 armored personnel carriers of the Vietnamese army. On other occasions when Communist agents were arrested, the Viet Cong threatened Buddhist monks and compelled the pagodas to demand the release of the *Communists by insisting that they were Buddhists subjected to religious persecution* [italics mine].

In four villages occupied by the Viet Cong, the Communists outfitted known Viet Cong sympathizers in Buddhist robes and insisted that they be given refuge in the pagodas. If the senior monks in the pagodas refused their demand, the Communists took the monks away and put Viet Cong agents—dressed as monks—in their place.

On one occasion the Viet Cong themselves burned a historic pagoda, only recently renovated, and then forced local Buddhist leaders to call out the provincial Buddhist Association to complain about the "outrage" against Buddhists, which they blamed on Catholic government agents.

This remarkable statement by Thich Huyen Quang attracted almost no attention because it remained only a short time on the bulletin board of the new Buddhist Institute. It had been ripped down almost instantly by adherents of Thich Tri Quang, the Machiavellian leader of the Buddhist extremists. Its revelations were contrary to the propaganda line of the extremists denying any such infiltration.

Actually the brutal tricks described in the monk's statement were employed with suitable variations in the Communist penetration of all South Vietnamese religions. Indeed, in Hanoi there is an entire governmental department engaged in projects for penetrating South Vietnamese religions and ethnic minorities.

Father Cao Van Luan, former rector of Hué University, has cited chapter and verse to me about tactics used by the Communists to infiltrate the Catholics.

One Viet Cong document (captured in 1962) contained elaborate instructions to the would-be infiltrators of religious circles on the value of resorting, "when necessary, to strong denunciations of the Communists"—denunciations designed to camouflage their real identity and to establish the "anti-Communist" trustworthiness of the agents in question.

In the fall of 1964 speculation in Saigon centered on the degree to which the militant Thich Tri Quang, by now Vietnam's acknowledged specialist in masterminding government coups, was or was not actively collaborating with the Viet Cong. No Vietnamese or American could prove that he was a Communist or that his motives were pro-Communist. Proof, in the Occidental sense, presumably would require a plaintiff to produce an authenticated Communist-party card of membership, complete with photograph and fingerprints. But that Communist ends were being served by Buddhist-instigated street mobs and Buddhist-abetted intrigues among the military was undeniable.

I asked in a dispatch from Saigon of November, 1964: "Is a Vietnamese government of integrity and capability to be brought down once again by a numerically tiny minority of knife-wielding, rock-throwing hoodlums manipulated by Buddhist political priests of dubious purposes who use the privileged sanctuary of a few pagodas for instigating chaos?

"Is this the way to run a war—or even a capital city?"

The target of those autumn riots was Prime Minister Tran Van Huong, a Confucianist, a man of great force of character, shining honesty, and vast courage. He was more deeply respected by the diplomatic colony than any Vietnamese leader before or since. His government with but one exception was entirely made up of Buddhist, Confucianist, and Cao Daists—that is, non-Christians.

His crime? According to Thich Tri Quang and Thich Tam Chau (in this period the two rival monks had temporarily patched up their quarrels and were working together), Prime Minister Huong was "oppressing Buddhists" and followed "execrable" policies in ordering the police to break up the bloody street riots perpetrated by their followers.

But the charge of "oppressing Buddhists" was merely another ridiculous pretext for turmoil-making. Prime Minister Huong was no more guilty of *religious persecution* than had been General Khanh or President Diem.

The right to riot has never in history been equated with religious freedom, and yet this is what the monks in effect were proclaiming in public statements.

What they were demanding in private was more revealing of their true aims. It was no less than an end to the separation of pagoda and state; in the classic manner, what they had in mind was a feudal concept.

In an interview with me Prime Minister Huong said:

"This Thich Tri Quang and his faction want to create a state within a state. I have a complete dossier on their demands. They came into this office and demanded that 'their men' be given five key jobs, including that of Minister of the Interior. They demanded that the government give them important gifts of real estate. They demanded that the Buddhist Institute be given monopoly over certain forests so that they could go into the lumber business. They want to be given important licenses that will give them monopolies on imports from China. I have refused them all these things. I have also stated that there should be separation of church and state. And so this particular faction of Buddhists oppose me. But it is important to remember that the Buddhist Institute represents a tiny, if noisy, minority of the Buddhist faithful. This clique is dominated by men from Hanoi [Thich Tri Quang and Thich Tam Chau were both born north of the Seventeenth Parallel]. They are increasingly resented for their tactics here in the South."

Huong had been chosen Premier by the Vietnamese Military Council after serving as Saigon's mayor. He had startled the more staid Vietnamese as mayor by bicycling to and from work. He had been a schoolteacher and at one point taught French in Saigon University. His anti-Diem credentials were impeccable, for he had served a brief period in prison after issuing a stinging condemnation of the Diem regime in a manifesto published in 1961.

In a nation of men who have learned to bend, like bamboo, with the political winds, Premier Huong's candor and firmness were not only welcome but also astonishing. If discretion is the better part of valor, this valorous man was dangerously indiscreet.

He stated flatly that documentary evidence seized by his police showed that the Communists, in collaboration with certain members of the Buddhist Institute, had tried to turn street demonstrations into "armed insurrection."

"Had they succeeded," Huong said, "the Viet Cong would at this moment be running the country."

Evidence gathered by the authorities showed, the Premier said, that the riot-bent mobs streaming out of the Buddhist Institute compound have been "armed not only with knives and guns but grenades, including a type manufactured locally by the Viet Cong."

But, I asked, if there was evidence of collaboration between Thich Tri Quang and the Viet Cong, why wasn't the monk brought to trial for treason?

The Premier looked at his hands intently for what seemed at least a minute, marshaling his thoughts and searching for precise words. Then slowly he began: "Thich Tri Quang is very clever. One has to be very careful with him. He acts like a Communist. He talks like a Communist. The things he does help the Communists. But you Americans want absolute proof. And evidence is not the same as absolute proof. We can prove that Thich Tri Quang held a secret meeting with Viet Cong leaders near Cap Saint Jacques [November 1–4]. But Thich Tri Quang is capable of saying that he was down there trying to convert the Communists to Buddhism—and some people would believe him! He has convinced some of the more naïve of our young generals that he is merely trying to advance the cause of militant Buddhism. He intrigues very skillfully with the more ambitious young generals, setting one against the other and inciting them against me. Indeed, many Vietnamese generals court Thich Tri Quang's favors because they imagine him to have some special power over the Americans."

This was a point Premier Huong was anxious to drive home.

"Thich Tri Quang owes a great deal to the Americans," he said. "In 1963 in the drive against Diem, he fooled the Americans into thinking he could speak for a lot more Vietnamese than was the case. Thich Tri Quang's followers number no more then a few thousand and they are mostly Buddhist youth. But the mere fact that the American embassy convinced itself that his power was real gave him stature. Sometimes the Americans act as if Thich Tri Quang was a shadow government. Some of your officials are forever pressuring me into making concessions to him to gain his favor. The fact that one-sided concessions to Thich Tri Quang will only generate counterdemands from other groups seems to escape these Americans. Some at the embassy are disillusioned now with Thich Tri Quang but fear to say so out loud; they do not want to be called anti-Buddhist. Would they support me if I had Thich Tri Quang arrested on charges of treason? In any case, it is not just a simple matter of dealing with Thich Tri Quang. It is a matter of dealing with world opinion, the American embassy, and some Vietnamese generals who seek to enhance their position by gaining this monk's favor. He works in the shadows. He will not be easy to deal with."

In this period, when Huong stood firm against Thich Tri Quang, the world had become used to the sight of Saigon hovering between farce and tragedy. It had been doing so since the day in April, 1964, that Thich Tri Quang declared war on General Nguyen Khanh with his absurd charge that the general's Buddhist-dominated government was persecuting the Buddhists "even more than Diem."

Thich Tri Quang was an expert at tailoring his pretexts to suit the political season. He was something of a fashionable conspirator, keenly aware of shifting opinion in America and elsewhere and the outer limits of what was both credible and possible in Vietnam.

After the Bay of Tonkin incident of August, 1964, general Khanh persuaded the generals to give him emergency powers and to make him President. He argued that such authoritarian powers were essential to rule that anarchic country. Sick of the turmoil and ever-present threats of new coups, the U.S. embassy backed Khanh to the hilt in his effort to make himself a "strong man," in fact as well as in name.

But Thich Tri Quang saw Khanh's proclamation of emergency powers as the perfect pretext for unloosing the mobs. Buddhist street toughs concentrated on the charge that the Khanh regime had become "undemocratic." But the regime had never been "democratic." It had no electoral base. The concentration of power in Khanh's hands had but one defensible rationale: to provide him with the necessary authority to control his unruly country so that he could bring an end to the jockeying for power in Saigon and get on with fighting the war.

This goal was supported by the Catholics, Cao Dai, Hoa Hao, and moderate Buddhists. And when the minority of Buddhist extremists started preparations for anti-Khanh riots, alarm spread through these groups. They were fearful of any more "successes" for Thich Tri Quang because they deeply suspected him as a neutralist, at best, and a Viet Cong sympathizer at worst.

The anti-Communists ordered counterdemonstrations.

The inevitable clash between the demonstrators was diabolically exploited by the Viet Cong and the results added up to a shameless descent into violence and brutality.

At one point a jeep with broadcasting equipment sped up to a Catholic school to announce repeatedly that students of a nearby Buddhist school were "preparing to attack you." Then the jeep roared over to the Buddhist school to announce that the "Catholics are preparing to attack you." Neither group was in fact planning anything—until the jeeps appeared. When the students rushed into the streets to what they imagined was their own defense, anarchy and agony gripped the city.

Even battle-hardened war correspondents were appalled at the nightmare of blood and cruelty.

A Japanese photographer told me of his frustration at seeing truckloads of police look the other way when a captured youth presumed to be Catholic was led toward the central market. There a mob of hooligans, who may or may not have been Buddhists, rushed the prisoner. A ten-year-old boy plunged a dagger into the prisoner's thigh. The victim tried to run away but was stopped before he went twenty steps. A bicycle was thrown on top of him and the mob jumped up and down on it. Finally the victim struggled up, dragging a broken leg behind him, but was cut down again and clubbed to death.

According to the Japanese eyewitness, cruelty was rampant and was inflicted indiscriminately by the swarming mobs. In another incident a mob of suspected Catholics cornered a presumed Buddhist. At the command of a known professional agitator, the mob pulled out wicked-looking sharpened sticks and started gouging the prisoner. His agony was terminated when a twelve-year-old boy split open his head with a hatchet. And that is how he was found by his parents, body sprawled in a pool of blood, the hatchet still lodged in his skull.

The exact composition of the mobs could not be accurately determined. A Vietnamese-speaking Filipino reporter told me, "It is wrong to say this was a Catholic-Buddhist battle. It was a political battle. Several times Viet Cong agents worked up a mob to attack a youngster by shouting, 'This boy is the son of the cruelest oppressor in Vietnam.' Often the victim was not a Catholic at all but a non-Christian like the rest."

From all the evidence, Communist agents did indeed handle much of the riot choreography. Many mobs moved in military formation, signaling one another by blowing whistles and beating drums.

Why didn't the police and army intervene?

First, for three gory days they had orders not to. Later General Khanh explained this seemingly callous disregard for life and property by saying that he hoped to win the favor of the Americans with a display of his determination not to "repress" demonstrations. He intended at the same time to prove to the Buddhists that he was "different from Diem." During this *"laissez faire"* period, therefore, troops and police were idle bystanders, accessories by default to bloodshed and murder.

By the time this interlude of anarchy and grief had ended in Saigon and the port city of Danang in the North, perhaps one hundred Vietnamese were dead or wounded. General Khanh's attempts at "liberality" had been translated into a license to murder and commit arson and other more devious crimes. His refusal to order the authorities to repress the street mobs brought a death toll that made many a Saigonais long for the good old authoritarian days when Diem's police kept control of the streets and the only fatalities were those monks who took their own lives.

But in August, 1964, it was not the riots that caused the general to step out of power. For Khanh finally came to his senses, faced up to his responsibilities, and gave orders that police bring the streets under control. He relinquished his emergency Presidential powers and political authority itself as the result of a macabre ultimatum delivered to Saigon military headquarters on the evening of August 26.

The bearers of the ultimatum were Thich Tam Chau and Thich Tri Quang. The two monks were received at headquarters by Colonel Pham Ngoc Thao, then press aide to General Khanh. They brought with them the text of a radio address that Thich Tri Quang demanded that General Khanh must deliver over Saigon radio before morning. The speech, as prepared by the monks, contained the announcement that General Khanh would retire from the political scene to make way for civilian rule (a demand that might at first glance seem sensible, until it is remembered that within a few months the same two monks intrigued with military man Khanh to get rid of the Prime Minister Huong's *civilian* rule).

After two hours of conversation with Thich Tri Quang and Thich Tam Chau, General Khanh capitulated. It was now one A.M., but even so he directed Colonel Thao to telephone Ambassador Taylor and Deputy Ambassador Johnson and ask them to come down to military headquarters for an emergency discussion.

When Colonel Thao protested such an unconditional surrender to the two Buddhist leaders, General Khanh replied: "I had no alternative. They told me that if I did not act on their demands they would have two monks burn themselves to death before noon tomorrow."

General Khanh plainly feared that a revival of the suicides—the self-immolations that had scorched international headlines—would lead to a repetition of the press campaign that had made Ngo Dinh Diem the object of revulsion in much of the world.

When Ambassadors Taylor and Johnson learned of the suicide threats in their post-midnight rendezvous with Khanh, they both counseled against capitulation to Buddhist blackmail, but to no avail. At three A.M. Khanh went on the air to announce that he would relinquish the powers that nearly everybody agreed were necessary to hold the nation together.

It was plain that what Vietnam needed then, and now, was a strong man who would exercise more power—not less—in forcing the squabbling parochial national factions into line.

Americans ought to be reminded that our own democracy was not preserved in times of great national crisis without painful restrictions of freedom. Abraham Lincoln put twelve thousand political prisoners in jail during the Civil War. It is utterly hypocritical for Washington to give lip service to the notion that Vietnam's problems can be solved by more democracy or turning the country over to "civilian rule" when the inescapable truth is that the military represents the only cohesive source of power, the only viable entity, left in Vietnam. It had been obvious since the death of Diem that what Vietnam needed was a tough but fair military dictator, benevolent enough to avoid the cruel excesses of power, who would brook no opposition to what was necessary to win the war.

Crosby Noyes, the astute foreign editor of the Washington *Evening Star,* summarized the problem in writing that one of the troubles with the war in Vietnam was that "there is no nation to fight it."

"In this unhappy situation," Noyes wrote, "there is one quite obvious remedy. Much as the Americans hate to face the fact, the only practical way of making a non-nation function with reasonable order and efficiency is to impose order through a government that is strong enough, and where necessary, ruthless enough, to keep the warring factions and self-serving pressure groups in line. Until November 1963, Vietnam had such a government. No doubt, in certain respects, the regime of Ngo Dinh Diem was less than admirable by Western Democratic standards. No doubt it was unpopular with certain elements of the population and, since its leaders were predominantly Catholic, notably unpopular with the militant minority of Buddhists. Yet with all their faults, Diem and Nhu ran the war effort as it has not been run since last November 1. . . ."

In August, 1964, Thich Tri Quang and Thich Tam Chau successfully forced General Khanh to relinquish (ostensibly at least) political power and return to his post of commander-in-chief of the armed forces. His retreat marked the first time since the death of Diem that the threat of suicide by fire had served as a lever of political power.

Although the bloodshed in Saigon and Danang got the headlines, it is possible that history will record that Thich Tri Quang's extremists did their most lasting damage in the countryside.

Operating from the Tu Dam Pagoda at Hué, Thich Tri Quang formed the so-called "National Salvation Councils," which had an ominous predilection for taking vigilante action against proven anti-Communists.

Thich Tri Quang's maneuvers in 1964 were clearly aimed at destroying the will of the regularly constituted authorities to resist the Viet Cong. The interference of the Buddhist extremists in police and army attempts to control the Viet Cong reached alarming proportions in Central Vietnam.

In the fall of 1964 a distinguished foreign observer wrote this account of what went on:

If a Communist agent who is arrested in Central Vietnam claims that he is a Buddhist being persecuted, he is likely to be released. The authorities will apologize to the local Buddhist Association. The official who made the arrest will be reprimanded, maybe dismissed. This has happened often enough in some provinces since last November 1 to make police and military fearful to take action against suspected Viet Cong Communist collaborators. They know that if they do, the provincial Buddhist Association may shoot off a telegram to the Unified Buddhist Church in Saigon. Buddhist leaders will complain to the government. A couple of Saigon daily papers will run sensational stories about "repression of Buddhists," and the Saigon government usually surrenders to the pressure. For example, in Duy Xuyen district [near the Seventeenth Parallel], which is heavily infiltrated by Communists, 400 persons were held between July 20 and August 5 [1964] for investigation and re-education. This timing has significance because usually on July 22 [the anniversary of the Geneva accords] the Viet Cong tried to stage maximum trouble. Of the four hundred put in the re-education camp, only *ninety* were Buddhists, *forty* were Catholics and the *rest* were simple Ancestor Worshippers. But the provincial Buddhist Association claimed that *all* were Buddhists and they were being persecuted for their religion. At Thich Tri Quang's demand, Khanh (who was still premier and still under the illusion he could appease this monk) fired the district chief and the division commander. General Khanh even made a special trip to Duy Xuyen on August 9 to express regrets and donate 50,000 piastres to "victims of persecution." He did so despite the fact that the investigations at the re-education camp brought information as to the whereabouts of *six Viet Cong arms caches*.

Additionally, Thich Tri Quang's national-salvation councils spread much confusion and fear in the areas around Hué by taking the law into their own hands, threatening district leaders (especially those of the Catholic faith) and sometimes forcing them to flee for their lives. Thich Tri Quang's Buddhist youth once kept a Catholic lieutenant imprisoned in a movie theater for four days on charges of having participated in the roundup of the Viet Cong suspects in Duy Xuyen district.

What was the American reaction to this Buddhist campaign of terror and turmoil that plainly served the ends of the Viet Cong?

The United States was in a painful dilemma, and this was especially true while Henry Cabot Lodge* was serving his initial tour as ambassador (August, 1963–July, 1964). How could Lodge admit that Thich Tri Quang was the villain of the piece (if war and political stability mattered) when he had given him asylum for two months in the U.S. embassy? Indeed, in Saigon there was for all too long a widespread impression that Thich Tri Quang was a hero of sorts to the Americans, an impression that Thich Tri Quang skillfully fostered. Some of the young foreign-service officers at the embassy were very taken—and taken in—by this monk. Several specialists in the Vietnamese language had reported (incredible as it may seem) that Thich Tri Quang was "friendly to Americans and our purposes," and they had a natural reluctance to admit that their original estimate (made during his two months in the embassy in 1963) may have been far wide of the mark. History is a chronicle of the compounded mistakes of proud specialists and experts.

In any case, the United States embassy, which during the summer and fall of 1963 had been moralizing at every turn about Diem's arbitrary ways, maintained a significant silence about the witch hunts conducted in the post-Diem era. The shock to the Vietnamese body politic had been severe enough when the successive military juntas turned the bureaucracy upside down with massive firings and hirings.

---

* Lodge's close relationship with the radical Buddhists is among the reasons that his reappointment in July, 1965, was controversial and initially caused dismay among strong anti-Communist groups such as the Catholics, Hoa Hao, and Cao Dai.

Then came the Buddhist drive to banish and purge all "Diemist" officials. In the reign of terror that ensued, thousands of Vietnamese anti-Communists were purged, jailed, and even executed for having done nothing more than obey the legitimate orders of their legitimate government.

U.S. silence about these cruel witch hunts did not raise our moral stature in the minds of thinking Vietnamese. What is worse, our silence was taken in some quarters as acquiescence and thus encouraged the instigators of the witch hunts.

As of this writing the United States has remained totally silent concerning the arrests of professors, officials, and students, all staunch anti-Communists, who have been held without trial for nearly two years. When the reign of terror was at its peak, in mid-1964, this incredible double standard did much to expedite the spiraling decline of law and order.

Why did the United States look the other way at the height of these assaults upon justice?

Did the United States have a guilt psychology? Having signaled the downfall of Diem, did the United States feel unable to protest the persecution of those who served him in the anti-Communist struggle?

With regard to the Buddhist extremists the first sign of official U.S. anxiety came after Ambassador Maxwell Taylor arrived in Saigon in July, 1964. After taking a hard look around, Taylor remarked that Thich Tri Quang was "a dubious character" and might have ambitions to be the "Makarios of Southeast Asia."

The eye-opener for the Americans should have come in late summer of 1964, when Thich Tri Quang began attacking the United States openly and viciously. In the Buddhist journal *Hai Trieu Am* (Voice of the Ocean Tide) Thich Tri Quang accused the United States of stirring up religious feelings in the northern city of Danang. It was the United States, therefore, Tri Quang maintained, that was responsible for the "shocking atrocities" there. He was referring to the burning of a Catholic village by mobs claiming to be Buddhists. During the riots at least eight Catholics, including two children, and one Buddhist lost their lives by beheadings, beatings, and stranglings. Three of these had been dragged in desperately wounded condition from the recovery room of the American-controlled hospital and stabbed to death in the street outside.

But Thich Tri Quang tried to place the blame on the Americans, asserting that "for ages past, before the Americans arrived here, Buddhists never destroyed or burned any houses." The Buddhist weekly also accused the Voice of America and American newspapers of stirring up religious trouble throughout Vietnam. It said there would not have been violence in the village outside Danang if American servicemen had not fired shots into the air when mobs tried to swarm into their billets inside the city.

In any case, Buddhist charges that the United States fostered religious hostility were a blatant contradiction of America's immediate objectives—political stability and an end to turmoil in the streets.

Indeed Thich Tri Quang's accusations were so mendacious and malicious, it seemed to me, as to raise doubts about the truthfulness of his earlier utterances, starting with the campaign against Diem and ending with his successful efforts to overthrow General Khanh and Premier Huong.

In Saigon a particularly frustrating incident in the late summer of 1964 convinced the U.S. military side of the mission that the Buddhist extremists were playing into the hands of the Viet Cong, even though some diplomats (especially those who had championed Thich Tri Quang a year earlier) remained of two minds.

The incident was connected with the U.S.-Vietnamese project Hoc Tap, designed to concentrate pacification efforts in the province immediately around Saigon, where an all-out effort to root out the Viet Cong was planned.

General William C. Westmoreland, who had taken over from General Harkins in early summer, reasoned that the best place to start flushing out the Viet Cong was in Saigon itself. The Vietnamese authorities had knowledge of the whereabouts of twenty-five key Viet Cong agents within the city's perimeter. But the Vietnamese police were so demoralized by repeated purges of their ranks that they had been quite literally afraid to take the responsibility of apprehending the Viet Cong. General Westmoreland overcame this reluctance by inducing General Khanh (still acting as Premier) to approve the project. Further, he had U.S. police experts work hand in glove with the Vietnamese authorities in building up the dossiers that would justify the seizure and arrest of the Viet Cong agents.

"This way," a U.S. official explained, "we tried to arrange things so that if anything went wrong, the Vietnamese could blame the Americans. They wouldn't have to risk their own political hides."

The police work was skillful and all twenty-five Viet Cong were duly picked up in coordinated raids throughout Saigon. General Westmoreland was gratified that a good beginning had been made on Operation Hoc Tap. His gratification lasted less than twenty-four hours, however. The day after the raids, he was flabbergasted to hear that all the Viet Cong agents had been released. From his shadowy command post, Thich Tri Quang had declared that the arrest of the Viet Cong agents represented "persecution of Buddhism." He threatened to start trouble unless they were released. The simple if alarming fact of the matter was that General Khanh feared Thich Tri Quang's trouble-making more than the Viet Cong agents.

It was a situation at once ludicrous and intolerable. U.S. officials were so dismayed that when Premier Huong took over the reins of government from Khanh (in October, 1964) and revealed his tough-mindedness in declining to bow to such Buddhist blackmail, some hope and encouragement seeped into the American establishment in Saigon. Thich Tri Quang, however, was infuriated and retaliated with a second round of post-Diem street riots.

At this point anti-Americanism was openly a part of the political game being played by Thich Tri Quang and his adherents. Not even American correspondents, once the heroes of the riot-prone Buddhists, were immune to harassments, both small (like being spat upon) and serious (like being robbed of wallets and cameras).

Explaining this hostility, General Khanh perceptively observed, "Those Buddhist demonstrators no longer have the American press on their side."

On my visit in November, 1964 (my second since the overthrow of Diem), I saw other signs of the erosion of Thich Tri Quang's position, notably in the growing opposition to his tactics within the ranks of his own coreligionists.

Most significant to me was the defection of the Xa Loi Pagoda. The Buddhist leaders at this pagoda expressed strong disapproval of the violence and intrigue of the extremists. Indeed, both Thich Tri Quang and Thich Tam Chau had been expelled from the Xa Loi Pagoda by its Buddhist congregation, led by Dr. Mai Tho Truyen, the head of Saigon's Buddhist Laymen's Association. This expulsion was a historic event because it was the Xa Loi that had been Thich Tri Quang's command post in the 1963 campaign against Diem. A year later he was specifically forbidden to set foot in the Xa Loi.

It was a strange experience to revisit the Xa Loi Pagoda after the expulsion of the extremists. During the 1963 Buddhist revolt the Xa Loi had been the scene of furious secular activity and much violence. On the pagoda steps, as one instance of the violence, a young Buddhist girl had sought to hack off her arm in a febrile and inspired act of protest. As the command post of the revolt, the Xa Loi telephone switchboard had served like lanterns in the church belfry of an earlier day to tip off the world, through calls to the press, about imminent suicides by fire. Its mimeograph machines had spewed out potent antigovernment propaganda. A year later all the trappings of a riot headquarters and other earthly pursuits were gone. The Xa Loi was once again a haven of serene meditation. The sound of religious chanting soothed the spirit, contrasting sharply with the previous year, when ceremonies were drowned out by antigovernment harangues shouted by hoarse-voiced monks speaking through rasping loudspeakers.

The expulsion from the Xa Loi was not a physical inconvenience to Thich Tri Quang because the Buddhist extremists were by now ensconced in the pagoda of the new Buddhist Institute, located about five miles distant from the Xa Loi and built on government-donated acreage. But the fact that Buddhist leaders of the Xa Loi were literally not on speaking terms with Thich Tri Quang's extremists was of major importance. The fissure helped to expose the phoniness of Thich Tri Quang's claim to speak for all Buddhists of Vietnam.

The deceitfulness of this claim was evident to those who bothered to contact Buddhists in the countryside. And the split with the Xa Loi dramatized the point. Dr. Truyen was known in Saigon to have an important following among the moderate (nonviolent) Buddhists in

Saigon and the surrounding Mekong delta. After Thich Tri Quang's expulsion from the Xa Loi the militant monk could not claim with any conviction to speak for these southern Buddhists who inhabited the most populous part of the country.

At the Xa Loi a senior monk said of the ouster of Thich Tri Quang: "We feel that he is a traitor to Buddhism. If the Americans knew anything about Buddhism they would not be fooled into thinking that this man has anything to do with our religion. The youngsters that hero-worship Thich Tri Quang are poor innocents who don't know what they are doing. They are being used."

What, I asked, did the monk mean exactly by "traitor to Buddhism"?

"There are many reasons for saying that," he replied. "The lord Buddha preached against hatred. Buddha said: 'Hatred does not cease by hatred. Hatred ceases by love. This is the eternal law. Even though others do not understand the folly of conflict, let us avoid it.' But Thich Tri Quang makes a business of stirring up hatred at a time when we should be binding up wounds instead of creating new wounds. Thich Tri Quang has started a hate campaign against Catholics and Diemists. But Buddhists have always gotten along with other religions. Buddha himself fraternized with persons of different beliefs. Buddha never demanded blind acceptance of his teachings and never condemned those of others. Buddha said: 'O monks, do not accept even my own words out of respect for me. You must examine them on the touchstone of your reason, as the goldsmith tests the purity of his gold by putting it on a fire.' Thich Tri Quang's campaigns of hatred are against the law of Buddha. As to Diemists, every educated Vietnamese served President Diem in one way or another. Thich Tri Quang himself was the recipient of favors from Ngo Dinh Can [Diem's brother], who gave money for the Tu Dam Pagoda. It is hypocritical to call others Diemists and exempt himself.

"Buddha also taught that truth is a supreme virtue. But Thich Tri Quang has spread slanders as widely as he has spread hatred. If he were some ignorant layman, it might be different. Thich Tri Quang has a brilliant mind. He knows that he is acting contrary to Buddha's laws. So we are suspicious."

"Why, in light of all this," I asked, "did you ask me not to quote you or use your name? Aren't the members of the Xa Loi anxious for the American public to know the truth?"

"There is reason to fear Thich Tri Quang," the monk replied. "He has sent his young Buddhists around to beat up several of us who opposed him. And so our superior has forbidden us to take the risk of incurring his anger. But one day everyone will perceive the truth. He has alienated many Buddhists already."

It was certainly true that at this juncture Saigon was thoroughly jaded and annoyed with the stage-managed riots of the Buddhist extremists.

I too soon began to find them boring. Tactics had changed very little since the anti-Diem riots. I even recognized in the crowds some of the same professional agitators of the previous year and found myself waving in recognition (only one waved back). The demonstrating "students" also included many who had seen thirty years of age many moons ago.

The true artists in the business of Vietnamese riot-making are distinguished by their talent for producing reasonably authentic martyrs. But even artists make mistakes, and during my second riot season a colossal one was made.

The martyrdom act in question opened in front of the Gia Long Palace, where the antigovernment demonstrators brought with them two students lying on stretchers and heavily bandaged from top to toe to bear out the assertion that they were critically wounded. Each stretcher was borne by four frail, beautiful Saigon girls, who, weeping tears of compassion, gently placed the stretchers on the ground in front of the mob that was threatening to storm the palace.

Unfortunately, when a tear-gas bomb went off in the vicinity, the beautiful stretcher-bearers were unnerved and dashed away from their wounded charges. This was not as heartless as it sounds, because lo and behold, the "critically wounded" students leaped from their stretchers and not only managed to sprint away at top speed but also *easily overtook and passed their girl bearers.*

I will say this for the "student" and "Buddhist" mobs of that era. They never attacked unless the odds were three hundred to one for their side. Another requirement was that the individual they pick on be unarmed.

For instance, one day near the railway station I watched four hundred student "rioters" close in on a thin, white-uniformed policeman. The toughness of these Saigon police can be deduced from the fact that they are whimsically referred to by the street hooligans as "white mice."

The "students" began by jostling this poor "white mouse" of a policeman. Then they took off his cap and played catch with it. Then they knocked him down and began to stomp on him. At this point I called to an American photographer to hurry over and watch the "fun." The approach of the camera is, I am convinced, what saved that poor "white mouse" from being killed.

The contrast between the words and the deeds of the Buddhist extremists would have been laughable except for the evil consequences of the deceptions they practiced. At the Buddhist Institute Thich Tri Quang and Thich Tam Chau would issue statements disclaiming any responsibility for the riots, then in the same paragraph denounce the Huong government for repressing the rioters.

When foreign correspondents visited the Buddhist Institute, curiously no attempt was made to hide the bustle of activity connected with preparation for the next day's riot. One day, after interviewing a Buddhist spokesman, four Americans watched two large vans drive into the yards of the Buddhist Institute, where monks joined in unloading masses of banners and placards that appeared in the demonstration of the following day. In another corner of the yard Buddhist youths were seen sharpening the ends of long, wicked-looking sticks.

Many of the riots took place in the vicinity of the Buddhist Institute, whose walled compound served as a kind of privileged sanctuary for the rioters. I know most Americans will think I am being frivolous when I say that in order to avoid wasting time I got into the habit of telephoning the Buddhist Institute each morning to learn the time and place of the riot for the day and was politely provided with the information as if I had called to ask when I could attend church services. But it's true.

Riots were easy to arrange, and they followed a familiar pattern. The Buddhist Institute would let it be known that a protest demonstration was to be held. Since these were against the law, police would be dispatched to the general area. They would be attacked by a hail of rocks and then rushed—and sometimes overwhelmed—by the mob. Inevitably troops and tear gas would have to be called to the rescue.

In one riot I witnessed two plastic Viet Cong-made grenades being thrown from a roof, injuring a dozen persons and causing the imposition of martial law and a strict curfew. For a brief time order prevailed in the streets.

The government's action to curb violence was seized upon by the Buddhist Institute to issue long, impassioned denunciations of the "brutal dictatorship" of Premier Huong. Some newspapers echoed the Buddhist charges. The Saigon press—a total of fifty-six different newspapers—was largely bought and paid for by various special-interest groups, very much like the French press before World War II. In point of fact, after many years of riot-watching in many different parts of the world, I will attest that the Vietnamese police and military were incredibly forbearing; they endured with stoical restraint the most outrageous provocations, including vicious assaults by the gangs armed with stones and chunks of metal.

"It is all done for the benefit of American television," said a concierge of the Caravelle Hotel as I returned hot and weary from a day of riot-watching. "The American people will get the wrong idea of the Vietnamese people. Those rioters don't represent anybody. You Americans pay too much attention to the violence perpetrated by a few thousand people. Most of us don't even know—and don't care—that a riot is going on until we read about it in the papers."

And it is true that the riots had more impact in world headlines than on life in Saigon.

Landing in Hong Kong one morning, I was greeted with bold headlines shouting: "Saigon riots rock Huong government." I had covered that riot the day before, and all it had rocked was about four square blocks around the Buddhist Institute. Traffic in that part of town had to be detoured. Perhaps one thousand persons were involved. The rest of Saigon went blithely about its business as usual.

The utterly artificial nature of these "riots" was brought home to me one day after quiet and order had been restored to the streets near the Buddhist Institute. I stood in the midst of the rock-strewn street talking to a young tough about what was going to happen next. His "rioters," perhaps a hundred strong, were lined up outside the Buddhist Institute gate. Opposite them were several scores of paratroopers who had been rushed to the scene. Suddenly two cameramen—one European, one Vietnamese—dashed up. They had missed the riot and wanted to recoup. One shouted, "God-dammit, look fierce—throw something!" The rioters obliged. Rocks began to fly at the paratroopers. A short distance down the street, other rioters, unaware that this was a staged performance for the cameras, promptly went into action. All hell broke loose within seconds, forcing the troops to use tear gas to quell an altogether senseless outburst started by the zeal of two professional cameramen.

In January, 1965, relations between the United States and the Buddhist extremists appeared to reach rock bottom.

According to a British diplomat: "The neutralist and pro-Communist factions were feeling very cocky. The Pleiku incident [attack on the American compound] had not yet occurred. Nobody expected the decision to bomb the North. Thich Tri Quang thought that this was the moment to build up neutralist pressure and drive the Americans into a mood of exasperation and humiliation that would cause you to get out. He said as much to one of our men [presumably a British secret agent], who has an anti-American cover."

Early in January a statement from the Buddhist Institute derided American aid as merely "the defecation of capitalism." Thich Tri Quang's Buddhist toughs simultaneously opened a house-to-house campaign in the effort to enlist Vietnamese by word of mouth in a Yankee-Go-Home-movement. They vilified the Americans as "enemies" and "oppressors" of the Vietnamese people.

In mid-month a crowd led by three hundred yellow-robed monks marched on the U.S. embassy cursing and shouting slogans against the "American-Huong dictatorship." Four blocks away hooligans commanded by four monks blaring orders over battery-powered bullhorns assaulted the United States Information Agency, smashing its glass doors and windows.

During these events monks and nuns "fainted" repeatedly before the newsreel cameras, only to sprint nimbly away when tear gas was fired in their direction. One monk "stabbed" himself, only his body bore no wounds when he was taken to the hospital.

Sixty of the most violent monks were jailed. Not so curiously, not a single one of them could recite a single Buddhist saying. This was so brazen a masquerade that the Vietnamese authorities were emboldened to issue warnings about Viet Cong agents using holy robes to disguise their subversive purposes.

The anti-American outburst in the northern city of Hué was even more violent than that in Saigon. In that former imperial capital some four thousand students and hoodlums sacked the two-story U.S.I.A. headquarters, splintering furniture and bookshelves. Then they burned five thousand books.

Hong Van Giau, the head of the Hué Buddhist Student Association, later explained in a remarkable interview with the Washington *Post* that the decision to attack the library had been taken after consultation with Thich Tri Quang and was really quite "moderate" because no Americans had been physically hurt. The "only damage," he said, was to property.

"When Thich Tri Quang is at the Tu Dam Pagoda at Hué," Giau was quoted as saying, "we meet almost daily to talk over plans. We meet together with the Buddhist hierarchy, and after a common agreement has been achieved, *we then make a decision about force*; we could not do it alone because if you cannot reach joint agreement, *you cannot agitate other groups* [italics mine]."

The arrogance and conceit of the radical Buddhists were no better illustrated than by a communiqué that appeared in January on the bulletin board of the Buddhist Institute pagoda. In this communiqué the Buddhist Institute boasted that as a result of its "work" at least two thousand officers of the Vietnamese army would lay down their arms and refuse to fight if Thich Tri Quang and Thich Tam Chau ordered them to do so.

How had the Buddhists infiltrated the Vietnamese army?

The process dated back to the summer of 1964, when General Khanh was still under the illusion that he could appease his most vocal tormenter—Thich Tri Quang—by yielding to his demands. One of these demands was for the right to assign Buddhist chaplains to every army unit.

Three-man Buddhist-chaplain teams (in reality political cells) were soon thereafter attached to the army. The Buddhist chaplains could hardly wait to show their hand and almost at once started distributing tracts telling soldiers that they need not obey their officers if they felt they were acting in the interests of "colonialist Americans" or if they were "unfaithful to the Buddhist cause." Several Vietnamese army commanders became so irate that they expelled the politicking chaplains. Thich Tri Quang's claims of having subverted four regiments were no doubt exaggerated. Still, it was another example of the capacity of this militant minority to make trouble out of all proportion to its true importance in the Vietnamese scheme of things.

By the end of January the majority of the U.S. mission were of the opinion that a showdown between the government and the Buddhist extremists was in order. Premier Huong was advised that the United States would stand behind him totally in resisting Buddhist pressures, the latest being a widely advertised fast to the death on which Thich Tri Quang and Thich Tam Chau had ostentatiously embarked at the Buddhist Institute.

Even *before* the fast had started the Buddhist Institute issued an accusing communiqué stating, "The American ambassador and his lackey [Prime Minister Huong] want to let Buddhist leaders die off and Vietnamese Buddhism perish. Taylor must bear responsibility for the oppression, terrorism, and cruelty to Buddhism that has never been seen before." (Thus Taylor, by the Buddhist sliding scale, was also more of a monster than Diem!)

The challenge was clear. In the previous August Thich Tri Quang and Thich Tam Chau had forced General Khanh to surrender power by threatening him with two suicides by fire, and he preferred to step down rather than risk the grisly incident and its consequences.

Now the two monks were trying to force the Americans and Huong to do their bidding by threatening their own deaths by starvation.

It seems quite appropriate to ask how any country can be sensibly run if its leaders bow to this kind of political blackmail from persons without either the responsibility or the right to speak for any but a handful of their own followers. Blackmail is an endless, insidious process—and unlimited in its power to intimidate and frighten—if responsible authorities refuse to stand against it.

Huong understood this but was without the power to sustain a long resistance against the blackmailers unless the army leaders supported him. The policy of abdication of responsibility displayed by Khanh in August was not followed by Huong: the Prime Minister courageously ordered his police and troops to keep order and minimize turbulence, and they succeeded admirably, considering the extent of provocation. The riots, which dwindled to nothing during the period of martial law in December, could not have overthrown Huong of themselves any more than the riots at the University of California at Berkeley at the same time could have toppled Governor Earl Brown. These street disorders and the Buddhist hunger strike were decisive only in that they served as the pretext for General Khanh to throw out Huong and once again seize power for himself and the Armed Forces Council. An opportunist of some patience and wile, General Khanh had long awaited his chance to reenter the political arena, and he thought that by tossing Huong's scalp to the Buddhists he would achieve his ambitions. He took the precaution (he thought) of obtaining a written agreement from Thich Tri Quang and Thich Tam Chau promising they would go into exile if he would act to dispose of the Huong regime and thus spare them the embarrassment created by their pledge to starve themselves to death if it were not overturned.

As soon as Huong had been done in, however, the two monks boldly reneged on their bargain. "Khanh cannot rule because he is too bad a man," said Thich Tri Quang, totally ungrateful for the gift of Huong's ouster. And a month later the young Turks of the Armed Forces Council agreed and sent Khanh into humiliating exile as a roving ambassador temporarily assigned to the United Nations in New York. He was the twentieth general officer so banished from his native land.

The measure of Thich Tri Quang's self-confident mood in the winter of 1965 was the fact that he hesitated less and less to show his true colors. In interviews with the Hong Kong *Standard* and *Le Monde* of Paris, he revealed that he favored a neutralized solution for South Vietnam. Now, this may have been all right for a De Gaulle to advocate, but it was an advocacy that had been considered treasonous in South Vietnam.

The surfacing of his true feelings had its disadvantages because it alarmed many experienced and influential correspondents who had originally put Thich Tri Quang down as a trouble maker but now suspected something more sinister.

In late January Keyes Beech of the Chicago *Daily News* wrote from Saigon:

The United States is fighting a two-front war in Vietnam—one against the Communists and another against the Buddhists.

That statement must be immediately qualified, however. The war may really be a one-front affair after all, for Buddhists and Communist objectives dovetail at least eighty per cent of the time.

Of the five governments South Vietnam has had in the last fourteen months, the Buddhists have overthrown every one that showed some promise of coping with the war against the Communists.

If a Communist spokesman can be believed, the Communists have been manipulating South Vietnamese Buddhists and students ever since the spring of 1963 at the birth of the movement that overthrew the Diem regime.

Wilfred Burchett, Australian-born Communist sympathizer and newspaper correspondent, told me as much last November in the neutralist capital of Phnom Penh. Burchett said the anti-Diem rioting was only a foretaste of what was to come. Events have enhanced his reputation as a prophet. . . .

In February, 1965, Richard Critchfield, the distinguished Asian correspondent of the Washington *Evening Star,* reported that "many diplomatic observers in Saigon have long been convinced that Tri Quang was an instrument of the Communist policy to end American influence in Vietnam in circumstances that would leave little possibility of salvaging the Western position anywhere in Asia."

The drama of the Buddhist extremists took some strange turns in the winter, spring, and summer of 1965.

By February Dr. Phan Huy Quat, a physician and long-time member of the Saigon establishment, had been named Prime Minister. The selection was made by the Armed Forces Council at the specific demand of Thich Tri Quang. With "his man" at the helm, Thich Tri Quang now preferred to work mainly behind the scenes. In this period the militant monk abandoned the direct-action methods of riot and arson and sought to bring down his various quarry via pressure exerted through the Prime Minister.

His prime target in the spring of 1965 was Brigadier General Pham Van Dong, 46, a solidly professional and pro-American combat veteran who served as mayor of Saigon during the worst of the Buddhist-inspired violence. General Dong was one of the few officials who consistently declined to fold up in the face of Buddhist blackmail and threats of suicides by burnings. In April Premier Quat caved in under Tri Quang's pressures and fired Dong.

Thich Tri Quang often accomplished his purge missions through the intervention of his principal disciple in the armed forces, General Nguyen Chanh Thi, a flamboyant, unstable leader of the First Corps area, in which Hué, the monk's headquarters, is located.

Acting on Thich Tri Quang's "suggestions," General Thi managed to purge many staunch anti-Communists from key posts and to replace them with Thich Tri Quang favorites. In the course of two months, Thi's men were placed in charge of the pivotal Twenty-fifth, Ninth, and First divisions in the Mekong delta. He also named the head of the thirty-thousand-man national police force and the internal-security apparatus.

At the same time, Thich Tri Quang organized in both Saigon and Hué a subrosa peace movement. Training centers were set up to instruct and equip monks for the campaign of propagandizing the countryside with demands for immediate peace.

In April a sixteen-year-old novice monk burned himself to death at the Buddhist Institute, leaving behind a note demanding "peace in Vietnam." The next day a twenty-five-year-old nun tried to do the same but was stopped by a relative. Such burnings were regarded as having the blessing of Thich Tri Quang.

Nonetheless, the U.S. embassy remained reluctant to recognize, publicly at any rate, the potent poison spread inside the Vietnamese body politic by the Buddhist minority exerting pressure directly on Premier Quat.

Correspondent Richard Critchfield of the Washington *Evening Star* wrote from Saigon in this connection, "Despite this accumulating evidence, the United States is reluctant to admit that the extremist Buddhist minority is today serving as an alarmingly effective fifth column in undermining the anti-Communist struggle in South Vietnam. Ambassador Maxwell Taylor's inherent soldierly distaste for Vietnam's often seamy political intrigue coupled with his opposition to undercover counter-subversion operations has left the United States virtually defenseless in combating Buddhist infiltration here.

"One senior anti-Communist Vietnamese military leader when asked to account for Washington's tolerant attitude toward the Buddhist extremists shrugged: 'It's high politics. If they're really that naïve in Washington, then we are lost.'

"Many responsible Vietnamese believe the handwriting on the wall is now clear: The Buddhist military alliance [Thich Tri Quang plus General Thi] hopes to remove all determined anti-Communist elements from power by political sleight of hand and then confront the United States with an ultimatum to get out of South Vietnam."

Fortunately, even if Washington, for whatever reason, failed to face up to the fifth-column potential of the Buddhist minority, the Vietnamese people saw the danger. Anti-Communist leaders among the Cao Dai, Hoa Hao, and Catholics reacted with increasing alarm to Premier Quat's purges from within of honorable Vietnamese. Significantly, they were joined in their protests (peaceful) by anti-Communist Buddhist moderates like Dr. Truyen of the Xa Loi. The political crisis that these anti-Communist groups created was too much for Quat, who in June voluntarily stepped aside and handed the reigns of power back to the military. The new leaders of Vietnam now were Major General Nguyen Van Thieu, a Catholic convert, and Air Commander Cao Van Ky, a Buddhist.

President Thieu, a calm, intelligent, mild-mannered man, was unquestionably dedicated to the cause of repelling the Communists. Air Commander Ky was a flamboyant idealist of conspicuous courage.

He wore lavender scarves and wrote poetry, but he also led bombing missions over North Vietnam. His popularity with his men was well established.

The U.S. embassy, which was not pleased at Ky's appointment, nonetheless approved the spartan program he outlined in accepting the premiership. His program was designed to eliminate everything from reckless speculation in the price of rice to the prevarications of the smutty Saigon press. Freedom is sweet, but the Saigon press was the bane of every responsible American in Vietnam because it spread outrageous rumors, tipped the enemy on military movements, and generally behaved in an abysmally irresponsible manner, which in most societies would have been deemed intolerable in time of war.

The stamina or survivability of the Thieu-Ky junta, with its ten-man directorate, could not be measured when it took power. But Thich Tri Quang began his intrigues early. At a meeting in Hué in early June Thich Tri Quang called a meeting of Buddhist youth to discuss the question of whether the campaign against the military government should be based on the pretext that it was undemocratic or on the pretext that President Thieu was a member of the Can Lao (the party which, in the Diem days, united the most dedicated anti-Communists of Vietnam.)

As it happens, President Thieu was not a member of the Can Lao, but that was not a deterrent factor to the Buddhist extremists, whose allegations often were woven of whole cloth. As an example, Ambassador Taylor never "cruelly oppressed" Buddhists, but that did not prevent the Buddhist extremists from accusing him of it.

A prime weapon in Thich Tri Quang's chaos-courting hands were the jealousies and quarrels among the generals themselves.

The main task of Thieu and Ky at the outset was to stay united and keep their flanks protected against Thich Tri Quang, using his own disciple, General Thi of the First Crops, as the cutting edge of the ever-present coup threat. In August, 1965, Thich Tri Quang gave an interview to the *Far East Economic Review* in which he publicly assailed the Thien-Ky junta. "I am against this government," the monk is quoted as saying. According to the *Review*, Thich Tri Quang said he would support efforts to topple the junta.

The President and Prime Minister also would be tested by whether they fell into the habit of further appeasing the ethnic or religious pressure groups. The tragic history of 1964 and 1965 has shown that appeasement, like blackmail, feeds on itself and whets the appetite of the unappeased. By placating the Buddhists with purges of their blacklisted officials, Quat stimulated worried anti-Communists to demand his own ouster. And so the vicious circle goes.

The overwhelming majority of Thich Tri Quang's coreligionists—the moderate and devout Buddhist—feel a sense of revulsion at his cruel and bloody tactics. In contrast to his equivocal statements, his espousal of a neutralist regime that would undoubtedly include the unneutral Viet Cong, most thinking Buddhists oppose flatly and publicly the Viet Cong. In late spring of 1965, one monk—Thich Nguyen Tu in Binh Dinh province—burned himself to death in protest against the seizure of his pagoda by the Viet Cong.

Certainly a return to the rule of law and the separation of church and state are among the precepts that the United States ought to support in Vietnam. It surely must actively erase the impression that Americans favor the minority Buddhist extremists.

No Vietnamese leader has a chance of restoring a semblance of stability until the Buddhists go back to the pagodas, the Catholics go back to the churches, and the military go back to fighting the Viet Cong instead of each other.

The United States had best face the fact that Thich Tri Quang and the Buddhist extremists will in the future, as in the past, oppose the government—any government.

Why?

The most persuasive analysis came from an experienced British diplomat:

A defensible case can be made for the theory that Thich Tri Quang will sooner or later seek to undermine any stable government in Vietnam. If it looks like the tide of war is flowing the United States way, he might make overtures of good will—the more easily to do the nicely lulled Americans in later. After all, Tri Quang told General Taylor that he favored American bombing of the North, and then went straight to the French to explain that he was only lulling Taylor's suspicions so as to have a free hand to press on with his undercover campaign for peace at any price—or rather peace at the Communist price. A man who will do things like that will do anything. Tri Quang takes the long view. He is patient. He has been a revolutionary for a long time. He has great instinct for waiting until the time is ripe.

If Thich Tri Quang wants to deliver Vietnam to Neutralism or Communism under his own leadership, it would explain the mystery of why in the spring of 1964, he dropped a political bombshell by raising the false issue of religious persecution on the part of the Khanh government, which was after all, dominated by Buddhists. Such a charge was ridiculous in light of all the concessions—indeed the favoritism shown to the Buddhists by Khanh's regime.

It was equally ridiculous to charge religious persecution to Premier Huong, a fair and tolerant man if there ever was one.

But the cry of "Buddhist persecution"—as Tri Quang well knows—brings on almost Pavlovian reaction in the outside world, where most people are too uninformed and too naïve to believe that a Buddhist monk might make up such accusations out of whole cloth to gain his own ends. So it is an effective way of harassing the government. Such ambitions would also explain Tri Quang's constant demands for purges of officials—not just Catholics, but Confucianist, Cao Dai, Hoa Hao, Ancestor Worshippers, Muslims, etc.—who were guilty of nothing except faithfully fighting against the Communists under Diem. And mark you, it is of great significance that Tri Quang's intended victims were always the toughest of anti-Communists. In appeasing Tri Quang with purges of persons innocent of any breaking of any known law, both post-Diem military juntas created tremendous morale problems in the military and civil service, which are being denuded of reliable personnel. Vietnamese reason that if—after the fact—it becomes a crime to have carried out orders of one head of state, it can, similarly, become a crime ex post facto to have served another. They are scared to take responsibility. Chains of command break down. Perhaps the officer who gives orders today will be purged tomorrow. Can his subordinate take the risk of doing his bidding? And that is why, if the constant purges demanded by Tri Quang continue, the structure of government will be so weakened as to make it easy for the Viet Cong to take over from within.

You Americans had best realize that Thich Tri Quang is the enemy of everything your country is trying to accomplish in Vietnam and act accordingly.

It was an informed, wise bit of advice. But Washington had heard it before; and often before, it had been heard, but not heeded, like the reprise of a tune that conjured up a disagreeable memory.

CHAPTER 14

Our Vietnam Nightmare

> A man who knows he has made a mistake and does not correct it makes another mistake.
>
> —The Sayings of Confucius

A disillusioned Allied diplomat in a bitter moment once described American policy as: "Friendly to the neutrals, neutral to the enemy, and hostile to its friends."

And how sadly and truly that description of American policy fits United States actions in Vietnam.

It's not that *America wanted* to play the enemy to its friends in Vietnam. As the months, years, *coup d'états,* and crises went by it became appallingly evident that the United States simply did not know who its friends were in that tormented country or how to distinguish them from its foes. Incredible? Of course it's incredible. And that's what gives the situation in Vietnam its persistent nightmarish quality.

That is also why in Vietnam the United States for so long played the role of the Ugly American in the worst possible sense.

History may well write that in Vietnam, as in the popular novel *The Ugly American,* there were the good Americans, the idealistic

Americans, and the perfectionist Americans, who in their missionary zeal to impose their own Western concepts of right and wrong on that lovely and tragic Oriental country nearly did Vietnam in—but only for its own good.

What are we in Vietnam for?

We are not, theoretically, in Vietnam as conquerors. As compared to the situation in Japan and Germany, we do not have the right, theoretically, to treat the Vietnamese as a beaten foe whom we can remold to suit our political heart's desire.

We are in Vietnam, theoretically, to help the duly constituted authorities and the people combat the Communist armies—officers and enlisted men—sent south by Ho Chi Minh in massively mounting numbers to terrorize, bomb, burn, trick, and bleed the Vietnamese nation into submission to the Communist North, because, among other things, if the North left the South alone, Free Vietnam would thrive and prosper and put Ho Chi Minh to shame just as surely as West Berlin puts East Berlin to shame.

But what did the United States do? It allowed itself to forget that it was in Vietnam as an ally, not as a conqueror. In the fall of 1963 Washington went into the business of hiring and firing governments. We not only forgot the one overriding priority, the war effort, but also, for the first time in history, conspired in the ouster of an ally in the middle of a common war against the Communist enemy, thus plunging the country and the war effort into a steep spiral of decline.

Even the State Department, which played such a dominant role in signaling the downfall of Diem, was finally to admit—albeit somewhat indirectly—the tragic outcome. In the White Paper of February, 1965, the State Department says in typically clinical tones: "the military and insurgency problem was complicated by a quite separate internal political struggle in South Vietnam which led in November, 1963, to the removal of the Diem government. . . . There have been a number of changes in the leadership and composition of the Saigon government in the ensuing period. *These internal developments and distractions gave the Viet Cong an invaluable opportunity and they took advantage of it* [my italics].

What had happened? Very simple. The good Americans had acted on the very false assumption that somehow an Oriental country that had never in the twentieth century experienced nationhood or known peace could nonetheless develop "instant democracy" and operate responsibly in the middle of a war, acting with the smoothness and patriotic dedication that is expected in a country like Great Britain, where it took many hundreds of years and many wars to make responsible parliamentary government possible.

Such a false assumption is a bungle that history does not lightly forgive. The impossible, if well-meaning American demands for the trappings of democracy brought near chaos instead.

America had heard mutterings of discontent about Diem's undemocratic ways almost from the moment his regime was born. But the U.S. government finally turned on him partly because it was bamboozled into believing that Diem was, among other excesses, indulging in the evils of religious persecution. We had the arrogance to play God in Vietnam. And yet our ignorance was so abysmal that we fell for a hoax perpetrated by a tiny, militant, totally untypical group of Buddhist extremists led by Thich Tri Quang, who then and subsequently served Communist ends. Some American officials came to call Thich Tri Quang the "Makarios of Southeast Asia." But this does an injustice to the Cypriote leader, Archbishop Makarios, who at least never deliberately deceived his own coreligionists, inspiring them to tragic suicides by fire as a technique of political pressure and personal aggrandizement. A robed Machiavelli with incense, Thich Tri Quang had the United States so tightly wrapped around his demagogic finger that Washington blindly placed the blame, not at Thich Tri Quang's door, where it belonged, but at Diem's.

But, as I have pointed out, the record then and later clearly showed that Diem repressed nobody for *religious reasons*.

In 1963 the attitude in Washington was such that almost anybody who took to the streets in Vietnam was deemed to be in the right and Diem in the wrong. The mistake was made of thinking that temporary detention of a few thousand students and Buddhist extremists (who had never helped or would then help the war effort) could decisively damage morale in the countryside, where the people couldn't have cared less about the urban disturbances except, occasionally, to deplore them. The habitual carping and plotting of the teahouse intellectuals and the generals was taken as a black mark against Diem, when in point of fact they represented an endemic psychological disease whose virulence would increase when Diem's strong hand was removed.

The supreme irony of it all is that since the anti-Diem *coup d'état* that Washington signaled in hopes of better times, American officials have privately come full circle. As one small example, the United States in recent months has lost any illusion that a Vietnamese riot makes right. By now Washington has concluded that in the light of the indiscipline, factionalism, irresponsibility, and endemic plotting characteristic of the educated Vietnamese, no person can keep control of the situation in Vietnam without resorting to virtually the same tight rein that Diem used. In other words, Diem was right and we were wrong. A strong authoritarian hand was not a whim but a dire necessity.

In 1965 it might have been comical—if it hadn't been so tragic— to hear a top State Department official declare in private conversation that "the kind of military strongman we need in Vietnam is one who is astute and wily enough to jockey power among the young generals so as to prevent any single one of them from having sufficient strength to even think of trying a *coup d'état*." But when Diem had indulged in such jockeying, he was accused of "interfering with the war for political reasons" and impeding its progress. Partly because of his skill at preventing concentrations of power among the military, Diem had managed to rule nine whole years without succumbing to any *coup d'état*. No successor government has yet been able to stay in power for nine months.

Nowadays, the longing for "instant democracy" has given way to a longing for "instant stability."

But how can you make policy based on the assumption that a certain amount of authoritarianism is necessary in Vietnam when you don't dare say so out loud? Can you imagine the American Secretary of State saying: "We've made such a confused mess in Vietnam that we either support an efficient dictator for the duration or that country goes under and we lose Asia"?

Can you image good, perfectionist, idealistic Americans even admitting that what's good for modern America may not work just at this instant in time in Oriental Vietnam? What would Senator Morse think of an American policy unabashedly dedicated to the support in this emergency of the unspeakable—a military dictatorship?

Or perhaps we could follow this policy without quite proclaiming it out loud.

There is always the alternative of frankly recognizing that the disasters following the Diem overthrow betrayed America's profound ignorance of Vietnamese realities. As Confucius wisely said, a man (or nation) who makes a mistake and does not correct it makes another mistake. One clearly indicated corrective course of action for our past mistakes is to acknowledge that we should henceforth respect the sovereignty of Vietnam in fact as well as in form. Vietnam's rights as a sovereign state clearly entitle it to install a measure of authoritarian rule and curb civil liberties (as we ourselves have done in wartime) if the Vietnamese leaders decide that the emergency demands it. We should forgo the practice of making political and economic warfare on an allied country—especially a country caught in the agony of subversive war—because it does not follow our dictates about "changes in policy and personnel." Even with regard to the war effort the United States should not, despite its great power, go beyond the normal rules of allymanship, which are to make demands (as distinguished from urgent suggestions) only if the common war effort is visibly, and not just theoretically, jeopardized. And before we complain about this or that Vietnamese general it would be well to make sure that we understand exactly what we are about and that our case is foolproof and that we are not imposing Western values on Oriental situations. Nor should we publicly humiliate and excoriate a wartime ally because it does not follow our dictates in such things as street demonstrations and police handling of rioters, whatever their religion, ethnic group, and complaint.

The United States should realize that we gravely injure a proud new nation by this kind of international nagging and hurt its standing before its own people and wound its pride. National leaders are developed by the exercise of responsibility, which is impossible if we insist on treating them as puppets on our string. Proud and stubborn allies may be difficult, but they are better than obsequious and spineless allies.

In Korea, proud and stubborn Syngman Rhee often balked spectacularly at American policies. Like Diem, the Korean President was often reviled by important segments of the American press that condemned him as a "dictator" and scoffed at his plea that in wartime a strong authoritarian hand was necessary. But in Korea, even though sorely tried, the United States never turned on the old Korean patriot. And whatever may be said of Old Man Rhee, he ruled his people and held his country together in a way that would not have been possible if a mere American puppet had been in his place.

President Johnson once called President Diem the "Winston Churchill of Southeast Asia." This may annoy the devotees of the great Englishman and is perhaps an exaggeration. Clearly, however, Ngo Dinh Diem towers so far above any of his shallow and opportunistic successors that there is no comparison.

Whatever his faults, Diem obviously struggled in his own Oriental fashion to impart a rough justice and to improve the lot of his people. His critics grant him that much and the record bespeaks the fact that he did more for his own people in a short time than any other contemporary South Asian leader.

Better than we ever could, Ngo Dinh Diem knew his own people with all their faults and virtues. Most important of all, he profoundly understood the nature of the Communist struggle, for like the many anti-Communist nationalists allied with him, he had been coping with Red terrorists all his adult life. Diem was a twenty-nine-year-old province chief when he first sent his agents to penetrate Communist cells in his bailiwick. Thus he could swiftly identify the Communists —indentification remains a requirement in countersubversion—and round them up when they surfaced to start trouble. If Diem's successors in the provincial capitals had been as diligent and crafty as he, the Communists might not have later acquired such a momentous capacity to terrorize and kidnap Vietnamese nationalists, including Diem (by then he was no longer in a position of authority).

The Americans who believed more civil liberties were the sure answer to Vietnam's problems used to accuse Ngo Dinh Diem and his brother Ngo Dinh Nhu of being "as bad as Communists" for practicing such "dirty tricks" as using secret agents and secret police to serve their countersubversion purposes.

But what kind of reasoning is that? Is England as "bad as the Communists" because it employs real-life James Bonds by the score?

The American accusations have a highly hypocritical ring inasmuch as the C.I.A. has itself been training agents for secret subversion and infiltration of the Viet Cong inside South Vietnam.

Granted that dirty tricks are inevitable in a fight for survival, the goals and philosophy of a nation should be given great weight in history's verdict. Diem's humanist philosophy was the antithesis of Marxism-Leninism. Like Adlai Stevenson, he believed that "Communism is the corruption of a dream of justice." As to Democracy, Diem once referred me to Plato's definition: "Democracy is a charming form of government, full of variety and disorder, and dispensing a sort of equality to equals and unequal alike."

"But," Diem said, "to make democracy work even remotely as it does in England and America, we in Vietnam must lessen the inequality between our people—between the Montagnard and the Vietnamese, between the villager and the Côte d'Azur elite, who are more French than Vietnamese. And the time for variety and disorder comes when wars are won."

In judging America's decision to depose this man whose indomitable will to fight the Communists remains unchallenged, history will surely and wryly note that we did so under pressures that posterity will find strange indeed.

The pressures came from Buddhist extremists who at best tolerate and at worst oppose the war effort, from students and intellectuals who have made a specialty of avoiding the draft, and from military men whose post-Diem intrigues and squabbles nearly drove their country into the ground. It was the kind of bargain to bring rejoicing to the hearts of pacifists, defeatists, and friends of the Viet Cong, wherever they might be.

For all these reasons, the record of our recent dabblings in Vietnamese internal affairs certainly justifies the greatest skepticism about further attempts to play God out there.

"The Americans—sometimes they know not what they do in matters of Oriental religion, politics, and psychology," Prime Minister Huong said. "We are indebted to your country for coming to our aid. But the Americans should find out what kind of people inhabit the country they are fighting for. Americans think every member of the yellow race who burns incense is a Buddhist. . . . But most incense-burners are ancestor-worshipers [Confucianists]. . . . Maybe fifteen percent of Vietnamese go to the pagodas. . . ."

At this juncture Prime Minister Huong was reacting to a press-conference remark by Secretary of State Rusk *in the fall of 1964* stating that eighty percent of the Vietnamese were Buddhists. Even at that terribly late date our Secretary of State had not been properly informed on the ethnic and religious composition of the country for which we were shelling out one million dollars a day!

As for the Buddhists, it was an insult to a great religion, rooted in the doctrines of compassion and nonviolence, to believe that those rock-throwing, hate-spouting Vietnamese extremists in monks' clothing were genuinely representative of the admirable middle path taught by the Enlightened One. As for the anti-Catholic attacks instigated by Thich Tri Quang, they are in total opposition to the tolerance preached by Buddha. Indeed, Buddha compared a man who condemns other religions to "one who looks up and spits at heaven." Articulation is not representation, and neither is the capacity to make trouble. But in the depth of our ignorance we thought the extremist trouble makers represented the majority sentiment in Vietnam, which was emphatically not the case. Additionally, for a long time we were reluctant to face up to the grim reality that the Communists had infiltrated Buddhism as they had every other element and institution of Vietnamese life.

This reluctance was pronounced among the younger foreign-service officers at the Saigon embassy, and they were the ones mainly in personal contact with the Buddhists at the working level. The U.S. ambassador based his decisions in considerable part on reports of conversations, analysis of Buddhist-controlled newspapers, etc., submitted by Vietnamese-speaking junior officers.

Gradually I began to comprehend, at least in part, their attitude. It was a backlash of the McCarthy era. Ironically, a very good case can be made to support the theory that McCarthy was the greatest American benefactor the Communists ever had. By his techniques of character assassination and his cruel and unsupported accusations during his witch-hunting days, McCarthy hurt many innocent Americans. As revulsion grew, the pendulum swung to the opposite extreme. As a result of some upside-down logic, the mere fact that McCarthy had accused people unjustly of being Communists produced a feeling that there was something wrong and illiberal about calling *anybody* a Communist or even Communist-serving.

In Vietnam I heard a young foreign-service officer turn in anger on a newspaper friend of mine who had observed (with considerable understatement) that the turmoil and intrigue fostered by Thich Tri Quang must be a delight to the Communists.

"You're as bad as McCarthy," said the young man. "There is no *proof* that Thich Tri Quang is a Communist."

"Perhaps so," said the newsman, "but there is no *proof* either that Viet Cong are Communists. They don't carry Communist-party cards. The way we can tell that the Viet Cong are Communists is when they start shooting at us. And Tri Quang and the Buddhist extremists have been shooting rocks, knives, and grenades at the authorities in Saigon. So whether he carries a party card or not, that is proof to me that Tri Quang is serving Communist purposes."

In the Diem period we were trapped in part because of our naïve idealism. It never occurred to the direct, openhearted, well-intentioned Americans that a person in Buddhist garb could deliberately and deviously invent charges of religious persecution, use suicide squads to trick his own coreligionists, create turmoil, and enhance his own power—all with the ultimate aim of toppling the legitimate Vietnamese government, ridding Asia of the Americans, and making a deal with Hanoi.

But the overwhelming bulk of the evidence points to precisely such ends and means.

In Morris West's novel on Vietnam, *The Ambassador,* the wise Zen Buddhist asks the ambassador in the opening chapter: "What will you do when they ask you to kill the cuckoo?"

At the end of the book the ambassador has the answer: "I found it. I killed the cuckoo."

For Americans of conscience (if that is not too old-fashioned a word), the answer stirs dark memories of Vietnam.

Can we Americans escape the feelings of blood on our hands after grasping the height of moral arrogance implicit in the U.S. decision that led to the overthrow and murder of an *Oriental* ruler because he did not live up to our dubious *Occidental* concepts of how to run an *Oriental* country?

In total war there is no such thing as legality, Winston Churchill once said. But even in total war it is customary to shoot your enemies —not your friends.

In Morris West's novel, Mel Adams, the fictional embassy counselor, gives this warning: "If we do intervene, by tacit or open guarantee to a group of military plotters, we become conspirators. Even if we appear to be advantaged by a change of regime, in the end we are not. We destroy our status and impugn the integrity of our national purpose. If the Vietnamese President is killed during the coup, we would become by that fact accessories and guilt partners to a political assassination. The policy [overthrow] is morally wrong, historically unsound, and totally dishonorable."

At the end of the novel the ambassador cries out: "How then can we say how they must live and what they must believe to be content. There is murder in this. Destruction and sowing of hate. I know, I was the instrument of it." He thus went to the heart of the danger of an Occidental stranger presuming to judge and condemn an alien ruler of an alien land whose psychology, customs, and realities an American has the greatest difficulty penetrating.

And if the overthrow of a friendly allied leader is morally wrong, historically unsound, and totally dishonorable, it also has disastrous *practical* consequences of a kind that not many Americans yet understand.

The tragedy had its repercussions in many places besides Vietnam.

It was no accident that on November 4, 1963—two days after Diem's overthrow and murder—Prince Norodom Sihanouk of Cambodia announced that he would reject further American economic or military aid. At the time, the Cambodian royal army was trained by Americans and half of its support came from U.S. funds.

During my visit to Cambodia shortly after the coup against Diem a royal adviser explained the Prince's decision this way: "Sihanouk hated Diem and Nhu. This was inevitable. Vietnam is Cambodia's historic enemy. But the Prince is *légitimiste*. When he saw what the Vietnamese military did to Diem and Nhu with the help of the Americans, he made a decision. It was to deprive the American military of any power or connection with the Cambodian military so that the U.S. could never try its intrigues here. He saw that Diem and Nhu had been friends of the United States. After what your country did to them, Sihanouk saw no point in having such 'friends' here."

The generals who plotted the coup were sullied to some extent by U.S. involvement and encouragement of their actions. They had, after all, played the game of a foreign power in committing treason against their leader, one of their own. For this reason they were regarded with a certain contempt by nationalist Vietnamese. And when they were overthrown in their turn it caused not a flicker of concern.

"If the generals had done it on their own," said a Saigon philosophy professor, "it might have been different. But everyone knew they hadn't dared to move until the Americans urged them to do so. From that time on the battle was unequal. It wasn't a very fair contest."

Deep national pride probably explains why most Vietnamese to whom I have talked feel that it was better, if a choice had to be made, for Diem to be murdered by his generals than for him to have accepted Ambassador Lodge's offer of haven at the U.S. embassy pending exile.

Explained the Saigon professor: "If Diem had sought help of a foreign power, he would have undermined everything he stood for. It would have destroyed the faith of the people in his integrity and character. It would have been craven and cowardly for Diem to seek help from the Americans; more so, because they had betrayed him. He kept faith with his principles concerning Vietnam's national sovereignty. He surrendered to the Vietnamese generals, not foreigners. History will applaud this. It may be that the Americans would have treated Diem more gently than the generals. But as a Vietnamese it would have been wrong for Diem to put his trust publicly in out-siders. As a Vietnamese, he surrendered to Vietnamese. The generals killed him and the onus is on them."

Strange as it sounds to a Westerner, the violent overthrow of the Diem regime struck at the deep feelings of filial piety that dominate many tradition-minded Vietnamese (as opposed to the Gallicized Vietnamese).

As explained by the Confucian scholar Ch'u Chai: "Filial piety, as taught in Confucianism, is not merely a domestic virtue, but diffuses its influence through all actions of life. It originates with the bonds of common parentage and extends to other relationships. The humanists made the virtue of filial piety the chief *cornerstone* of the social structure."

In Vietnamese tradition the head mandarin of the nation was owed respect and obedience even as the male head of the family was owed respect and obedience.

Since World War II the pendulum of American policy has swung, out of necessity, away from the isolation of the 1930's. Power, pride, and the Cold War have dictated this course. But in Vietnam the pendulum swung to an opposite and ugly extreme of deep, meddle-some, and unforgivable intervention in the affairs of another country. It was all the more unforgivable because for a few months in the spring and summer of 1963 the war was approaching a turning point. It was not yet being won; still, for the first time, by a consensus of informed, objective witnesses, there was light at the end of the tunnel. Gains were being made in important areas of the countryside. For more than twenty-five years free people had been on the run from Communism in Asia. The last big Communist victory had been Dien-bienphu, in 1954. Could any aim have higher priority than turning the tide while the turning was good and demonstrating at last that the Peking-Hanoi-style wars of liberation were not invincible?

Will history be any kinder to us when it is written—as it surely will be—that the policy-makers dominating that historic hour did not really know what they were doing or comprehend the terrible alternatives they were forcing upon themselves and upon the Vietnamese people?

Those who perpetrated the *coup d'état* argued that the Diem overthrow merely unmasked how badly things had been going all along. It is understandable that the Vietnamese military junta would make these self-serving assertions. In their desperation, Big Minh and his generals needed *something* to explain their dismal performance. But the arguments by their coup-inciting American counterparts cannot be supported by the record.

Granted that some of Diem's province chiefs painted too glowing a picture of progress in such ventures as the strategic-hamlet program. But the Americans and British knew the state of the program was exaggerated before the *coup d'état* occurred; that is why they successfully pressed the Diem regime to decree a slowdown. But these exaggerations were marginal, not decisive, to the balance of gains and losses in the countryside as a whole. What really hurt the strategic-hamlet program was the vacillation of the junta, the confusion of the bureaucracy, and the massive escalation of Viet Cong power, not inherent defects in design or implementation. Yet, as of this writing there are still five thousand strategic hamlets that are regarded as going concerns, compared to eight thousand that were operational (on paper) under Diem.

In the controversies that swirl about Vietnam, the decisive points of comparison are these:

In 1963 Vietnam was able to export three hundred thousand tons of rice. Supplies flowed smoothly from the farmers in the countryside to points of shipment abroad on the wharves of Saigon.

In 1965 Vietnam had to import rice because the roads into the city had been cut so badly that it was impossible for the farmers to get their grain to Saigon.

In 1963 the coastal area from Saigon to Hué was clear and traffic moved back and forth along the mandarin road (Highway One); the North-South Railway was functioning; roads connecting the Mekong-delta rice bowl in the South were open.

In 1965 neither Highway One nor any important feeder highways were open, nor was the railroad. An airlift had to be instituted to five major cities in the coastal area. The Mekong delta was largely cut off from Saigon so far as road traffic was concerned.

In the summer of 1963 the average number of Viet Cong attacks was two to three hundred a week. Few were larger than company or battalion size. The heaviest weapon was usually the machine gun.

In the summer of 1965 the Viet Cong were often making six hundred or more attacks a week; many were conducted by two and three regiments at a time; and weapons included mortars, flame throwers, recoilless rifles, and artillery.

In midsummer 1963 Ho Chi Minh publicly hinted in a radio broadcast at a negotiated modus vivendi with South Vietnam.

In midsummer 1965 Ho Chi Minh rebuffed all offers of unconditional discussions on grounds that the Viet Cong victory was certain.

In the summer of 1963 the Viet Cong were unable to seize and *hold* for more than twenty-four hours any strategic hamlet.

In the summer of 1965 the Viet Cong seized and *held* hundreds of strategic hamlets, sending five hundred thousand peasant refugees fleeing to safer, government-held areas. The Communists had the capacity to capture and occupy district capitals and provincial capitals.

This tragic deterioration came about in Vietnam because we repeated there the mistake we had already made once before in Asia after World War II. The previous mistake was in China.

Our bungles in Vietnam demonstrated anew that the national interest of the United States dictate that we ask only two things of allied governments: Do they work? Do they serve our purposes better than any available alternative?

It is admittedly not always easy to be clear about the alternatives in light of the strange double standard that dominates the thinking of many of our intellectuals and some of our press. Under the double standard a kind of relentless microscope is applied to magnify and bring out into the open the shortcomings, failures, and defeats of our avowed friends, whereas those of our avowed enemies are given short shrift or overlooked.

How many inches of newspaper type have been devoted in the past decade to the religious persecutions, concentration camps, grinding agricultural failures, and industrial scandals in the Red "Paradise" presided over by Ho Chi Minh in North Vietnam?

Dismally few.

President Diem would have considered himself blessed had the Western press given his errors the same once-over-lightly.

Indeed, for many years much of the Free World was given to incredible romanticism about Mao Tse-tung in China and, for a briefer time, Fidel Castro in Cuba, both of whom were portrayed as modern-day Robin Hoods in agricultural reformers' clothing.

If there is any leader of the Free World who has been as greatly romanticized in the West as these leaders of the Communist World, the name escapes me.

In China in the late 1940's the vital question for the United States was simply: Was Mao Tse-tung, an avowed enemy of all our country stood for, better for our purposes than Chiang Kai-shek, an avowed friend?

Even today Chiang Kai-shek is not by any means a model of Jeffersonian democracy. This is, of course, deplored by those who naïvely insist that the American type of government ought to be as applicable in Taipeh as in Kansas City.

But there are few persons nowadays who would consider the world better off with Mao rather than Chiang in Peking.

In Vietnam the choice was between Diem and political and administrative chaos.

Hindsight?

Nonsense!

There was no mystery about Mao Tse-tung for those who would take their magnifying glasses off the warts on the noses of our friends and pass a little time examining the warts on the noses of our enemies.

As to Diem, many months before the *coup d'état* I quoted Robert Thompson, the British adviser, as having predicted, along with many others, that "the overthrow of the Diem regime in the middle of a war would set back the war at least twelve months, perhaps forever."

If Ho Chi Minh himself had been writing the script, he could scarcely have asked for better than the chaos and lawlessness brought about by the political reign of terror that followed the death of Diem and Nhu.

No wonder Ho Chi Minh took the turmoil in the South as a signal to intensify to a spectacular degree his military intervention. Ho Chi Minh and Ngo Dinh Diem had long ago taken each other's measure and had wary respect for each other.

According to an Australian journalist, with communist sympathies, Ho Chi Minh greeted news of Diem's overthrow with the remark, "I could scarcely believe that the Americans would be so stupid." But when the realization sank in, the most unbenevolent Uncle Ho escalated the war by putting a whole new army in the field of South Vietnam. Could the Americans really have expected that Ho Chi Minh would resist the opportunity of applying maximum pressure at the time of Vietnam's maximum weakness?

And so as Communist power grew and Free Vietnam weakened, the Americans were confronted with the awful choice of making a humiliating retreat or paying an increasingly high price in men, weapons, and risks.

Proof there can never be, but it can be convincingly argued that the United States would not have been confronted with such costly choices if it had put Vietnamese realities above considerations of image and "reform" and had stuck with the Diem regime, which had established its capability of ruling its own people and consolidating control over the countryside. Since November 1, 1963, the record has been retreat, retrenchment, and rebellion.

Have Americans learned that they cannot afford to be arrogantly moralistic to the extent of sacrificing the imperfect but friendly leaders on our side—and on a false charge at that—to the benefit of the hostile leaders of the Communists?

Surely we must find a balance between the kind of isolationism that says, on the one hand, to hell with the rest of the world, and the kind of interventionism that on the other goes so deep as to overthrow the leaders of a friendly country that is deep in a fight for its existence.

We are paying in Vietnam for seeking to impose our own values, our own methods, our own style of democracy in a strange country that resents our demands because it does not understand them or understands them imperfectly. A wise and great country must resist the temptation to try to reshape its ally in its own image on the grounds that what suits us must suit others equally.

What we did in Japan and Germany we did by virtue of our absolute victory plus our absolute mastery over those prostrated nations. We reap disaster when we treat Vietnam like a conquered country, hiring and firing governments like puppets.

Deep down, the people of the Orient feel the same way about the Quislings of the East as do the people of the Occident about the Quislings of the West.

The principal way that America can reshape countries that are friends (an aim of highly dubious value) is by example and by persuasion in those cases where we are confident we understand the culture, psychology, history, and values of a people. Vietnam was never one of those cases, and that explains why American pressure there was often exerted at the wrong times, at the wrong places, and for the wrong purposes.

Action against our Communist enemies is one thing. Pressures on Fidel Castro make sense from the point of view of our nation's security. But violent and painful pressures to reform our friends are based on the highly debatable proposition that Uncle Sam has the wit and wisdom to know more about what's best for a given country than its own leaders. Washington disagrees with De Gaulle (the last of the Western mandarins). But history is likely to say that the great Frenchman knew more about his own people and his country's necessities than his American "advisers."

In 1964–65 in Vietnam the tragic and vicious circle was completed when some Americans, including many who had cried the loudest for Diem's scalp, began using the coup-ridden political situation as an excuse for urging "disengagement" from Vietnam, offering as an excuse its hopeless instability—the instability that the United States itself had done the most to create. It's like ordering a man's hand chopped off and then condemning him to death because he is physically disfigured. And if we were to withdraw, it would be tantamount to a condemnation of death for Vietnam and all those brave peasants and teachers and doctors who have committed themselves in the belief that America keeps its word.

President Johnson summed up our obligation magnificently in his famous Baltimore speech of April, 1965, in which he answered the question "Why are we in Vietnam?":

"We are there because we have a promise to keep. Since 1954 every American President has offered support to the people of South Vietnam. Thus, over many years we have made a national pledge to help South Vietnam defend its independence. To dishonor that pledge, to abandon this small and brave nation to its enemies, and to the terror that must follow, would be an unforgivable wrong.

"We are also there to strengthen world order. Around the globe, from Berlin to Thailand, are people whose well-being rests in part of the belief that they can count on us if they are attacked. To leave Vietnam to its fate would shake the confidence of all these people in the value of an American commitment; and in the value of America's word.

"The result would be increased unrest and instability—and even wider war. . . . There are great stakes in the balance. Let no one think for a moment that retreat from Vietnam would bring an end to conflict. The battle would be renewed in one country and then another. The central lesson of our time is that the appetite of aggression is never satisfied. To withdraw from one battlefield is to prepare for the next."

Or as Winston Churchill put it, "A great power's security can never be purchased by throwing smaller nations to the wolves."

Long before the Viet Cong monsoon offensive of 1965 it became inevitable that Americans would have to join in fighting the conventional war that the battle in Vietnam had largely become. If anything, President Johnson put off the intervention for far too long.

"The President wants to do what's necessary, but he doesn't want to split the country," explained McGeorge Bundy, director of national-security affairs. Translated in public-opinion-poll terms, this is what is known as doing only what is politically palatable at home. It is piecemeal commitment.

Perhaps the delay was politically necessary, but it was costly militarily: we allowed the situation to deteriorate dangerously before American troops finally went into combat, so the effort to blunt and defeat the Viet Cong aggression was to be more costly than if we had acted earlier.

Why the delay?

For one thing, American intervention didn't fit the script. The United States had been saying this was Vietnam's war; they had to do the fighting. We could help, but we couldn't win their battles for them, not in a war supposedly fought on guerrilla, or insurgency, lines.

It is still true that we *cannot* fight it *for* them. But we have to win the battle *with* them.

The argument that the commitment of American troops would smack of colonialism lost its force when it became starkly plain that without such combat support the Vietnamese army would be overwhelmed. From the point of view of enemy propaganda, the commitment of American combat troops changed nothing. The Communists had been calling us colonialists from the moment that it looked as if our aid might be effective in helping South Vietnam fend off aggression. The limited nature of our objectives—to give the South Vietnamese a chance to live free of Communist violence—was well comprehended by the Vietnamese army. It was realized that the United States would like nothing better than to withdraw its forces from Vietnam—if it could. Indeed, the deepest anxiety of the Vietnamese generals was that American public opinion might cause the United States to abandon the struggle. Even as is the case in West Germany, which is forever demanding reassurance that the United States forces won't leave them to face the Russians alone, so did the Vietnamese constantly ask for tokens of U.S. determination.

The bombings of North Vietnam and the commitment of the United States marines and other ground troops finally stilled the nervous nellies among the Vietnamese who went into a dither every time Walter Lippmann wrote a column calling for disengagement from the Asian mainland or Senator Morse got on his feet in the Congress to advocate the impossible—*honorable* retreat.

The Johnson administration had trouble recognizing the necessity for deployment of American combat troops partly because there had been so much loose talk about the "dangers of getting bogged down in a land war in Asia."

The late General Douglas MacArthur has been massively misquoted and misunderstood on this point. During his lifetime, I made a point of talking to the general personally about Indochina because in Washington I had heard sentiments ascribed to him that sounded out of character. After his death I double-checked my understanding with Major General Courtney Whitney, his devoted friend and military aide.

To set an important historical point straight, General MacArthur never once believed or advocated that we should *surrender* Indochina rather than get "bogged down" in a war on the Asian mainland. He did strongly believe and argue that American troops should never again be committed to ground warfare in Asia if the responsible military commander in the field was to be forced to fight with one hand tied behind his back—in other words, if the enemy were again, as in Korea, to be granted a privileged sanctuary and America were to renounce the use of its most decisive military instrument: nuclear weapons.

General MacArthur did not think nuclear weapons would have to be used in Southeast Asia. But he thought it dangerous psychologically to assure the Communist enemy that he could count on immunity from such weapons; such assurance could only embolden the aggressor. In other words, the United States shouldn't deprive itself of the inhibiting effect that mere fear of the use of atomic weapons might induce in the enemy.

And in point of fact, in the war in Vietnam, both Peking and Hanoi have been put on notice that there will be no privileged sanctuary in matters of geography or weapons.

Another problem was that the United States persistently underestimated the numbers of Communist soldiers poured into South Vietnam by Hanoi. While Washington debated about what to do, the Communists confronted the Americans with the *fait accompli* of massive escalation. Part of our trouble was the mania for *proof*. A

Viet Cong unit was not held to exist unless two prisoners were taken in battle. In other words, the Viet Cong unit became real only if it was committed to battle and actually *lost two prisoners*. This is idiocy. The whole point of military intelligence is to deduce *in advance of battle* the enemy's strength and whereabouts.

In the past two years the tragedy of the Vietnamese army has been that it was "piecemealed," to use the military jargon, nearly to death as battalion after battalion was mauled by the vastly superior forces the Viet Cong was able to concentrate.

The Vietnamese army was very thinly strung out because, unlike the Viet Cong, it had to defend many fixed positions inside the country—the big cities, airfields, ports, etc. When American troops took over defense of static positions, this released some, but not enough, Vietnamese for combat.

Nobody ever knows exactly how many Viet Cong are in South Vietnam at any one time. But in 1965 there were some knowledgeable military men who felt that the Viet Cong actually outnumbered the Vietnamese army units that were combat-ready. Yet in wars of this kind the defenders need a ratio of ten to one over the aggressor.

The devastating Communist attack of November 2, 1964, on the big Bien Hoa airbase destroyed five B-57 jet bombers and damaged fifteen others and gave dramatic warning that Hanoi was shifting the war into a high and dangerous gear.

Washington's failure to retaliate for that Viet Cong attack brought the first major disagreement between Ambassador Maxwell Taylor and President Johnson. The ambassador correctly regarded the audacious attack on Bien Hoa as a Viet Cong probe of U.S. determination and will. If the United States did not clearly and instantly retaliate in some way (by bombing a similar installation in North Vietnam, for instance) the Viet Cong would be encouraged to attempt even bolder attacks on American-held bases.

President Johnson refused to act on recommendations for instant retaliation for reasons connected with the political campaign then coming to a close.

Johnson's campaign was based in part on the alleged "recklessness" of his opponent, Senator Barry Goldwater, in the debate on Vietnam. Johnson was loath to order a retaliatory bombing raid that, in the heat of an emotion-charged campaign, would give his opponent an opening to say: "See who's trigger-happy now. Is Johnson less 'reckless' than I'm charged with being?" Later on Senator Goldwater was in fact to comment wryly: "When I advocated bombing North Vietnam, this was recklessness. When Johnson does it, this is statesmanship."

In truth, some of the suggestions made by Goldwater, who was at the time a major general in the Air Force Reserve, reflected military judgments of highly responsible officials in the Defense Department. Unfortunately, Senator Goldwater had a knack of expressing his ideas in ways that shocked his hearers into thinking he was indeed both war-happy and reckless.

That Vietnam became a political issue made it all the harder for Johnson to face up to the necessary military decisions, especially when these were precisely what Goldwater had advocated.

In late December President Johnson was still telling reporters in background meetings that he was resisting the unanimous pressures of the joint chiefs to intercept the supply routes by air bombardment and naval blockade.

"I'm not going to get in any deeper and I am not going to get out," the President would frequently say.

Then came the Christmas bombing of the American hotel-billet in Saigon and the February, 1965, mortar attack on the American compound and air base at Pleiku, in the central highlands, with heavy loss of life and property.

The Viet Cong thus forced our hand. Until Bien Hoa there had been a tacit gentlemen's agreement under which the Viet Cong rarely made massive sustained attacks on strictly American installations, which until the spring of 1965 were theoretically defended by Vietnamese irregular forces, such as locally raised militia.

The attack on Pleiku dramatically exposed new enemy calculation and aims. First, it showed that the Viet Cong had become so strong in manpower and improved weaponry that the Vietnamese militia could no longer cope with the attacks and could no longer be counted on to defend American-occupied installations. Second, the Viet Cong would make such American-held installations not only fair game but also priority game.

The alternatives were starkly simple. We could either surrender these positions or provide American troops to defend them. The Vietnamese army had no manpower to spare.

It was with heavy heart that Johnson ordered the bombing of North Vietnam. Contrary to the majority of his advisers, who believed that Peking would not intervene massively, Johnson could not escape the dread of that eventuality.

"We could lose two hundred thousand men if that happened," Johnson remarked to his aides on more than one occasion.

The President was frustrated at the internecine quarrels of the squabbling factions in Saigon.

Trying to get the Vietnamese to pull together, Johnson observed, "is like standing on a piece of paper in the sea and trying to keep your balance." (How Diem would have agreed!)

The President had hoped to have political stability in Saigon *before* ordering attacks on the North. Gradually he saw that this might mean waiting forever.

The bombings of the North were intended to have an effect beyond mere retaliation for the massacre at Pleiku. The purpose was psychological as well as military. The bombings were intended as a signal to Hanoi that it was wrong in its conviction that American determination to save South Vietnam could be broken in the same way that the French will to fight had been destroyed a decade earlier.

Air power alone could not halt North Vietnamese infiltration. But as Captain Ba, the Viet Cong defector, had remarked to me, "There was no need to make infiltration so comfortable for us." And the American air action made infiltration not only uncomfortable but also costly and dangerous.

Even so, Hanoi's lifeline to the South could certainly not be decisively cut until the United States got over its belief that it was impossible to police the border between South Vietnam, Laos, and North Vietnam. Nothing is impossible if a nation as advanced in technology and inventiveness as the United States is willing to apply its know-how and instrumentation and muscle to the task.

Or as a Japanese general remarked after V-J Day in 1945, "Americans don't fight jungle war. They bring in their bulldozers and bulldoze the jungle away." And in the war with Japan that's exactly what we did do on countless Pacific islands. It is an example of what was necessary in Vietnam in at least some of these crucial border regions, for only in that way could the crossing points be brought under surveillance.

In the interior of Vietnam, near Ben Cat (about twenty miles from Saigon), is a one-by-two-mile piece of jungle inhabited by nothing but pythons, monkeys, and Viet Cong. It has been a launching point for vicious Communist attacks that have taken countless lives. Once our B-52's bombed it to break up an impending attack, and it was beautiful shooting that placed bombs inside a target one-mile-by-two in area! But this devilish patch of jungle is a good example of a Viet Cong haven deserving of the bulldozer.

The Viet Cong made important changes in their political tactics in 1965. In the early days of the war they had been very correct toward most of the peasant population. Nothing was "stolen." The peasants were ordered to pay taxes in piastres and donations of rice. Terror was selective—the village chief, the schoolteacher, the doctor, not the poor ordinary peasant who tilled the paddies (unless he was suspected of collaborating with the Americans).

Beginning with the bloody battle of Dong Xoai, in May, 1965, the Viet Cong abandoned the "correct" (by their standards) attitude toward the people. In the twelve hours or more that the Viet Cong held Dong Xoai, the district capital, the guerrillas stole everything in sight—pots, pans, mattresses, clothing. Then, using flame throwers, they cruelly and wantonly burned down half the wooden houses in the town. It was irrational and brutal, because no government forces were in that particular area.

Said one shocked U.S. adviser: "The Viet Cong flame throwers in Dong Xoai did more damage than our Napalm ever has. We have hit selective targets but we have never burned down half a town that contained no enemy forces of any kind."

Why the scorched-earth policies? Was this a deliberate order from Hanoi in hopes that massive terror would be more demoralizing than selective terror? Or was Hanoi running out of deeply indoctrinated, disciplined cadres?

The answer may include both possibilities. For the numbers of voluntary deserters from the Viet Cong skyrocketed in 1965. In the last week of May, 1965, a record total of 2,265 Viet Cong surrendered under the government's *chieu hoi* (open arms) amnesty offer and 354 were hard-core regulars bringing in forty-three individual weapons and thirty-seven grenades.

In the summer of 1965, however, Hanoi remained totally cocky and confident of victory.

A diplomat who talked with Ho Chi Minh in that period commented: "General Giap beat the Caucasians once before. He is confident that what he did to the French he can do to the Americans."

Unfortunately there were some Americans who felt the same way and suffered from a Dienbienphu syndrome. They felt a kind of hopelessness about trying to win a jungle war.

But the Communists, with all their emphasis on proper historical context, made a massive misjudgment precisely because they failed to read history correctly.

At the time of Dienbienphu France was a weak power at the end of its resources. The revolving-door governments in Paris betrayed continuing ferment. Inflation and all the other ills of a weak economy prevailed throughout the land. French public opinion looked on Indochina as a war that was literally bleeding the nation to death. And so when Pierre Mendès-France took the reins of government he was driven into the kind of negotiations that must always be avoided—those conducted in a mood of desperation. In 1954, at Geneva, France surrendered half of Vietnam.

History can perhaps forgive a weak power, depleted and demoralized, for ignoring the interests of its allies, for deserting its comrades-in-arms in Indochina, and for closing its eyes to the consequences of withdrawal in Asia. France could argue that it had no other choice.

Our situation is far different.

The United States is obviously not a small European power at the end of its military, economic, and political resources. It is a great global power whose might is undiminished. Simultaneous to the war in Vietnam, our gross national product has gone up and up, and so have living standards. President Johnson is so confident of the future that he thinks that he can fight both the war in Vietnam and the war on poverty and at the same time build the great society!

History will judge a powerful United States by entirely different standards from those used on an exhausted France. The United States cannot permit savage reprisals to be worked on anti-Communist Vietnamese. It cannot allow them to die by battalions to save American lives and property. It cannot offer the Soviet Union political concessions at the price of its European allies* in order to win its help in ending the Vietnamese war. It cannot be indifferent to the extension of Chinese Communist power in Asia.

As to negotiation, despite all the noisy debate there are no *fundamental* differences inside the country about the *idea* of negotiation. Nobody would oppose negotiations that would end the fighting, set up enforceable peace terms, preserve the rights of our friends in South Vietnam, and leave intact the honor and prestige of the United States. The choice is not "negotiations" or "no negotiations." The question is: What kind of negotiations?

It is clear that negotiations can be meaningful only when the North Vietnamese and their Chinese sponsors have fully comprehended the difference between a powerful United States at the peak of its economic and military strength and an exhausted France at the nadir of its economic and military fortunes.

It is plain that it may take some time to persuade the Communist leaders in the North that this country has the power and will to do whatever is necessary to live up to its pledge to compel North Vietnam to leave South Vietnam alone. And here the West must learn from the East the quality that the Orient possesses in abundance—the quality of patience.

So volatile is the situation in Vietnam that anything can happen.

* French Prime Minister Mendès-France persuaded the Soviet Union to intervene with Ho Chi Minh in 1954 in return for scuttling the European Defense Community (EDC) treaty.

Suddenly, without any official public hint from Hanoi, the guerrillas might be given the signal to creep out of South Vietnam over the Ho Chi Minh trail and head north.

Or the Communists might start a peace offensive of the talk-and-fight kind. It is Mao Tse-tung's theory that mere talk of an armistice puts inhibitions on the bourgeois countries that can be turned to Communist advantage. An air of sweet reasonableness also helps to enlist the unaligned world in the business of putting pressure on the United States to "make concessions." If such a phony peace offensive begins, watch out! Remember that in the war against the French the biggest Viet Minh offensive—the final attack on Dienbienphu—took place in the late spring of 1954 while the Geneva parley was going on and "peace negotiations" were in progress.

It is also possible that the battle could go on for a decade, as it did in Malaya.

What the American people should keep in mind is that the scale of expenditures is not in the least prohibitive in proportion to the goal: putting a halt at long last to the steady expansion of the Communist empire that since World War II has been gobbling up territory at the rate of about fifty square miles an hour and has in the Occident brought the Red flag over all of East Europe, East Germany, and East Berlin and in the Orient over North Korea, Tibet, and North Vietnam.

Painless peace there is not. The United States, if it has the will, can keep up its operations in Vietnam on a steadily rising scale, year after year, and decade after decade, if that is vital to our interests.

And the American people should remember also that there is no conceivable way in which the Viet Cong can win if we remain determined to do whatever necessary to prevent it. They can't push us into the sea. They can't destroy our military power. They can win some battles. But they can't win the war.

And this remains true, even if the Chinese come in. The Chinese swarmed into Korea and we deprived them of victory there. The supply lines in Korea were far shorter than is the case in Vietnam. Further, there is not a responsible military officer who fought the war in Korea who is not convinced that the Chinese would have been driven back to their own borders had it not been for the restraints placed on the military such as making Manchuria into a privileged sanctuary. In the war in Vietnam there will be *no* privileged sanctuaries.

The only way that the Communists could make the United States welsh on its commitment to Vietnam is if American public opinion in the 1960's were to become as demoralized as French public opinion in the 1950's. This is something the Communists are working very hard to accomplish, and there are a great many Americans unwittingly serving the Viet Cong objective of undermining the nation's will and stamina. But articulation is not representation in America either, and it is hard to believe that the people of this country would adopt a policy of scuttle and run.

Our Vietnamese nightmare was in great part one of our own making. And our responsibility for creating the nightmare that followed the anti-Diem *coup d'état* only heightens our obligation to bring it to an end.

Senator Mike Mansfield has now joined the chorus* of those proclaiming the overthrow of Diem to have been "a great tragedy" that turned the tide of war so drastically downward that America was forced to begin paying the price of its mistake by shedding its own blood in the battle against the Viet Cong. By labeling the Diem overthrow a mistake, Senator Mansfield may have helped to swing American policy from its unhappy past of being "friendly to the neutrals, neutral to its enemies, and hostile to its friends."

Dangerous as such prophecies are, I believe America will in Vietnam somehow muddle through—with the accent on the muddle.

*The chorus includes, in addition to President Johnson, Vice-President Hubert Humphrey, General Eisenhower, General Maxwell Taylor, Admiral Arleigh Burke, Senator Thomas Dodd (D., Conn.), Congressman Clement Zablocki (D., Wis.), General Lucius D. Clay, and thousands of Americans in our armed forces who were in Vietnam at the time.

ABOUT THE AUTHOR

Marguerite Higgins was born in Hong Kong, graduated from the University of California and the Columbia School of Journalism. In 1942 she began reporting for the *Herald Tribune* and was sent abroad as a war correspondent in 1944. In 1947 she became Chief of the Berlin Bureau and, in 1950, Chief of the Tokyo Bureau. Thereafter, until 1958, she covered the war in Korea, where, in 1951, her dispatches won her a Pulitzer Prize for International Reporting. In 1958 she became the *Tribune's* diplomatic correspondent in Washington, is now in the Washington bureau of *Newsday,* and writes for more than sixty newspapers including the Washington *Evening Star,* the Chicago *Daily News,* the Boston *Herald,* the Seattle *Times,* the Philadelphia *Inquirer,* and the Houston *Post.*

Miss Higgins has had several books published previously, among which are: *Red Plush and Black Bread, Tales of the Foreign Service* (with Peter Lisagor), and *War in Korea.*

She is married to General William Hall and has two children.

In September, 1965, Miss Higgins left for her tenth visit to Vietnam.